Contents

Foreword

It doesn't seem all that long ago, when people and organisations who showed concern for the environment and the natural world were considered just a trifle 'cranky'. Not any more. There is increasing public awareness of environmental issues and of the dangers that come from upsetting the ecological pyramid, and increasing concern at the loss for all time of species of flora, fauna and indeed sadly, entire habitats. There is enormous support for protecting and conserving as much as possible of our natural heritage.

Much of the credit for this public appreciation of what is happening around us belongs to the scores of organisations that have been established to protect or conserve various elements of our natural heritage. Almost entirely charitable and supported by volunteers, these organisations have done immense work in educating the public, raising funds to preserve species and to purchase and maintain valuable habitats. Some of the evidence of their success can be seen on the pages of the five regional editions that together make up *The Macmillan Guide to Britain's Nature Reserves*.

British Gas is delighted to sponsor these regional editions, for the Company has itself a long-standing commitment to protect the environment. Of course the product it supplies, natural gas, is the least pollutive of the fossil fuels, burning without soot, smoke or smell, and contributing least to the acid-rain problem and the greenhouse effect. Much of the progress made in Britain with clean air in the 1960s and 1970s was because of natural gas.

Similarly the transportation of natural gas need make little impact on the landscape – or indeed the townscape. The first natural gas pipeline was laid from Canvey Island, Essex, to Leeds and was completed in 1963. Since then, some 3,400 miles of underground transmission pipelines have been laid, networked across the country, transversing environmentally sensitive moorlands, forests, mountains and bogs as well as some of the country's richest farmland.

The British Gas pipeliners have restored the routes to their former status and in some cases have improved conditions with the advice of local naturalists. Although the Company has its own teams of specialists, it takes considerable heed and co-operates closely with local expertise on environmental matters.

The Company's onshore terminals and other vital installations are invariably sited in rural areas – sometimes in places that are outstanding in terms of habitat. However this has always been taken into consideration with natural landscaping and screening and the planting of indigenous trees and shrubs. Indeed, there is actually a nature trail round the perimeter of one of the onshore terminals. Another terminal also was built a half-mile from its ideal position in industrial terms, to accommodate wildlife considerations.

Within the boundaries of gas installations across the country there is an enormous variety of wildlife which has been allowed to develop without the hindrance of man. A typical example is in Derbyshire where a test centre for controlled explosions, combustion and venting of gases in confined spaces has also become a veritable treasure of wildlife. Among the flowers are yellow toadflax, rose-bay willowherb, white field rose, ladies bedstraw and wild orchids as well as the better-known oxeye daisies, foxglove, primroses and cowslips. In this environment the abundance and variety of the flora has attracted a good population of butterflies: red admirals, tortoishells, peacocks, commas, brimstones, white and painted ladies, and if the chatter of wildlife is momentarily silenced by the occasional experimental controlled explosion, the chances are that it will be broken afterwards by the raps of one of the three species of woodpeckers there – green, greater-spotted and lesser-spotted. While the few staff based at the site are regaled by the cabarets given by hares, stoats, weasels and rabbits, their favourite residents must undoubtedly be those stars of the nocturnal world – badgers.

The enclosed land around the Company's compressor stations have also become mini-reserves in their own right and nature lovers working on these installations have reported some interesting sightings.

At one compressor station the Company is establishing an experimental wildflower meadow and conservation area, with the involvement of the local branch of the British Trust for Conservation Volunteers. The site is becoming a haven for a wide variety of species to thrive, in a part of the country where intensive farming, the use of chemical fertilisers and pesticides, the grubbing of hedges and woodland, and the drainage of wetlands have resulted in a serious loss of natural habitat.

British Gas is just one of the many industries proving that if we go about things the right way, industry and nature can co-habitate. It takes a little bit of extra effort and it costs more too. But we think it's a small price to pay for saving something that we have enjoyed for future generations.

Introduction

The publishers are grateful to British Gas plc whose support for these regional guides have made their publication possible.

The entries are based upon detailed work and research by Valerie Thom, and since revised and rewritten by Linda Bennett. Their work would not have been possible without the unstinting co-operation of the Royal Society for Nature Conservation, the Scottish Wildlife Trust, the NCC and many other bodies concerned with conservation.

Our basis for inclusion of a site is that members of the public should have access either by common law rights, or by membership of a club or trust which gives access by right of membership by special permit. (All sites in the latter category are marked *Permit only* in the text.) Exceptions have been made on two criteria; where we believe that an endangered or rare species would be threatened by publication of any information about the site where it is found, or where the owner of a site at present allowing access to a limited section of the public would be unwilling to continue such arrangements if an account were published here. We have taken the best advice available on these delicate issues, but in the last resort have made our own judgement.

Our aim has been to be comprehensive and 500 sites have been added to the 1984 list. We have taken pains to ensure that the information was accurate at the time of compilation in mid 1988. It has not been possible to evaluate and include all the sites owned or managed by the Forestry Commission, the Woodland Trust, the Ministry of Defence, and the various water authorities. Readers should apply for information to the appropriate addresses (see p.129).

Every entry has been shown to a representative of the owner or managing body to ensure accuracy and the text has been read by two other advisers in addition to our own staff.

In Scotland we have followed the modern regions, though dividing Highland and Strathclyde into two to make them less unwieldy. The geographical area of each section is coloured green on the map.

Each section is introduced by a well-known naturalist living in the area and possessing an extensive knowledge of its characteristics. The longer entries in each section have been selected for their perspective on the magnificent diversity of habitats in Britain, and because they are large enough to sustain much public use; many of them offer interpretative facilities. The increasing emphasis on and support for wildlife in cities is reflected in this Guide.

Readers will no doubt wish to support the work of the trusts and other organisations involved in the management of many of the sites included here. The addresses of the relevant bodies are on p.129.

At a time when public interest in our natural heritage has never been stronger, but when paradoxically threats to its future seem to be gathering force, we hope that this Guide will encourage both the sensitive use and enjoyment of Britain's wildlife.

How to Use the Guide

Entries are arrranged alphabetically under counties or regions. The precise order is shown in the Contents list.

Each county or regional section contains a map showing sites open to the general public, with details of size, population, physical features, climate and major land use. An introduction highlights the main points of interest and characteristics of each county or region.

Factual information is given at the beginning of each entry, in this form:

```
    1           2      3
    SC 946562: 43ha: Great Bookworthy BC
  4 Limestone cliffs, grassland, heath and scrub
  5 Restricted access to old quarry: apply to warden
  6 Booklet and nature trail leaflet from car park
  7 Spring, early summer
```

Key

1 Ordnance Survey map reference (every OS map contains clear instructions on how to read it) or, in the case of very large sites, reference to the map. For sites marked *Permit only* apply to the managing body (see addresses on p.129) unless otherwise stated.
2 Area in hectares, or length in kilometres, as appropriate. (One hectare is approx. $2\frac{1}{2}$ acres; one kilometre is approx. five-eighths of a mile.)
3 Manager/owner of site (for key to abbreviations, see p.128).
4 Brief description of site.
5 Details of any restrictions.
6 Availability of leaflets or other information.
7 Best season(s) for visiting site.

Sites with access limited to members of trusts or other bodies, or to holders of special permits, are not shown on the map or given OS references.

Cross references to other sites mentioned in the text are shown in CAPITALS on their first mention in any entry. These may include sites not in this region but which may be found in the other companion books in this series (see p.10).

A list of addresses of nature conservation trusts, wildlife organisations and other managing bodies of sites is on p.129.

Borders

The Cheviot Hills are the natural frontier between England and Scotland, and visitors who come to the border at Carter Bar feel instinctively that they are entering a different land. To the east the ridge of the Cheviots points to the igneous massif of Cheviot itself, and to the west stretch successive ranges of hills, while to the north, across some odd, hummocky toothills, lies a clear view of the great expanse of the Tweed Valley. Far to the north again, the line of the Southern Uplands forms another natural frontier. The Borders Region can be seen as an independent unit built round the great river system of the Tweed, with its many tributaries pointing into hidden valleys in the hills.

The Border towns with their woollen industry stand at river crossings, their ruined abbeys testament to the riches of the valley. Not far away lie the historic houses of the great landed estates of the Borders, many now open to the public; they offer not just art and landscape, but wildlife in their parks and woodlands among prosperous agriculture. The Borders are famous for their green, sheep-grazed hills, but today Borderers are learning to acccept afforestation as a competing use for this hill land.

The Silurian rocks of much of the Tweed Valley have been subject to extreme folding, which explains the rolling landscape with many a hollow to hold the mosses or mires so prized by naturalists. There is also a broad band of Devonian old red sandstone, easily recognisable in the architecture and red soils from Jedburgh to the Berwickshire coast. Evidence of volcanic activity is conspicuous in the triple peaks of the Eildon Hills and other isolated 'laws', and in spectacular coastal cliffs at St Abb's. The rainfall varies from over 1000mm on the western moors to 600mm in the Merse of Berwickshire. Severe frosts are a feature of the inland valleys, and a cold east wind with sea haar (mist) is prevalent on the Berwickshire coast in spring. The region is relatively sheltered, however, and the encircling hills often break a layer of cloud to dapple the landscape with sunshine.

The short coastline is rocky, with the highest cliffs in eastern Scotland. On the cliff ledges between St Abb's and Fastcastle seabirds nest in such numbers that they are of international importance. Offshore the exceptionally clear coastal waters support a marine life that is unusually rich for the generally murky North Sea; this interest is already acknowledged by the expanding scope of marine reserves around Eyemouth and St Abb's. The passage of bird migrants is very evident in spring and autumn, and the mixed habitats of the ST ABB'S HEAD reserve are a happy hunting ground for birdwatchers. Steep grassy slopes among the coastal cliffs provide some of the richest grasslands remaining in the Borders, and here cowslip, early-purple orchid and wood vetch occur in abundance, as well as more maritime flowers.

The importance of the Tweed river system has received formal recognition by the Nature Conservancy Council. It contains many fish in addition to its famous salmon, but the otter which was widespread until a decade ago has now almost disappeared and mink have become common. Kingfisher are scarce, but the winter wildfowl are impressive with a large population of whooper swan. The vegetation of the lower reaches is somewhat marred by aliens, including forests of giant hogweed and the gaudy Indian balsam. In the upper reaches there are many fine river valleys including the Tweed itself at Tweedsmuir, Yarrow with St Mary's Loch, Ettrick, Teviotdale and the Jed Water. All these valleys have a varied wildlife interest and dipper are frequent everywhere, while ring ouzel breed by the higher burns. However, the wet meadows full of globeflower that were a feature of such areas as Teviothead a century ago have been lost to agriculture.

Large lochs are scarce, consisting of St Mary's Loch in the west, and HOSELAW and YETHOLM Lochs together beneath the Cheviots. These last two are reserves and hold large wintering wildfowl populations including geese and wigeon. Elsewhere the wildfowl move between smaller lochs and the rivers in response to the availability of food supplies and to disturbance.

The mosses of the Borders are nationally important but relatively unknown: six of them are included in the Scottish Wildlife Trust reserves. Raised bogs, valley bogs, basin mires and fen are all well represented and occur at a variety of altitudes and in different water regimes. Unlike the long-lost ancient fens of the Berwickshire Merse, none of these mosses with their associated carr of willow and birch is large enough for its bird life to be exceptional, but they support a wide range of specialised plants and insects including some rare water beetles. Characteristic plants include greater spearwort, coralroot orchid and holy-grass. Most of the mosses have been disturbed by drainage and digging in the past, but perhaps the greatest threat today is the run-off, from adjacent arable land, of fertiliser and sprays.

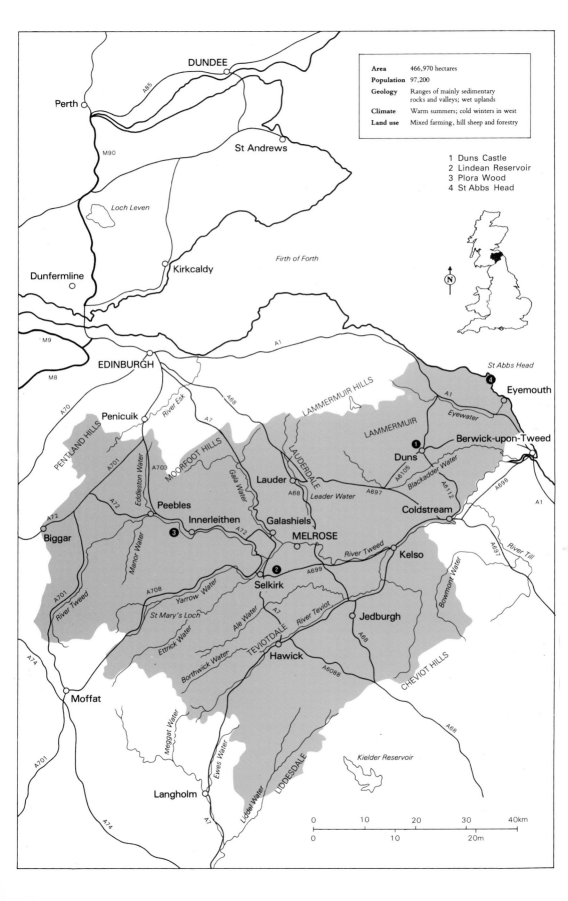

Area	466,970 hectares
Population	97,200
Geology	Ranges of mainly sedimentary rocks and valleys; wet uplands
Climate	Warm summers; cold winters in west
Land use	Mixed farming, hill sheep and forestry

1 Duns Castle
2 Lindean Reservoir
3 Plora Wood
4 St Abbs Head

N

DUNDEE
Perth
A85
St Andrews
M90
Loch Leven
Firth of Forth
Dunfermline
Kirkcaldy
M9
M8
EDINBURGH
A1
LAMMERMUIR HILLS
St Abbs Head
Eyemouth
4
A70
Penicuik
River Esk
A68
A7
LAMMERMUIR
Eyewater
A1
PENTLAND HILLS
A701
Eddleston Water
A703
MOORFOOT HILLS
Gala Water
LAUDERDALE
1
Duns
Berwick-upon-Tweed
A6105
Blackadder Water
A6112
A72
Peebles
Lauder
A68
Leader Water
A697
Coldstream
A698
A1
Biggar
A72
Manor Water
3
Innerleithen
A72
Galashiels
MELROSE
River Tweed
Kelso
A697
River Till
A701
River Tweed
A708
Yarrow Water
Selkirk
2
A699
Bowmont Water
St Mary's Loch
Ale Water
A7
River Teviot
Jedburgh
A68
Ettrick Water
Borthwick Water
TEVIOTDALE
Hawick
A6088
CHEVIOT HILLS
Moffat
Meggat Water
Ewes Water
Kielder Reservoir
A68
A74
Langholm
A701
A7
Liddel Water
LIDDESDALE
A74

0	10	20	30	40km
0		10		20m

Throughout the Borders one may still find rocky hillsides that have escaped the plough, where superb banks of rock-rose are mixed with fragrant thyme and locally with maiden pink. Mountain pansy is also abundant and butterflies such as common blue may be plentiful; the number of species is limited, but sometimes includes Scotch argus. These grasslands now need more protection.

Ancient deciduous woodland is rare in the Borders and is generally limited to fragments on steep river banks and up the hill burns; centuries of border warfare and intensive sheep farming have contributed to this. Way-marked countryside walks developed by the initiative of the Borders Regional Council lead through several of the remaining woodland areas, as by the Whiteadder at Abbey St Bathans, the Tweed at St Boswells and again at Neidpath Castle by Peebles. Red squirrel are still common in these areas.

There are nationally important moorlands including the superb landscape of the Tweedsmuir Hills, the wild wastes of the Langholm to Newcastleton Hills, the grouse moors of the Moorfoot Hills, Kielderhead Moor high on the Cheviots and the lowland Greenlaw Moor. Wild goat and mountain hare inhabit the high tops and, on a few crags, raven and peregrine still nest. These hills appear well rounded, but they conceal many a steep-sided cleuch with hidden botanical riches lying within.

Some of the new conifer forests have been planted with sympathy to the wildlife interest by leaving a proportion of open ground, especially along the burns. Here the inevitable roe deer have prospered together with, more locally, the even more damaging sika deer; among birds that have found a place here are black grouse, long-eared owl, crossbill and siskin. Such gains to wildlife do something to balance the continuing losses of many habitats to agriculture.

MICHAEL E. BRAITHWAITE

Bemersyde Moss

Permit only; 27ha; SWT reserve
Marsh, shallow loch
April–August

Willow carr and continuous reed canary-grass and sedge marshland surround a central mosaic of open pools and marsh vegetation on this rather wet moss. Nodding bur-marigold and celery-leaved buttercup are among the less common plants present. Over 10,000 pairs of black-headed gull breed on the moss and grasshopper warbler is a typical species of the willow. Many wildfowl visit in winter, when the outflow is adjusted so that the open water area is more extensive.

Cragbank Wood

Permit only; 9ha; NCC reserve
Deciduous woodland
Apply to NCC Galasheils
Spring, summer, autumn

The wood is a mixture of ash, wych elm, alder and hazel with a wide diversity of associated flowering plants, ferns and lichens, which indicate the ancient, undisturbed nature of the site and include some species now extremely scarce in south-east Scotland. The dead and dying timber provides ideal habitat for many species of insect. Herb-rich grasslands at the edge of the wood add variety.

St Abb's Head is notable for its spectacular scenery, seabirds, plants and rich marine life.

Den Wood

NT 145522; 5.6ha; WdT reserve
Mixed woodland
Summer

A locally important woodland on the north-east
bank of the River Lyne, with many broadleaved
species.

Dunhog Moss and Hare Moss

Permit only; 4ha; SWT reserve
Peat bog and fen; loch with reedbeds
July–September

Both these small mosses are noteworthy for their
water beetles; 23 species have been recorded,
some of them relics of the ice ages. *Hydroporus
glabriusculus* is known in Britain only from this
site and a few other localities in the Borders
Region. *Hydroporus elongatus* is similarly restricted
but with one outlying site in Ayrshire. The
complex of willow carr and marshland at Dunhog
includes an interesting sequence from acid bog to
base-rich fen with sedge–bryophyte communities
and three species of tussock-sedge, all of local
distribution in southern Scotland. Grass-of-Parnassus is plentiful at Dunhog and there are
colonies of ringlet and Scotch argus butterflies
there. Little grebe and tufted duck breed on Hare
Moss, which was dammed in the 1960s to create
a lochan, and now has extensive reedbeds.

Duns Castle

NT 778550; 77ha; SWT reserve
Loch, mixed woodland and grassland
April–July

In late spring this mixed woodland reserve is a
riot of colour, with great drifts of early-blooming
wild flowers. In some areas ramsons carpet the
ground, elsewhere there is a sea of bluebells, or
vivid red campion or purple wood crane's-bill;
meadowsweet, foxglove and water avens continue
the succession. Even the conifer plantations here
have a green ferny floor. Beech dominates much
of the woodland but there are also fine mature
oak and ash and occasional stands of slender
poplars. In addition to the many well-known
woodland plants the reserve contains some less
familiar species, including toothwort and the
waxy-flowered common wintergreen.

The Hen Poo, an artificial loch of 7ha, provides
additional habitat diversity. Yellow iris, bulrush
and bogbean grow on the marshy margins and
the plate-like leaves of yellow water-lily float on
the surface. There are water shrew and tench in
the loch and otter occasionally visit, while badger,
roe deer and red squirrel occur in the woodland.

A network of rides and grassy glades criss-
crosses the whole area and these sheltered spots,
together with the variety of food plants present,
ensure that the reserve is rich in butterflies and
moths. Five species of tit have been recorded,
including the very local marsh tit. Pied flycatcher
breed regularly in the nest boxes provided and
chiffchaff are among the warblers present.

Gordon Moss

Permit only; 41ha; SWT reserve
Peat bog with scrub woodland
May–August

The superficially uniform lichen-covered jungle
over much of this moss conceals a considerable
diversity of habitat which is due to the effect of
old peat workings and to the presence of strong
springs of mineral-rich water. The woodland
includes birch, willow (six species), alder and
aspen and shelters roe deer and a varied bird
population. Six species of orchid, including coralroot orchid and lesser butterfly-orchid, occur;
lesser wintergreen, moonwort and greater spearwort are also present.

The site is a good locality for a number of moths
which are of limited distribution in Scotland;
these include small chocolate tip, miller, northern
drab, powdered Quaker and beautiful carpet.
Gordon Moss also supports a colony of small
pearl-bordered fritillary butterflies.

Hoselaw Loch and Din Moss

Permit only; 20ha; SWT reserve
Open water and raised bog
October–March: wildfowl; July: flowers

Situated at 200m and surrounded by farmland,
the 12ha Hoselaw Loch is an important refuge for
wintering wildfowl. Flocks of pink-footed and
greylag geese, mallard and wigeon use the open
water for roosting, and diving duck such as
goldeneye, pochard, tufted duck and goosander
feed there regularly. Curlew, lapwing and snipe
frequent the muddy shores in summer. The domed
peat of Din Moss is up to 10m deep and carries
heather, crowberry, bilberry and cranberry. Along
the edge a strip of alder, birch and willow provides
cover for roe deer and woodland birds. Where
bog and loch meet there is a rich fen vegetation
with cowbane and greater pond-sedge.

Lindean Reservoir

NT 5128; 14ha; Borders RC
Reservoir with island and woodland
Hide; leaflet from BRC; further information from BRC
ranger, tel. St Boswells 2330
April–August

The western end of this reservoir, also used for
angling, is managed as a nature reserve. The
mineral-rich water supports a good variety of
aquatic life. Some 200 flowering plants have been
recorded in the area, among them grass-of-
Parnassus, skullcap and early marsh-orchid. The
reservoir is locally important for breeding and
wintering duck; whinchat, sedge warbler and
linnet breed in the area.

Pease Dean

NT 790705; 31ha; SWT reserve
Mixed coniferous and broadleaved woodland
Steepest parts are dangerous
April–August: woodland plants; spring, autumn: migrants

The reserve has two arms: one follows the Pease Burn from close to where it enters the sea, the other follows the Tower Burn. The area nearest the sea is an open valley with grassland, gorse and alder beside the burn; upstream, where the two burns merge, the valleys become steeper. Here, on well-drained soils, there is ancient woodland of sessile oaks but elsewhere the soils have been enriched by leaching of minerals from the upper levels and there is a dense canopy of ash, elm and sycamore.

Plora Wood

NT 305366; 21ha; WdT reserve
Mixed woodland
Spring, summer

Much of the wood is now planted with beech and conifers, but it is an ancient site which still retains many of its interesting plants and animals.

St Abb's Head

NT 9168; 97ha; NTS SWT reserve
Sea cliffs and grassland
Visitors' centre open April–September from 10am to 5pm
Leaflet from NTS, SWT reserve ranger, or at car park
April–July: breeding birds; Spring, autumn: migration

Spectacular cliff scenery, a vast seabird colony, rich marine life and a varied flora make this a site of unusually diverse interest. Some 10,000 guillemot breed here, packed in serried ranks on steeply sloping ledges and the tops of stacks. Several thousand kittiwake cling to the smaller peaks and pinnacles; brooding razorbill, wings adroop, tuck themselves into the larger niches; and fulmar cackle from ledges surrounded by hanging gardens of common scurvygrass, thrift and sea campion.

Deep gaps or inlets give good cliff viewing in many places, while the headlands afford extensive views out to sea. In summer flights of gannet pass to and from their BASS ROCK (Lothian) breeding ground, but it is during migration periods, especially in autumn, that the greatest variety of bird species occurs. Sooty and Manx shearwater regularly pass offshore, as do arctic and great skua. The Mire Loch is visited by waders pausing there on their travels. The small passerines recorded include such uncommon visitors as red-breasted flycatcher, greenish warbler and yellow-browed warbler, wind-drifted across the North Sea to this prominent stretch of coast.

Behind the cliffs short-turfed grassland rolls in a series of humps and hollows down to the narrow ribbon of the Mire Loch in the valley bottom. Some of the humps are of mineral-rich rock; others give rise to acid soil and the vegetation is correspondingly varied.

The reserve's insect life is varied. Migrant species include Camberwell beauty butterfly and the large and spectacular death's head hawkmoth. More regularly seen are small copper, common blue and grayling butterflies and some of the larger day-flying moths, such as yellow shell, silver Y and colourful six-spot burnet.

Strong tides sweep along this exposed stretch of coast and help to ensure that the sea remains unpolluted. Skin divers and marine biologists take advantage of the good conditions to study the life of the submarine kelp forests which can be no more than glimpsed from land at very low tide.

St Ronan's Wood

NT 327370; 22ha; WdT reserve
Mixed deciduous woodland

This area is part of an important landscape in the Tweed Valley. St Ronan's Wood forms an attractive backdrop to the town of Inverleithen and contains many fine specimens of oak, beech, sweet chestnut and Scots pine. At the north end of the wood is St Ronan's Well, a mineral water spring, and to the west is an Iron Age fort with excellent views along the Tweed Valley. Access is from St Ronan's Terrace off the A72 in Inverleithen.

Whitlaw Mosses

Permit only; 19ha; NCC reserve
Valley fens
Access arrangements from NCC Galashiels
June–August
These fens in shallow valleys, fed by base-rich ground water, show succession from swamp communities through tall herb to willow scrub. The rich flora includes marsh-marigold, water avens, marsh hawk's-beard, round-leaved winter-green, cowbane, bog sedge and coralroot orchid.

Whitlaw Wood

NT 500132; 9ha; SWT reserve
Broadleaved valley woodland
Spring, summer

The underlying Silurian rocks of greywackes and shales are base-rich in parts and support elm–ash woodland with pockets of beech and oak; coppiced hazel is common, with bird cherry, rowan and blackthorn. The rich ground flora of primrose, early-purple orchid, woodruff, wood-sedge, goldi-locks buttercup and sanicle is enhanced by wet flushes running down the steep slopes with angelica and meadowsweet. Great spotted wood-pecker, woodcock and sparrowhawk all frequent the wood and an adjoining river enhances the reserve.

Yetholm Loch

NT 803279; 26ha; SWT reserve
Loch, willow scrub and marshland
No access to marsh
July: flowers; October–March: wildfowl

The marshland at the inflow end of the loch provides the principal interest of this site, which is enriched by drainage from the surrounding farmland. The vegetation types represented include willow carr and greater spearwort–bottle sedge fen. Great crested grebe, shoveler, teal and pochard breed regularly; winter visitors include whooper swan and pink-footed goose.

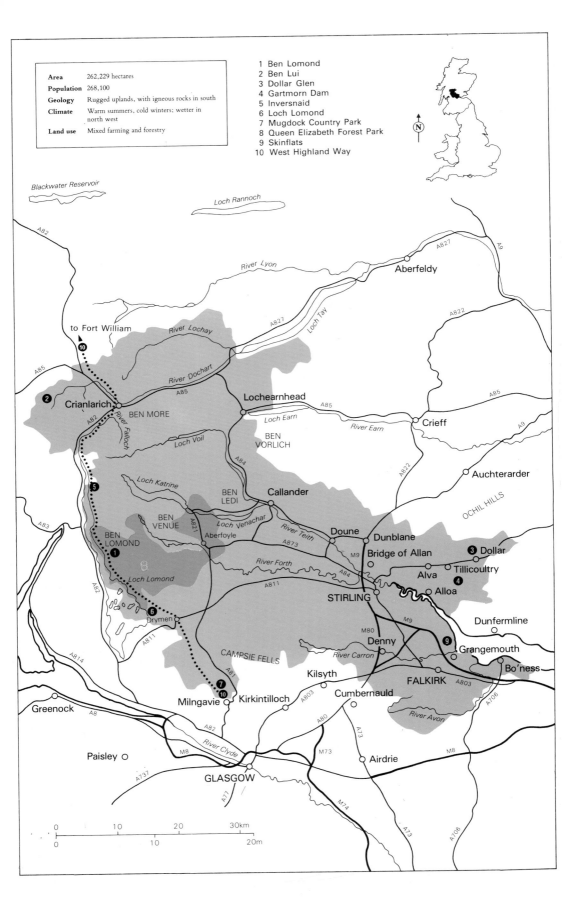

Area	262,229 hectares
Population	268,100
Geology	Rugged uplands, with igneous rocks in south
Climate	Warm summers, cold winters; wetter in north west
Land use	Mixed farming and forestry

1 Ben Lomond
2 Ben Lui
3 Dollar Glen
4 Gartmorn Dam
5 Inversnaid
6 Loch Lomond
7 Mugdock Country Park
8 Queen Elizabeth Forest Park
9 Skinflats
10 West Highland Way

N

Blackwater Reservoir

Loch Rannoch

River Lyon

Aberfeldy

to Fort William

River Lochay

River Dochart

Loch Tay

Crianlarich

BEN MORE

Lochearnhead

Crieff

River Earn

Loch Earn

BEN VORLICH

River Fillan

Loch Voil

Auchterarder

Loch Katrine

BEN LEDI

Callander

OCHIL HILLS

BEN VENUE

Loch Venachar

River Teith

Doune

Dunblane

Dollar

BEN LOMOND

Aberfoyle

River Forth

Bridge of Allan

Alva

Tillicoultry

Loch Lomond

STIRLING

Alloa

Dunfermline

Drymen

CAMPSIE FELLS

River Carron

Denny

Grangemouth

Bo'ness

Kilsyth

FALKIRK

Milngavie

Kirkintilloch

Cumbernauld

River Avon

Greenock

River Clyde

Paisley

Airdrie

GLASGOW

0	10	20	30km

0	10	20m

Central

The majestic peaks and shapely ridges of the southern Grampians, from Ben Lomond in the west to Ben Vorlich in the east, occupy almost half of Central Region and beckon the northbound visitor. However, the charm of these distant hills is only one of several attractions in a small area of Scotland in which scenic variety is the key to diversity of wildlife.

The changes in landscape from north to south are quite dramatic. North of the Highland Boundary Fault are windswept, towering bens and steep-sided, often loch-filled glens. These have been moulded by moving ice from a base of ancient sediments which were altered and contorted beyond imagination to form massive folds of schist, slate and grit, of which only the foundations now remain.

South of the bisecting fault are the abrupt humps of the Menteith Hills and the gentler terrain of the Braes of Doune, which are formed of sloping sandstone beds, liberally speckled with quartzite pebbles to form 'plum-pudding' rock. Continuing southward, these uplands suddenly give way to the flat Carse of Stirling, only a few metres above sea level, even at Aberfoyle. Its clay bottom is patched with peat mosses and incised by the meandering channel of the Forth, which snakes around the dolerite crags of the Stirling Gap. The Forth Estuary expands between levées which protect the eastern carselands of Falkirk and Clackmannan from the salt-laden tides.

Volcanic activity and faulting produced the precipitous south-facing scarp of the Ochil Hills east of Stirling, while later eruptions of lava created the cliff-edged massifs of the Gargunnock Hills and the Campsie Fells to the west. The Campsies terminate above Killearn in the sugar loaf of Dumgoyne, an old volcano. The smooth undulations in Falkirk and Clackmannan, here and there punctuated by heaps of colliery waste, are of glacial drift which covers the coal measures beneath. In the far south the relatively barren peatlands on the rolling Slamannan plateau yield a more accessible fuel source.

Such contrasts in land form and surface water assure the naturalist of a remarkably compact package of plant communities and wildlife habitats, perhaps unrivalled in the rest of Scotland. This is further enhanced by climatic variation; southern-based plants and insects find their northern outpost here, overlooked by hills which contain the southernmost limits of the arctic–alpine communities. Humid Atlantic air, which in a year drops over 2500mm of rain to the east of LOCH LOMOND, soon gives way to more continental influences east of Stirling, where 1000mm of rain in a year is the norm. Plentiful sunshine during the summer months ripens the farmers' hay and cereal crops two weeks earlier than in moist Strathendrick further west.

The hand of man, as elsewhere, has modified most of the native habitats, nowhere more than in the woodlands. In the Highlands especially, forests of oak, and in the far north Scots pine, were relentlessly felled over the centuries until only a few coppiced remnants of the oak were left to regenerate in the Trossachs and by Loch Lomond; mere vestiges of the Caledonian pine forest now exist near Crianlarich. The open hillsides of grass and heather which replaced the woodland support sizeable herds of red deer as well as the hill sheep and cattle, and spring fires indicate management of heather for red grouse on many estates. However, trees are once again growing in expanding conifer plantations, particularly in Strathyre and in the QUEEN ELIZABETH FOREST PARK, where red squirrel are regaining lost ground and capercaillie lek on forest roads.

The high tops above 800m are perhaps least affected by man and his livestock. Here, alpine turf and dripping rock ledges provide a paradise for botanists, notably on the northern hills of Breadalbane (see BEN LAWERS, Tayside), the Braes o' Balquhidder and on BEN LUI, where saxifrages, speedwells and a host of other plants nestle on the least accessible spots. Here too, the bird-watcher may be lucky enough to glimpse a soaring golden eagle or watch ptarmigan play hide-and-seek among lichen-covered rocks. Further south, the warmer southern slopes of the Ochils have a distinctive flora, while the wooded gorges on the fringes of these uplands, such as DOLLAR GLEN and BALLAGAN GLEN in the Campsies, have much of interest for all kinds of naturalists.

The freshwater lochs in the Highland zone, like Loch Katrine, utilised for its pure water, tend to be deep and cold. But where rivers flow in, valuable wetlands develop on the alluvial soils; the Laggan Fen area where the River Balvaig joins Loch Lubnaig contains several rare plants within its sedgebeds. In addition to the ubiquitous brown trout, char haunt Lubnaig's depths, and in the northern basin of Loch Lomond, the unique powan thrives. The small hill lochans have breeding ducks and gulls. Of the lowland lochs, the best known is the Lake of Menteith whose reed-bordered bays are a summer home to great crested grebe. The Endrick mouth on the Loch Lomond reserve has attracted many rare birds, but its large wintering wildfowl population and wetland plant communities are more important; so too are the large flocks of duck which assemble on the man-made GARTMORN DAM.

FLANDERS MOSS on the carse west of Stirling is the largest raised valley bog in Britain; here a feeling of wilderness is sensed despite the surrounding arable fields. The peat vegetation supports rare insects and a huge gull colony covers the northern part, outside the reserve area. Nearby, otter inhabit the banks of the Forth as they do most major streams; the Region's rivers with their wooded banks and flood-plain meadows add an important element to the lowland wildlife scene.

It is the Forth Estuary, teeming with invertebrate fodder for the nationally important numbers of its wintering wildfowl and waders on its mudflats, which deserves the final words. The out-of-season visitor should pay a visit to SKINFLATS when the incoming tide sneaks towards the saltmarsh edge on a February evening, sharpening the brilliant orange reflections of the refinery flares over Grangemouth. The sight of several thousand waders in massed flight against this backdrop brings into focus the urgent need to protect this most precious and vulnerable of the Region's natural assets.

W.R. BRACKENRIDGE

Ballagan Glen

Permit only; 5ha; SWT reserve
Wooded gorge with rock exposures
Part of the reserve is dangerous
April–June

More than 200 species of flowering plants and ferns have been recorded in this steep and well-wooded glen, which is of geological importance for its exposed Ballagan Beds, a series of narrow bands of variously coloured sandstones. These, forming part of the 45m high west wall of the glen, are very unstable and consequently dangerous.

About 150 species of mosses and liverworts occur. Where the sandstone boulders in the stream bed are kept constantly damp by spray from the falls the liverworts *Scapania aspera* and *Cololejeunea* and the moss *Eucalypta ciliata* are present.

Ben Lomond

NN 3602; 2173ha; NTS–FC reserve
Woodland and mountain heathland
Access by footpath from Rowardennan or Kinlochard
Late spring, summer

Ben Lomond, the most southerly of Scotland's mountains over 1000m, is also one of the most frequently climbed, being less than 50km from the centre of Glasgow. Lying within the QUEEN ELIZABETH FOREST PARK, the lower slopes of the Ben have been planted with conifers, but extensive areas of older oakwoods remain around the Rowardennan car park and to both north and south along the loch shore. These contain an attractive diversity of woodland birds, including treecreeper, wood warbler and redstart.

The upper slopes of the Ben belong to the NTS and are devoted to hill sheep-farming. On the ledges of the north-east cliffs, where sheep cannot graze, a luxuriant moss heath survives and in the wetter areas bog myrtle and willow scrub predominate. Birdlife is rather sparse but there are meadow pipits and grouse in the area. Both roe and red deer live in the woods and a herd of wild goats may occasionally be encountered.

Ben Lui

NN 2626; 2104ha; NCC reserve
Mountainous area
Intending visitors should notify warden at NCC, Ardchatham, by Oban

The northern cliffs of 1200m high Ben Lui are well known for their rich mountain flora. On and below the outcropping mica schists and limestone the vegetation is particularly luxuriant and interesting. On the cliff ledges are large patches of mossy, purple and yellow saxifrage, and round-leaved wintergreen occurs alongside roseroot, globeflower and alpine saw-wort. Mountain avens, mountain bladder-fern and alpine bartsia are particularly abundant.

Black Devon

NS 925929; 0.5ha; SWT reserve
Riverside woodland
April–September

The reserve contains a waterfall and deep pool and forms part of a wildlife site stretching along the Black Devon river. Despite its accessibility kingfisher, heron, dipper and grey wagtail are often seen beside the pool, while red and grey squirrel both occur, along with the very local Daubenton's bat. Less common plants include wood speedwell and green spleenwort.

Dollar Glen

NS 9699 24ha; NTS
Wooded glen
Paths can be dangerous after rain
April–June

Oak is predominant in the woodland clothing the steep slopes of the glen but there is also some ash, wych elm and sycamore. In spring ramsons, celandine, wood-sorrel and dog's mercury carpet the ground, with mosses and golden-saxifrage in the steepest and dampest parts of the gorge. The summer woodland birds include wood warbler and spotted flycatcher.

Flanders Moss

Permit only, 255ha, SWT and NCC reserve
Raised peat bog
Bog surface can be dangerous
Apply to NCC, Lochleven, Kinross
April–June

These are two of the least disturbed sections of the very extensive bog which once filled the upper Forth Valley. Much of the bog is wet, with *Sphagnum* actively growing in open pools and abundant cottongrass. Heather dominates the drier areas and there is a fringe of birch woodland, giving way to purple moor-grass and bog myrtle along the outer edge of the moss. Cranberry is quite widespread and bog-rosemary, a very local species, is present.

Gartmorn Dam

NS 9294; 67.6ha; Clackmannan DC
Reservoir with wooded island and shoreline scrub
Hide; visitor centre; leaflet from countryside ranger.
Gartmorn Dam House, Sauchie, Alloa, tel. Alloa 214319
All year

This locally important site for wintering wildfowl holds up to 1500 mallard in midwinter, over 100 tufted duck, and smaller numbers of teal, wigeon, pochard and goldeneye. Greylag geese and whooper swan occasionally visit and a few great crested grebe attempt to breed. Three species of orchid and a wide range of aquatic plants are found.

Inversnaid

NN 337115, 374ha, RSPB reserve
Woodland and moorland
Spring, summer

Lying on the eastern shores of Loch Lomond, Inversnaid is a mixture of heather-clad moorland, deep brackeny slopes and woodland, intersected by burns which tumble down to the Loch. The broadleaved woods have exceptional communities of bryophytes and lichens, and buzzards, wood warblers, pied flycatchers and tree pipits all breed. On the shores and beside the burns, dippers, common sandpipers and grey wagtails nest, and black grouse can be seen in the clearings among the bracken and birch. The WEST HIGHLAND WAY passes along the entire length of the reserve, providing excellent views of all the habitats.

Loch Ardinning

NS 564779; 142ha; SWT reserve
Mixed woodland, heather moor, loch
All year round

The main south-east part of the loch is a glacially formed kettle-hole. A dam across the outflow created a long, narrow arm north-west, densely populated with reeds, rushes and sedges and rich in invertebrate life. Water lobelia flowers in the shallows and tufted duck breed. South-west of the loch lies a wet wood of willow, birch and alder while Muirhouse Muir to the east includes local patches of cranberry, bog myrtle and bog asphodel supporting whinchat and cuckoo.

Loch Lomond

NS 3598; 28ha; NCC reserve
Islands and marshy shoreline
Access to mainland section restricted; contact reserve warden, 22 Muirpark Way, Drymen, for advice; organised groups intending to visit Inchcailloch should contact NCC, Balloch
Reserve leaflet from NCC, Balloch; Inchcailloch
Nature trail (4km) leaflet from village shop or boatyard, Balmaha
May–July: breeding birds and flowers;
October–December: wildfowl

This, the largest freshwater lake in Britain, is famous for the beauty of its wooded shores and islands, its unusual variety of fish, and the winter concentrations of wildfowl near its south east corner. All are represented within the reserve which includes the five islands of Inchcailloch, Torrinch, Creinch, Clairinsh and Aber Isle, the marshy hinterland around the mouth of the River Endrick and part of the mainland shore.

Inchcailloch, the largest island, carries a fine example of the woodlands typical of this southern end of the loch and found also in the nearby QUEEN ELIZABETH FOREST PARK. Sessile oak is the dominant species, with alder and ash in the damper areas, Scots pine crowning the rocky summits, and guelder-rose, willow and bog myrtle along the shore. The island lies astride the Highland Boundary Fault and so has a variety of soil types with their associated ground flora. Conglomerate sandstone underlies about two-thirds of the island and forms the main ridge; beneath the oaks great wood-rush flourishes. A band of serpentine separates this area from the old red sandstone to the north and provides conditions suitable for lime-loving plants such as maidenhair spleenwort, woodruff, dog's mercury and sanicle. Wavy hair-grass, honeysuckle, heather and bilberry dominate the ground cover on the more acid soils. These oakwoods support a large insect population and there are abundant caterpillars for the woodland birds. The density of wood, willow and garden warblers is particularly high; redstart, tree pipit, great spotted woodpecker and jay also breed.

The most notable fish is the powan, popularly known as the freshwater herring, which is of very limited distribution in Britain. Salmon, sea trout and brown trout are widespread, whereas roach and perch are confined to the richer waters of the southern end. The aquatic invertebrate fauna includes a number of species known from very few other Scottish sites.

A patchwork of swamp, lagoons, fen and willow carr lies to the south of the slow-flowing, meandering River Endrick. Reed canary-grass lines the drainage channels, mats of bogbean, nodding bur-marigold and cowbane float on some of the pools and others are overgrown with mare's-tail, water horsetail and tufted loosestrife. The swamp is colourful in summer with yellow iris, yellow loosestrife, purple-loosestrife, skullcap, marsh willowherb and marsh forget-me-not. Angelica, meadowsweet, bittersweet and cuckooflower flourish where the ground is slightly drier.

The wildfowl breeding population is not large but several thousand ducks and geese spend at least part of the winter in this area. Greylag geese and whooper swan occur regularly and up to 100 Greenland white-fronted geese are sometimes present. Tufted duck, pochard, goldeneye and a few shoveler use the area, with very much larger numbers of mallard, teal and wigeon. If low water levels, exposing the invertebrate-rich mud, happen to coincide with migration periods waders, too, are attracted to the Endrick mouth: over the years no fewer than thirty-two species have been recorded there.

Mugdock Country Park

NS 548775; 206ha; Central RC
Woodland, lake, grassland and moorland
Leaflets from visitor centre on site
All year

Situated below the Campsie Fells this area contains ancient oak woodland, a loch, ponds, grassland and moorland. This variety of habitats provides opportunities to see a wealth of animals and plants.

Queen Elizabeth Forest Park

See map; includes six sites
Guide, maps and leaflet on forest walks from David Marshall Lodge, open daily 9.30a.m.–6p.m.
April–October

To many people the Trossachs, on the eastern edge of this area, are the epitome of Highland scenery.

Much of the western section remains unplanted. Along the eastern shore of LOCH LOMOND are semi-natural oakwoods, in early May alive with bird-song. The ground cover varies. In some parts primroses nestle among the roots, and as the trees come into leaf the woodland is carpeted with lesser celandine, bluebell, dog's mercury and wood-sorrel. Elsewhere there is a jumble of mossy mounds and bilberry humps, with occasional clumps of heather and many small rowan saplings.

Above the band of conifers that backs the shoreline oakwood, the lower slopes of BEN LOMOND carry heather, cross-leaved heath and bracken, dotted with birch regeneration and straggling, shoulder-high bog myrtle. The flora is richest where streams come tumbling down the slopes, for example around the Bealach Buidhe burn. There globeflower, starry and mossy saxifrages and lesser clubmoss flourish, as do the tiny moss-like Wilson's and Tunbridge filmy-ferns.

Higher still on Ben Lomond, on both the upper grasslands and the crags and corries, the variety of arctic–alpines is impressive.

A few ptarmigan frequent the highest summits, and there are raven around the crags and ring ouzel in the corries. The lower moorland holds breeding curlew, skylark and meadow pipit, with occasional pairs of hen harrier and merlin. Northern eggar moths, a large day-flying species associated with heather moors, are one source of food for merlin chicks; their wings may be found scattered around the cock bird's plucking post, among the half-grown wing feathers of fledgling meadow pipits. Red deer and mountain hare are present in moderate numbers on the hills.

The woodlands are perhaps at their most diverse around Aberfoyle and Loch Ard, a mosaic of natural woodland and plantations that vary in age and species. Juniper among birch, spruce beside larch – such contrasts of form and colour belie the myth that afforested areas are monotonous. Species typical of coniferous woodland are found here: the thin, wavering song of goldcrest comes from every stand of well-grown spruce, and red squirrel shred the cones of Scots pine. Oak and birch harbour tree pipit and great spotted and green woodpecker. Roe deer and wren take advantage of both worlds, feeding in the more open areas and finding cover in the denser plantations.

The oakwoods in the park and around the east end of Loch Katrine include examples on both acid and mineral-rich soils. Some, long protected from grazing, have a very natural ground flora, while others, among them the Fairy Knowe wood near Aberfoyle, have been woodland sites for at least 200 years.

Where LOCH LOMOND'S shore is of sand and shingle, miniature storm beaches are formed by the wind-blown waves and are soon colonised by skullcap and gipsywort. Pied wagtail feed on insects along the 'tide-line'. Reed-fringed Dubh Loch, sheltered in contrast, holds little grebe and sometimes goosander; small numbers of wigeon, goldeneye and pochard are often on Loch Ard, Loch Chon and Loch Achray. Common sandpiper, dipper and grey wagtail are frequent along the streams and rivers, heron fish in shallows, and both water vole and otter are known to be present. Some of the lochs are of botanical interest, having marsh and fen communities of types that are scarce in this part of Scotland.

For many visitors the David Marshall Lodge (NN 520015) on a rocky knoll above Aberfoyle is the first stopping place. Its windows offer panoramic views of the hills and forests, and it contains an exhibition on the history and wildlife of the area. From here a short woodland trail leads through the forest to a waterfall. Heading northwards from the Lodge the Duke's Road climbs to a viewpoint above Loch Achray, passing abandoned slate quarries where a tunnel used by hibernating bats has been protected from disturbance by a metal grille. Stonechat are often perched on the gorse bushes along this route.

Not far from the viewpoint at NN 515033 a forest drive branches off right and winds for 11km past Lochan Reoidhte, with its white water-lilies, along the shores of Loch Drunkie, and down to Loch Achray.

The park as a whole offers a wide selection of walking routes, ranging from short circular trails to the five-hour climb to the summit of Ben Lomond and back. An attractive section of the WEST HIGHLAND WAY runs through Rowardennan Forest on Loch Lomond-side and among other cross-country routes are the paths from Aberfoyle to Callander along the Menteith Hills, and from Brig o' Turk through the hills to Balquhidder. There is also a wayfaring course in Achray Forest, and three centres organising pony treks along the forest tracks.

Skinflats

NN 9385; 410ha; RSPB reserve
Inter-tidal mudflats and foreshore
Access restricted; contact RSPB, Edinburgh for advice
September-March

This stretch of the upper Forth is of major importance for passage and wintering waders and wildfowl in an area increasingly subject to industrial development and disturbance. In winter it holds virtually the entire Forth population of pintail, an exceedingly local species in Scotland,

and a very large concentration of shelduck. Significant gatherings of knot, redshank, dunlin, curlew and golden plover, and a wide variety of species, including arctic skua, have been recorded.

Wallacebank Wood

Permit only; 16ha; SWT reserve
Deciduous woodland
Spring, summer

Wood millet, an unusual species in this region, Yorkshire-fog and creeping soft-grass dominate the ground vegetation in this oak woodland. The reserve is interesting historically as it is the site of the Wallace Oak.

West Highland Way

NS 896744 NN 113743; 152km; Central, Highland and Strathclyde RCs
Long-distance way through woodland, moor and mountain
Official guide and map from bookshops
All year

The first officially designated long-distance footpath in Scotland goes through woodland on the shores of LOCH LOMOND, over high moorland and through the wild and rugged mountainous country around GLENCOE (Highland South), and on via Glen Nevis to Fort William; the wildlife interest is correspondingly varied. Adequate planning and equipment are essential for anyone intending to walk the full length of the Way.

Wildfowl frequent the sheltered and marshy south east corner of Loch Lomond.

Dumfries and Galloway

A striking diversity of habitats is found here over a short distance: coastal mudflats, extensive salt-marshes, coastal and river valley oak woodlands, lowland grassland, lochs and south-flowing rivers, and heather moorland leading to uplands with arctic plant communities. The Region's south-facing aspect and geographical position have brought together a unique assemblage of plant and animal species at both their northern and southern limits. Its climate makes Dumfries and Galloway the Devon and Cornwall of Scotland; the coastal strip is mild and dry, but the hilly areas experience higher rainfall, days of snow cover and a quick decrease in temperature.

The Region consists of a line of uplands extending from eastern Wigtownshire to the Moffat Hills in Dumfriesshire. The lower Palaeozoic sediments are intensely folded, with major granite intrusions. Adjacent to the granite is a ring of outcrops of metamorphosed rock. The ridges of the Merrick (843m), the Rhinns of Kells (813m) and Lamachan (716m) all arise above the inner granite basin of the Loch Doon pluton.

The landscape of Galloway has been shaped by the long-continued effect of the rivers and the short-lived influence of the ice ages, and their melt-waters, on the foundation rocks. In the upland areas the forces of erosion are much more apparent than are those of deposition. Classic glaciation features are present at White Coomb in the Moffat Hills, with south-facing corries and a morainic dammed lake, and in the GREY MARE'S TAIL which is the best example of a hanging valley in the Southern uplands. Galloway is the site of an ancient icecap, and glacial troughs occur at Loch Doon and Loch Trool.

Below 303m are the lowlands where glacial deposition has been the chief landscape-forming influence. Extensive drumlin fields occur between Kirkcowan and Burrow Head, Wigtownshire, and persist eastwards towards Dumfriesshire where at Locharbriggs there are impressive kame deposits.

The upland areas were formerly devoted to sheep farming, but its pre-war decline enabled the Forestry Commission to buy very large land holdings. By 1980, 187,500ha was under conifer afforestation, 30 per cent of the region's land area. Throughout the region dairy farming is important; some areas now rear beef, and there is subsidiary arable farming especially on the low ground. Sheep and stock rearing tend to dominate the unplanted moorland areas.

Much of coastal Galloway, parts of the Stewartry, and Dumfriesshire consist of raised beaches. In early spring the coastal cliffs of the south west are covered with the blue shimmer of spring squill. The south-facing aspect of the coastline, shell-rich soils, and the occasional iron-rich podzols contribute to the unusual plant associations. Scots lovage is at its southern limit here and golden samphire at its northern one. Locally along the shingle are patches of oysterplant, a relic of former arctic plant communities.

The sand dune complex of Torrs Warren is of outstanding interest and importance. Solitary bees find the warm sandy soil ideal for egg laying, and butterflies such as pearl-bordered fritillary, dingy skipper and common blue are found here too. The coastal areas are the haunt of peregrine and raven; the latter was once common in upland areas, but afforestation and the removal of sheep have reduced its range and numbers.

The saltmarshes and mudflats of Wigtown Bay, Southwick Merse and the CAERLAVEROCK reserve are the feeding and roosting grounds of pink-footed, greylag and barnacle geese, wigeon, pintail, shelduck and thousands of waders. Up to 10,000 golden plover may career in the clear of a January day, or an elusive cloud of dunlin dance away from a peregrine or merlin. Banks of oystercatcher and trails of curlew occur throughout Inner and Outer Solway, but it is only at Carse Bay that large gatherings of knot and pintail occur.

At Glencaple and Drummains the tall reedbeds are bordered by the short sward of sea aster and sea arrowgrass, food plants of the wintering wildfowl. Southerness Merse is the most westerly point in the range of the coastal-breeding natterjack toad, but its stronghold is at Caerlaverock where it breeds in shallow pools and hibernates in sandy banks. The coastal pebble beaches of Galloway at Port William, the saltmarshes and the shingle all provide breeding habitat for waders.

The hinterland contains the agricultural landscape of the Rhinns of Galloway, the home of corn bunting, summering corncrake and in winter hen harrier which roosts nearby in the largest established roost in Britain. Farming threatens the lowland grassland, and DOWALTON is a sensitive jewel in a busy agricultural landscape. Field gentian, dyer's greenweed, bog pimpernel and dense communities of orchids flower on the floor of a drained loch amid the summer hum of hoverflies.

The dales and low hills occupy an extensive area which was once well wooded, but now the woodland is limited to remnants on inaccessible valley sides. On Shinnel Water, the woods are rich in bird cherry; Scaur Water has ash woodland and at Dryfe Water there is hazel. The size, composition and history of the relict oak woodlands of Carstramon, Cree, Caldons, Buchan and Glenhead enable them to make a unique contribution to nature conservation. Cree and Carstramon, considered as a unit, are the best example of this ecosystem and contain rich bryophyte communities. Dog's mercury and bluebell grow in profusion. The woodlands also contain pied flycatcher, redstart, green woodpecker, wood warbler and tree pipit, together with purple hairstreak, the localised and declining butterfly which flights in July.

In the lowlands, the glacial deposits and climate have encouraged blanket peat which at Raeburn Flowe still bears typical bog plant communities. Afforestation and peat extraction put the future of such rich ecosystems at risk.

At Lochmaben, Dumfriesshire, the Mill Loch is the habitat of vendace, a relict fish species, and the wetlands of CASTLE AND HIGHTAE LOCHS contain the localised narrow-leaved bulrush. The most extensive wetland within the region is the KEN–DEE complex, noted for its wintering wildfowl. In summer the site contains breeding shoveler and great crested grebe; its shores are surrounded by varied and rich wetland plant communities with numerous dragonflies. The nearby oak woodlands echo on summer evenings to the sound of reeling grasshopper warbler, the yaffle of green woodpecker, and the soft croaks of roding woodcock. The wetlands host that gem of the flood plains, the globeflower. Once again plants at their southern limits, such as spignel, and northern limits, for instance saw-wort, occur. The wetlands of the Upper Cree are dominated by bottle sedge and the river is the haunt of kingfisher, goosander and otter. Carlingwark contains winter gatherings of shoveler, tufted duck and goldeneye, and even the occasional American pied-billed grebe.

The undulating moorland of Grobdale–Laughenghie–Laghead represents probably the best golden plover, curlew and snipe breeding area in the mid-altitude parts of the region. Surrounded by afforestation, this habitat, which also contains ring ouzel, whinchat, kestrel, merlin, hen harrier, short-eared owl, peregrine and golden eagle, characterises the true open hill spirit of Galloway – but for how long?

In the western part of the region the recent increase in acid precipitation, on an acid geology where the main land use is conifer afforestation, gives cause for concern about the lochs and rivers. Afforestation near the edges of water catchment feeder streams exacerbates a water-quality problem at such places as Loch Dee. The increased acidification of waters threatens the successful breeding of trout, salmon and amphibians, together with a range of aquatic invertebrates which form links in the complex food chains. The proposed afforestation of a further 60,000ha by the year 2000 would have serious implications for the overall ecology of the area, in which agriculture, recreation and nature conservation all compete with forestry.

PETER G. HOPKINS

Caerlaverock

NY 0365; 5585ha; NCC reserve
Saltmarsh, foreshore and freshwater marsh
The mudflats are dangerous
No access to sanctuary area; recommended access points at NY 018653 and at Eastpark, NY 052656
Leaflet from watchtower or warden, Tadorna,
Hollands Farm Road, Caerlaverock
October–March

This great saltmarsh or merse is important as one of the largest unreclaimed saltmarshes in Britain, as the most northerly breeding site of the natterjack toad, and as a winter feeding ground for the entire Spitsbergen population of barnacle geese. It is a dangerous area as the flats are intricately laced with deep, muddy creeks which fill with alarming speed as the tide comes in. The wildfowl can be observed most conveniently and safely at EASTPARK wildfowl refuge, where special facilities are available. Visitors wanting to go out on to the mudflats should first seek advice from the warden.

Up to 5000 pink-footed geese sometimes roost on the merse in the first three months of the year, with small numbers of greylag geese. Also important for pintail, this is one of the few Scottish locations where flocks of 1000 or more are recorded. Several hundred mallard, wigeon and teal spend much of the winter in the area. Large numbers of waders also pass through, with as many as 24 species being recorded in one season. Oystercatcher are by far the most numerous, with the peak roosting numbers, in October, estimated at around 15,000.

Red fescue dominates the vegetation on the merse, which is dotted with sea asters and has unusually extensive populations of saltmarsh flatsedge and saltmarsh rush. These plant communities provide valuable grazing for cattle in summer as well as for geese in winter. On the western side of the merse the force of wind and tide is resulting in erosion, with great hunks of muddy turf being torn off and deposited on the flats below. At the eastern side, corresponding accretion is taking place.

The thriving colony of natterjack toad, a specially protected species, is based on the pools fringing the saltmarsh. These very vocal creatures find there the warm, shallow, unshaded water necessary for successful breeding.

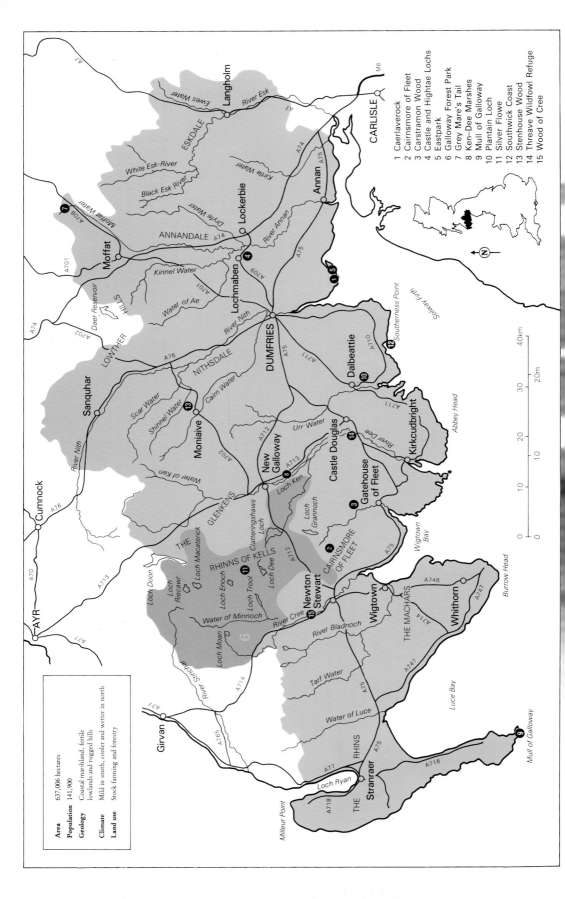

Area 637,006 hectares
Population 141,900
Geology Coastal marshland, fertile lowlands and rugged hills
Climate Mild in south, cooler and wetter in north
Land use Stock farming and forestry

1 Caerlaverock
2 Cairnsmore of Fleet
3 Carstramon Wood
4 Castle and Hightae Lochs
5 Eastpark
6 Galloway Forest Park
7 Grey Mare's Tail
8 Ken-Dee Marshes
9 Mull of Galloway
10 Plantain Loch
11 Silver Flowe
12 Southwick Coast
13 Stenhouse Wood
14 Threave Wildfowl Refuge
15 Wood of Cree

Cairnsmore of Fleet

NX 5266; 1922ha; NCC reserve
Granite uplands
Access restricted: contact warden, Falbae
Cottage, Falbae, Creetown for advice
Leaflet from warden or NCC, Balloch
June–September

The great granite hump of Cairnsmore, falls away
to the east in sheer cliffs and steep slab-strewn
slopes around a basin of undulating moorland.
On much of the lower ground the vegetation is
dominated by purple moor-grass, heather and bog
myrtle, with bog mosses in the wetter areas. Bare
white granite is exposed in many places higher
up, but on the long spur below the Knee of
Cairnsmore heather-covered peat banks stand
proud of the general ground level. No paths or
tracks penetrate the interior of the reserve.

The lower ground was formerly grouse moor;
more recently it has carried sheep and a flock is
still maintained. Past management has included
drainage, and stumps buried deep in the peat
demonstrate the previous existence of tree cover
on the site; present management is aimed at
encouraging a more widespread growth of heather.

The Cairnsmore of Fleet is now the only site in
the district including unafforested ground through
an altitude range from 167m up to the summit at
710m. The reserve is important for upland red
deer, feral goat, golden plover and raven.

Carstramon Wood

NX 592605; 83ha; SWT reserve
Ancient deciduous woodland
Spring, summer, autumn

The main tree species is sessile oak, with ash,
alder, hazel and birch in this, one of the most
attractive woodlands in Galloway renowned for
its display of bluebells. The wood is also good for
birds, and butterflies include purple hairstreak.

Castle and Hightae Lochs

NY 0881 and 0880; 137ha; Annandale and Eskdale DC
reserve
Lochs, reedbeds and woodland fringe
January–March

These lochs are of most interest after the shooting
season, when considerable numbers of greylag
geese, and sometimes also pink-footed geese,
come in to roost on Castle Loch. Smallish numbers
of mallard, wigeon and tufted duck are present
for much of the winter. Hightae Loch is rich in
invertebrates and there is a good variety of small
birds in the woodlands around the lochs.

Dowalton Marshes

Permit only; 61.5ha; SWT reserve
Willow carr and grassland on site of drained lake
Access to some areas restricted March–June
May–July: flowers; October–March: wildfowl

Both dry and wet meadow, as well as willow
carr, are represented on this reserve and the

correspondingly varied flora includes some 180
flowering plants. Among the more interesting
species present are brooklime, lesser water-
plantain, marsh pennywort, quaking-grass, dyer's
greenweed and several orchids. The drier patches
of woodland contain birch, elder, hawthorn and
wild roses; five species of warbler are among the
birds breeding there. In winter much of the carr
and the reed canary-grass is flooded and attracts
a variety of duck and also whooper swan. The
reserve is rich in dragonflies, hoverflies and
butterflies, although surrounded by intensively
cultivated farmland.

Drummains Reedbed

NX 984610; 5.5ha; SWT reserve
Reedbed and saltings
Hide
*April–June flowers, breeding birds; October–March:
wildfowl and waders*

Part of the Solway tideflats, this reserve includes
farmland, reedbed, saltings and mudflat, and part
of the tidal channel of the River Nith. Reed
bunting and sedge warbler breed in the reedbeds,
which serve as a winter roost for a variety of
species. The merse, with its sea plantain, sea aster
and common saltmarsh-grass, is grazed in winter
by wigeon and barnacle geese. The mudflats
support breeding shelduck and wintering pintail,
mallard, curlew, oystercatcher and dunlin.

Eastpark

NY 052656; 524ha; WT–NCC reserve
Farmland and tidal merse
Open daily 16 Sept–30 April (except 24 and 25 Dec) at
11a.m. and 2p.m., no access to merse; all visitors escorted
by warden; groups limited to 50, and those of 20+ should
book, tel. Glencaple 200. Observation buildings and hides;
educational display; binoculars for hire; leaflets from
Eastpark or Slimbridge (Gloucestershire)
Early October–end March

This extensive wildfowl refuge often holds the
entire Solway population of barnacle geese (up to

A bluebell glade in Carstramon oakwood.

8500) and a good variety of other wildfowl, waders and birds of prey. Most of the farmland around Eastpark was purchased by the Wildfowl Trust to ensure undisturbed feeding grounds, while the merse section lies within the Sanctuary Area of CAERLAVEROCK.

The barnacle geese start arriving from Spitsbergen early in October, reach peak numbers in November, and leave in mid-April. Pink-footed geese arrive later and only reach their maximum of around 3000 in late January or early February. Very much smaller numbers of greylag geese are also fairly regular in winter.

Among the most important and impressive visitors are whooper and Bewick's swan. Whooper numbers are highest in November–December, Bewick's slightly later. The flock of Bewick's swan has been gradually building up since the refuge was established; now over 70, it is by far the largest regular gathering of this species in Scotland.

Over 2000 wigeon and teal winter on the grassland and small numbers of pintail, gadwall, shoveler, pochard and tufted duck are regularly recorded; in recent years blue-winged teal and scaup have been observed. The waders most often seen are curlew, golden plover and lapwing, but many others visit occasionally including long-billed dowitcher, black-tailed godwit and green and wood sandpiper.

Fountainbleau and Ladypark

NX 986772; 5.5ha; SWT reserve
Wet woodland
Visitors should keep to the marked path
Nature trail (1km); leaflet from SWT
April–June

Deep drainage ditches criss-cross this woodland, which has a high watertable and frequently floods. As a result abundant rotten birches support prolific fungi and mosses. The decaying stumps are also important as nesting sites for the resident willow tits. Alder grows along the ditches, willows are widespread and a few oak, rowan and hawthorn grow in the driest areas. Marsh cinquefoil, marsh pennywort, marsh thistle, woody nightshade and water-pepper are characteristic plants of the wetter ground, with climbing corydalis and common St John's-wort on drier soil. In summer willow warbler, sedge warbler, reed bunting and redpoll are numerous; long-tailed tit, spotted flycatcher and tree pipit are also known to nest. Water vole and water shrew frequent the ditches and roe deer breed in the wood.

Galloway Forest Park

See map; includes eight sites
Guide from HMSO bookshops and forest centres; trail guides at Caldons and Talnotry caravan sites; further information from Clatteringshaws Deer Museum, open April–October, 10a.m.–5p.m., or recreation forester, Glentrool Forest, Bargrennan, Newton Stewart
All year

Rugged granite mountains, rushing hill streams with sparkling falls, and trackless wastes of bog combine to create an atmosphere akin to 'wilderness' in much of the unplanted section of the park. Such treeless hill country accounts for nearly 40 per cent of its 66,000ha and offers a great variety of walking routes.

The Merrick, at 843m the highest of the ten hills exceeding 600m, lies at the core of the Range of the Awful Hand, a five-fingered cluster of summits and glens. Crags and corries scar the northern and eastern faces of the Merrick, home of arctic–alpines such as dwarf juniper and starry saxifrage; dwarf willow and stiff sedge grow on the exposed ridges and parsley fern among the loose boulders below. From the summit the view eastwards takes in the much indented Lochs Enoch and Neldricken, lying in the basin of bogs and peat mosses which also holds the SILVER FLOWE reserve. Silvery granite sand lines many of the bays and gives the water an iridescent quality. Beyond lies the remote granite bastion of Mullwharchar.

Trees dominate the view westward too, crowding in around Loch Moan, with its big black-headed gullery, and along either side of the road leading from Bargrennan to Straiton. Here afforestation has had the greatest impact visually and on animal life. Much of the planting here with Sitka spruce and Japanese larch was carried out in the 1950s and early 1960s, so that trees now blanket the landscape. The moorland birds were forced out, to be replaced first by short-eared owl, whinchat and willow and grasshopper warbler, which find suitable food and nest sites among the rank growth associated with young plantations. As the trees closed up, creating a dark jungle of leafless twigs, these species left too. Today few birds are seen away from the forest edge, the rides and the few small unplanted enclaves.

In more recent plantings the ranks of conifers have been broken up, creating vistas, introducing a greater diversity of species, retaining areas of natural woodland, and leaving land unplanted around lochs and streams. Around Glen Trool substantial remnants of the original oak and birch woodlands survive at either end of the loch, at Buchan, Glenhead and Caldons. They hold a good variety of flowering plants and ferns and in summer are alive with birds such as wood warbler, redstart, tree pipit and pied flycatcher, the last often choosing nest boxes in preference to natural holes. The ground to the north is largely unplanted, comprising open rocky moorland of heather, purple moor-grass, rushes and bracken. The plantations stretch irregular fingers up the hillside.

On the eastern boundary, in Bennan Forest, the woodland strip along the shore of Loch Ken is predominantly alder, with birch and willow. Bog asphodel, bog myrtle, hemlock water-dropwort, sneezewort, angelica and greater bird's-foot-trefoil grow in this wet woodland, also the habitat of willow tit.

The Bennan Forest includes the oldest plantations in the park, dating from 1922, of Scots pine, European larch, Douglas fir, and Norway and Sitka spruce. Many are now mature and felling has started. Nightjar 'churr' in summer in the clearings and flit silently along the rides at dusk; green woodpecker breed here and little owl have been seen.

Red deer can be seen both in their wild state and in the big enclosure on Brockloch Hill, beside the A712 and not far from the Clatteringshaws Deer Museum. Between the deer park and Murray's monument an enclosure holds a flock of the multi-coloured feral goats seen on the remoter hills.

Other animals include red squirrel, fox, rabbit and mountain hare. Wild cat are absent but there are a few badger and otter have been increasing since otter-hunting ceased in the area. Mink are regrettably widespread but grey squirrel have not yet arrived. Fallow deer, originally from a deer park, occur only in Kirroughtree Forest. In recent years attempts have been made to re-introduce pine marten, once native. They have been seen on several occasions since and it is hoped that they may soon successfully establish themselves.

Dragonflies frequent many of the park lochs in late summer and early autumn. One of the easiest places to see them is beside Stroan Loch, near the southern end of the Raiders' Road Forest Drive.

Although most of the recreational facilities are along the southern fringe of the forest and around Loch Trool, opportunities for exploration and discovery are just as great in Carrick Forest to the north, with its scattered lochs of varying size and type, and in Clatteringshaws Forest to the east. Those who can spend several days on the hills and moors may sight hen harrier – there is a communal winter roost of around 30 birds in one boggy area; merlin – still present although decreased in numbers; or one of Galloway's golden eagles – sadly unsuccessful breeders in recent years. Short-eared owl, black grouse, buzzard and possibly raven may be seen, although the last has become scarcer with the absence of sheep carrion from the hills. Even short trips may reveal the unexpected – golden pheasant in Kirroughtree Forest, grass-of-Parnassus and fairy flax near Murray's monument, or even (as in 1976) a nuthatch in Glen Trool.

Grey Mare's Tail

NT 182150: 1016ha: NTS
Grass heath, cliffs, loch and waterfall
Paths and slopes slippery: take great care
Further information from NTS, Edinburgh,
or ranger on site in summer
April–August

Falling some 60m from the lip of a hanging valley, this is one of the highest waterfalls in Britain. Lush vegetation flourishes on the wet and inaccessible sides of the gorge; heather, roseroot, harebell, wood-rush, scabious, goldenrod, dog's mercury and wood sage are among the more obvious species. Where the cliffs give way to scree, however, all accessible plants are hard grazed by the multi-coloured feral goats, which scrabble their way across astonishingly steep slopes, starting a series of stone slides as they go.

Above the fall Loch Skeen lies in an upland basin, with lime-rich cliffs breaking the rolling grassland to west and south; these cliffs have an unusually rich flora for the southern uplands. Common gull nesting by Loch Skeen and raven playing above the cliffs are among the breeding birds of the area.

Ken–Dee Marshes

NX 6376 and 6869: 145ha: RSPB reserve
Marsh and deciduous woodland
Access restricted: visiting by arrangement only but
viewing possible from roadside
October–March: wildfowl; May–June: breeding birds

Loch Ken and the River Dee wind for 16km along the valley floor, fringed variously with marsh, woodland and fields. Peninsulas and bays scallop the shores and extensive mudflats are exposed at the northern end when hydroelectric activities lower the water level. The two areas comprising this reserve include a large canary-grass marsh, dotted with willows and seamed by open channels; wet meadows with birch, hazel and willow scrub; and fine open oak woodlands.

This is the wintering ground of the largest mainland flock of Greenland white-fronted geese, currently about 300 strong. Much larger numbers of greylag geese regularly roost on the river, while pink-footed, barnacle and bean geese and whooper swan all occur occasionally. Pintail and shoveler regularly nest and are often present in autumn among the dabbling ducks gathered near the north-end marshes. The muddy shallows there also attract waders passing along the natural migration route through the valley.

In summer the patches of wet meadow and adjoining marsh are alive with sedge and grass-hopper warbler. In these rough grasslands, once cut for hay, meadowsweet, valerian and marsh cinquefoil are abundant and there are good stands of such local species as spignel, saw-wort and wood bitter-vetch. On slightly higher ground gnarled old hawthorns and crab apples, and the occasional guelder-rose, are scattered through a jungle of bracken, birch, hazel and willow. This dense cover is favoured by the resident willow tits whose distinctive calls can be heard all year.

Although limited in area the mature oakwoods contain many fine trees and show signs of regeneration. Pied flycatcher and wood warbler breed in these woodlands and green and great spotted woodpecker occur in the vicinity.

Kirkconnell Flow

Permit only: 42ha; NCC reserve
Raised bog
Permit from warden, Tadorna, Hollands Farm Road,
Caerlaverock
May–July

The most important feature of this remnant peat moss is its extensive colonisation by Scots pine; birchwood is also present on some parts. Typical mire species are widespread and the reserve has a rich and varied insect population.

Knowetop Lochs

Permit only; 27.5ha; SWT reserve
Moorland with two small lochs
Nature trail (4km); leaflets, details with permit
April–July

Birch woodland separates the two small lochs, which are fringed with reedswamp, bog and willow carr. The surrounding moorland ranges from wet peat moss to grassy heath, and a belt of conifer plantation gives shelter to the north. There are four species of willow in the marshy thickets; whorled caraway, bogbean and intermediate bladderwort in the bog; petty whin among the heather of the drier moorland, and grass-of-Parnassus on the heath.

Four species of owl hunt over the reserve and many small woodland birds breed among the birches and willows. In spring blackcock display at a lek nearby, snipe drum over the bog and woodcock 'beat the bounds' of their territory. Whooper swan are regular winter visitors, as are several species of duck. Buzzard, kestrel, sparrowhawk and hen harrier are not uncommon birds of prey seen over the moors.

Mull of Galloway

NX 157305; 16ha; RSPB reserve
Sea cliffs
May–July

Rising to a maximum height of 87m, this rugged cliff supports a moderate-sized colony of seabirds, including cormorant, shag, kittiwake, guillemot,

razorbill and fulmar. Spring squill and purple milk-vetch are abundant on the cliff top; roseroot and Scots lovage are also present. Rock sea-spurrey, golden samphire, rock samphire and rock sea-lavender are at their northern limit here.

Plantain Loch

NX 841602; 4ha; FC
Shallow loch
July–September

This small loch is notable for the extensive colony of oblong-leaved sundew on its northern shore and for its dragonflies, many of which, trapped among the sundews, can be examined at close range. Species positively identified include common aeshna, four-spotted libellula, large red damselfly, common ischnura, green lestes, common blue damselfly and Scottish sympetrum; others probably also occur.

Silver Flowe

NX 4782; 191ha; NCC reserve
Blanket bog
Access restricted: contact warden, Falbae Cottage, Falbae, Creetown
May–August

Within this reserve, situated on the floor of a glacial valley in one of the remoter parts of the GALLOWAY FOREST PARK, lies the most varied and least disturbed area of acid peatland in southern Scotland. The seven distinct bog areas together represent a unique series of mire types.

Boggy peatland pools lie below the rugged hills in the heart of the Galloway Forest Park.

Colourful feral goats can be seen close to the road from Clatteringshaws to Newton Stewart.

Southwick Coast

NX 9155; 16ha; SWT reserve
Coast, marsh and wood
Path down track to Needle's Eye
All year

This area is of outstanding importance because of the vast flocks of geese (greylag, pink-footed and barnacle), duck and waders that overwinter. On the landward side a stranded cliffline supports a unique ancient oakwood. The presence of hazel and holly in the woodland bears testimony to its undisturbed character and the rich ground flora with early-purple orchid confirms this. Base-rich springs flush the lower slopes of the woodland and then flow into an area of brackish water fen, transitional to saltmarsh with sea lavender.

Stenhouse Wood

NX 795930; 18.4ha; SWT reserve
Deciduous woodland
Spring, summer, autumn

A fine colony of toothwort, which is parasitic on hazel and other trees, is found in this mixed deciduous wood. Oak, wych elm and ash are the most common trees and the understorey contains rowan, hazel, hawthorn and plentiful bird cherry. The woodland floor is dominated by dog's mercury, ferns and mosses.

Threave Wildfowl Refuge

NX 7462; 348ha; NTS
River, islands and marshes
Hide; further information from visitor centre at
NX 753605, leaflet from NTS
Open 1 November–end March

The marshes provide good feeding grounds for wildfowl, especially when they are flooded. Greylag geese, wigeon, mallard and teal are all regular autumn and winter visitors. A hide on the old railway at NX 745613 offers a good viewpoint; the Dee itself is best seen from NX 740619 or NX 744625 (access from Kelton Mains Farm).

Tynron Juniper Wood

Permit only; 5ha; NCC reserve
Shrub woodland
Permit from warden, Tadorna, Hollands Farm
Road, Caerlaverock
April–July

A dense growth of columnar and prostrate juniper is the main feature of this reserve, on which the regeneration of this species is being studied. A few ash and wild cherry are present among the juniper and the flora is quite varied. Juniper carpet and juniper pug moth have been recorded.

Wood of Cree

NX 382708; 239ha; RSPB reserve
Deciduous woodland, marsh, moorland
Spring, summer

There are references to the Wood of Cree as early as the thirteenth century and the reserve forms part of the largest remaining ancient woodland in the south of Scotland. Much of the area consists of overgrown coppice of birch, ash, hazel, rowan and willow, which were last cut in the 1920s. Most of the oaks are of a similar age – about 100 years old, as the woodland was all felled in 1875.

Despite the uniformity of age and lack of management, the wood is rich in birdlife. There is a large population of wood warblers, as well as redstarts, tree pipits, garden warblers and spotted flycatchers. A small number of pied flycatchers and willow tits breed here, both unusual species in Scotland. Tawny owls occur throughout the wood and buzzards and sparrowhawks occasionally nest. Dippers and grey wagtails can be seen along the burns cascading through the wood. The removal of the sitka spruce planted recently on the adjoining moorland will allow the meadow pipits, black grouse and whitethroats to stay here.

Bluebells, primroses, ramsons, cow-wheat and woodruff flourish, while in the marsh loosestrife, sneezewort and meadowsweet occur.

Among the butterflies seen on the reserve are Scotch argus and purple hairstreak.

Fife

In effect Fife is a large promontory dominated on three sides by salt water, and cut off physically from the rest of Scotland by these waters and the mass of the Ochil Hills to the west. This created an isolation that disappeared only with the building of the Forth and Tay road bridges during the 1960s, and made for a particular identity reflected in the past in its proud title, the Kingdom of Fife.

The county's southern shores are lapped by the tides of the Firth of Forth, which exhibits a wide range of habitat as it gradually widens from the infant Firth above Kincardine and flows east under the rail and road bridges. Here the estuary suddenly opens out, with Edinburgh in the distance to the south. On the Fife side are the regular series of villages and towns running east which prompted James VI of Scotland and I of England to describe Fife 400 years ago as 'a beggar's mantle fringed with gold', owing to the importance of these harbours and ports.

The islands of the Forth, in particular the ISLE OF MAY, have long fascinated both locals and visitors. Ranking with FAIR ISLE (Shetland) as one of the two most important east coast migratory points in Britain, since the 1930s this island's reputation as a place where a great variety of birds may be seen has spread far and wide, and the reserve is well worth a visit.

The FIRTH OF TAY, forming Fife's northern coastline, differs from the Forth. It is much more gentle and estuary-like, and the tide goes out a long way to reveal large sand- and mud-banks while trees reach down to the water's edge and reedbeds fringe the shores, the haunt of geese and shelduck.

The eastern littoral – exposed directly to the North Sea – presents a further contrast. The east coast of Scotland possesses few major sand dune systems and Fife is fortunate to have the unique TENTSMUIR at its extreme north eastern corner. At one time this was a wind-blown tract of wilderness, but though its character has been greatly altered by afforestation much of it remains full of interest, especially the eastern coastal strip at Kinshaldy just south of the reserve. This area's maritime plants, birds and insects are markedly dissimilar from those of MORTON LOCHS a few kilometres inland, with its pools, marshes and reeds favoured by wildfowl.

Just to the south is the EDEN ESTUARY, echoing to the cry of rare migrant waders, not far from St Andrews and its famous golf links. From here the coast is rock-girt around most of the East Neuk, and the shore walk brings such strange rock formations as the Rock and Spindle, and compact salt-marshes full of uncommon plants. Rounding Fife Ness and continuing up the Forth the cliffs and braes of Kincraig present a fine spectacle in scenic, wildlife and geological terms; the columnar basalt outcrops and the classic sequence of raised beaches are particularly remarkable. Further west the influence of man is much more pronounced and industrialisation looms large, but this has unexpected wildlife benefits in the large numbers of wintering duck that frequent the offshore waters.

Inland, man's effect on the landscape is even more marked. Until recently much of it was scarred by ugly pit bings and spoil heaps, products of an intensive coal mining industry; but these have now very largely gone, thanks to an imaginative land reclamation policy, to be replaced by such attractive open areas as Lochore Meadows Country Park, which includes a small nature area. The reclamation of other derelict land and its conversion to agriculture emphasises that Fife is predominantly a farming region. While there is still a fair amount of woodland much of it is now coniferous, and arable fields and pasture land dominate. There are no rivers to speak of – the Eden flowing through north east Fife is no more than a wide burn – but several lochs and reservoirs provide the freshwater environment necessary for a diversity of wildlife. Of the few raised bogs remaining, that at BANKHEAD MOSS has been made into a reserve. Moor and heath are now but fragments except in the Lomond Hills, which overlook much of Fife.

The twin peaks of the Lomonds are low by mountain standards, reaching a mere 519m, but they are of considerable interest. Though much affected by grazing and planting they still retain good areas of moorland and rough ground, with rocky outcrops here and there. The Lomonds Hills form a natural lung for Fife and there is a ranger service to give assistance and promote conservation.

To anyone standing on either peak, the broad effect of glaciation on much of the landscape is clear. During the ice ages the glaciers moved west to east, and these flows created an undulating topography pleasing to the eye. To the north east lie the eastern outposts of the Ochils, falling to the Tay on one side and sheltering the fertile Howe of Fife to the south. Both hills and strath are composed of old red sandstone, whereas the inland hump of the East Neuk is capped by dolerite sills and old volcanoes such as Largo Law (as are the Lomonds themselves). These volcanic features also occur in the south and west of the region, but here the underlying rocks belong to the carboniferous, its large coal measures now mostly exhausted. Scarps appear here and there, notably in the Cleish Hills which form part of the boundary between Kinross and Fife.

Owing to its comparative geographical isolation Fife tends to have a microclimate of its own – the fact that the weather in Edinburgh can be quite different from that in Dundee has played no small part in moulding both Fife and Fifers. This is particularly true of the coast, where a low shivering haar or sea fog at times blots out visibility all day while inland the sun is blazing down! Fife can also be subject to biting easterly gales, but its sheltered position does mean that rainfall is low and it shares with East Lothian some of the driest and sunniest spots in Scotland.

The old Kingdom of Fife thus provides a varied range of landscape, scenery and habitat for the lover of both coast and country, especially those with an interest in natural history and wildlife. Although there are as yet comparatively few declared reserves, there are many areas worthy of that status and all have much to offer.

G. H. BALLANTYNE

Bankhead Moss

Permit only; 9ha; SWT reserve
Raised bog
May–September

One of the few surviving in Fife, this peat bog is encircled by farmland. The peat is 7m deep at the centre and, although raised above the surrounding land, carries open pools with at least six different species of actively growing *Sphagnum* mosses. There is a rich growth of lichens among the heather-dominated ground cover. Scattered Scots pine and birch regeneration is taking place towards the centre of the moss and birch woodland is well grown around the fringe.

Cameron Reservoir

NO 470112; 64.4ha; Fife RC reserve
Open water
Access to hide restricted to Scottish Ornithologists Club and Scottish Wildlife Trust members
Winter

The most important pink-footed goose roost in north-east Fife, other wildfowl include tufted duck, mallard, greylag geese, wigeon, teal and goldeneye.

Dura Den

NO 415145; 12ha; WdT reserve/private
Woodland
Most of wood is private but it is all visible from the road and the footpath
Spring, summer

Calciferous sandstone, outcropping as cliffs from the steep wooded sides of a valley cut by the Ceres Burn. The woodland supports a diverse flora and a variety of typical birds and small mammals.

There are several large bat roosts and pipistrelle, brown long eared and Daubenton's bats can be seen in the evening.

Eden Estuary

NO 4819; 891ha; NE Fife DC reserve
Estuary with sandbanks and mudflats
Access points at West Sands (NO 497195) and along shore from Kinshaldy car park (NO 498243)
April–June: breeding birds; August–May: waders and duck

Sandbars and low dunes protect the mouth of this small estuary and make it very sheltered in comparison with St Andrews Bay. Much of the estuary itself is also sandy, but the flats become muddier towards Guardbridge. The reserve is fringed by a number of small but botanically interesting salt-marshes, brackish reedswamps and sand dunes.

The estuary supports large numbers of waders, especially bar-tailed godwit, redshank, dunlin, oystercatcher and knot. It is one of the very few Scottish sites regularly holding more than 100 grey plover and black-tailed godwit, and is visited briefly by many wader species on migration, particularly in autumn. At high tide the waders roost either on Shelly Point, on the north side of the estuary, or on the saltmarsh near Guardbridge. Over 1000 eider sometimes gather off the Eden mouth and many of the birds nesting on TENTS-MUIR bring their ducklings down to the estuary. Rafts of common scoter can often be seen in St Andrews Bay and several hundred mallard, teal and wigeon use the area in winter. Shelduck, which breed around the estuary, are at their peak in March, when the numbers present are of international importance. Common seal regularly visit the Eden and haul out on the sandbanks between Shelly Point and the river mouth.

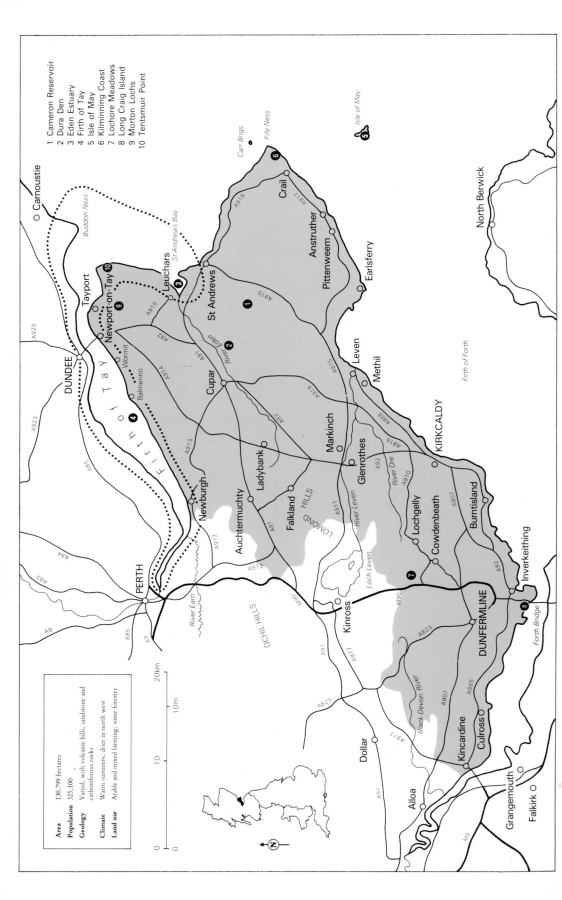

Area   130,799 hectares
Population 325,100
Geology   Varied, with volcanic hills, sandstone and
            carboniferous rocks
Climate   Warm summers; drier in north west
Land use   Arable and mixed farming; some forestry

1 Cameron Reservoir
2 Dura Den
3 Eden Estuary
4 Firth of Tay
5 Isle of May
6 Kilminning Coast
7 Lochore Meadows
8 Long Craig Island
9 Morton Lochs
10 Tentsmuir Point

Carnoustie
Buddon Ness
Fife Ness
Carr Brigs
Isle of May
St Andrews Bay
DUNDEE
Tayport
Newport-on-Tay
Leuchars
St Andrews
Crail
Anstruther
Pittenweem
Earlsferry
North Berwick
Wormit
Balmerino
Newburgh
Cupar
Ladybank
Auchtermuchty
Falkland
Markinch
Glenrothes
Leven
Methil
KIRKCALDY
Burntisland
Lochgelly
Cowdenbeath
Inverkeithing
DUNFERMLINE
Kinross
Dollar
Kincardine
Culross
Alloa
Grangemouth
Falkirk
PERTH

Firth of Tay
Firth of Forth
River Eden
River Earn
River Leven
River Ore
Black Devon River
Loch Leven
Forth Bridge

OCHIL HILLS
LOMOND HILLS
FALKLAND HILLS

A929 A923 A85 A9 A93 A94 A913 A912 A911 A91 A977 A823 A907 A985 A92 A90 M90 M9 A910 A955 A915 A916 A921 A919 A91 A92 A914 A918 A917 A915

N
0   10   20km
0   10m

Firth of Tay (Tay–Eden Estuary)

See map; includes eight sites
Estuary with sandbanks and mudflats
April–June: breeding birds; August–May: waders and duck

The Firth of Tay, with its off-lying Abertay Sands, has long been important for wildfowl and waders and is now recognised as the only site in Britain to hold an internationally significant gathering of eider; the flocks of 15,000 or more on the outer Firth in winter represent 1.3 per cent of the north west European population and 20 per cent of the British stock. In addition the estuary itself attracts nationally important numbers of grey geese and of several wader species, while the contiguous St Andrews Bay and EDEN ESTUARY also hold significant populations of duck and waders.

From Perth to just above its confluence with the Earn the Tay is narrowly confined between steep slopes and fringed with scrub and marsh; this stretch of the river holds comparatively few waterbirds. From Earnmouth to Kingoodie the estuary gradually widens, revealing at low tide a vast expanse of muddy sand, which is divided into discrete banks in a number of places by deep channels.

Many waders feed over the mudflats, especially in autumn and particularly around Invergowrie Bay. Large numbers of redshank, dunlin and oystercatcher are often present, with smaller numbers of bar-tailed godwit, curlew, lapwing, golden plover and knot. Some less common waders, such as black-tailed godwit, ruff, curlew sandpiper and spotted redshank, are also recorded quite regularly. This can be a difficult area to observe but reasonably good views can be obtained around Kingoodie and Port Allen. The extent of the mudflats makes it pointless to visit at low tide, when the birds at the water's edge are far beyond comfortable viewing range.

Many thousands of geese also use this section of the estuary, but only for roosting. The pink-footed geese generally roost over the Dog Bank and Carthagena Bank, while the greylag geese are concentrated around Mugdrum Island, off Newburgh. Most of the pink-footed geese flight off at dawn to north or west, to feed over the rich farmlands of the Carse of Gowrie, Strathmore and Strathearn. The greylags generally fly less far and often feed on the steep grass fields on the south bank of the Tay. There are several points along the minor road from Newburgh to Balmerino which give good views of the flighting geese.

Complaints about the damage caused by the geese are quite often and sometimes justifiably made by local farmers particularly in April. Migrating geese pass through in successive waves that may total 20,000 or more, each batch pausing for a day or two to feed ravenously on the young spring grass before setting off again.

At Dundee the Tay narrows again for about 5km. Common seal are regular visitors to this stretch and can often be seen off Riverside Drive or hauled out on the sandbanks between the road and rail bridges. In winter the sewage outfalls at the Stannergate and near Monifieth are popular with goldeneye, tufted duck and mute swan. In summer this stretch of the river is heavily used for recreation.

East of Tayport both shores are stony with mussel beds for a short distance before giving way to the sands of Barry on the north and of TENTSMUIR on the south. Here again the shores attract waders, including sanderling and knot. The extensive dunes and dune slacks of the Barry Links, lying behind Buddon Ness Point, are of considerable botanical interest and the area also

Morton Lochs: management has increased both habitat and species diversity.

holds an important breeding bird population. Barry–Buddon is used as an army firing range and so has been protected from the recreation pressures experienced by other dunes and beaches nearby.

The Tay's famous gathering of eider is found right at the mouth of the Firth, around the outer Abertay Sands. Because the birds sit well offshore for much of the time and the nearest land is very low-lying, shore-based observers have found it impossible to make realistic counts of these great rafts of duck; over the years estimates ranged from 2000 to 'uncountable masses'. Subsequent aerial counting showed that eider numbers here were at least as high as had been guessed, with over 15,000 birds present in the autumn of 1979.

Incidents of oil pollution in the Firth of Tay demonstrate just how vulnerable a great concentration of seaduck can be: over 2000 eider died as a result of just one oil tanker leak. As the Tay wintering eider flock includes a substantial part of the very important Ythan Estuary breeding flock (see SANDS OF FORVIE AND YTHAN ESTUARY, Grampian), as well as birds that nest in the immediate area, it is vital that the east coast population is protected from pollution of any kind.

Further offshore, the bay is an important area for scoter; both common and a few velvet occur regularly. Red-throated diver are also regular in autumn and winter and can often be seen close inshore near the Eden mouth.

From the mouth of the Eden fine beaches stretch to north and south. Those to the south are crowded with holiday-makers in fine weather, while those of Tentsmuir Point, at the north, are accessible only after a long walk or, in the case of organised groups, by vehicle through prior arrangement with the warden. The beach at Kinshaldy, which can easily be reached from the Forestry Commission car park at NO 498243, offers good opportunities for both seawatching and exploring the dune fringe.

Isle of May

NT 6599; 57ha; NCC reserve
Cliff-girt island
Access by boat from Crail, Anstruther or Pittenweem; summer day trips dependent on tides and weather
Permission required to carry out research on island: contact NCC, Edinburgh Bird observatory, Cupar, with limited residential accommodation: contact Isle of May Bookings Sec., c/o 9 Oxgangs Road, Edinburgh EH10 7BG
May–July: breeding birds; April–May and August–October: migrants

Since a bird observatory was set up in 1934 many thousands of birds have been ringed here, the hundreds of species involved including many 'first records' for Scotland. During the last 30 years some very striking changes have occurred in the breeding populations and also in the island's vegetation. These have been the subject of detailed studies, whose findings are now being used in managing the island's flora and fauna.

Forty years ago much of the Isle of May was carpeted with thrift and sea campion; then, 8000 pairs of four species of tern nested and there were only 800 pairs of gulls. By 1972 the terns, thrift and sea campion had largely gone, unable to survive alongside the 34,000 herring gull and 5000 lesser black-backed gull occupying the island. A gull control programme reduced numbers and in 1979 terns laid on the island for the first time since 1957. There are now 300 pairs of Arctic and common tern.

Some of the other changes have been equally spectacular and even more difficult to explain. Puffin numbered only seven pairs in 1955; now they are by far the most numerous species, with the estimated 18500 occupied burrows stretching to the centre of the island and young birds en route to the sea occasionally wandering into the various buildings. Shag too have shown a vast increase; over 1700 pairs now build their untidy nests on the low cliffs where only six pairs were present in 1934. Nineteen thousand pairs of kittiwake and guillemot also breed, with two thousand razorbill and a steadily expanding population of fulmar.

When strong east winds combine with poor visibility at peak migration times dawn often reveals an astonishing number and variety of tired birds. There could be a big fall of a relatively common species, such as brambling; an assortment of waders; or something really rare – perhaps a Sabine's gull, scarlet rosefinch or gyr falcon.

Rona, the northern tip, is the breeding ground for a large colony of grey seal. Interesting insects occasionally turn up, dragonflies for example, or a large influx of painted lady butterflies, or the rare humming-bird hawkmoth – recorded in 1980 for only the second time this century. The vegetation, both land-based and marine, is still yielding new records after many years of study.

Kilminning Coast

NO 633090; 8ha; SWT reserve
Coastal grassland
Spring, summer, autumn

This stretch of coast is interesting geologically; a wave-cut platform of calciferous sandstone is backed by a good example of a raised beach. There is a variety of interesting plants including a stand of wind-pruned blackthorn scrub. The reserve is a good area for viewing seabirds from the nearby BASS ROCK (Lothian) and ISLE OF MAY.

Lochore Meadows

NT 153953; 24ha; Fife RC reserve
Woodland and ponds
Leaflets available from Park Centre
All year

The pools provide a breeding area for coot, tufted duck and mallard as well as occasionally pairs of shelduck; pochard and wigeon also occur. The alder groves attract siskins, redpolls and mixed flocks of tits and finches. Raptors and waders visit the reserve on passage. Otters occur in the River Ore and roe deer are regular visitors.

Long Craig Island

NT 127123; 0.1ha; SWT reserve
Island
No access but may be viewed from shore at North
Queensferry
Spring, summer

The small, rocky, basalt island lies beneath the
Forth road bridge on the north side of the Firth
of Forth. It is an important nesting ground for
terns with 30 to 60 pairs of common and Arctic
and up to five pairs of roseate terns.

Morton Lochs

NO 4626; 24ha; NCC reserve
Man-made lochs, marsh and woodland
Three hides, one open to the public (suitable for the
disabled) and two accessible to permit holders only;
apply NCC, Edinburgh; booklet on rehabilitation
management from NCC
*April–June: breeding birds; August–January: waders
and wildfowl*

Originally created for fish-rearing, these lochs at
one time attracted large numbers of waders and
wildfowl and had a high conservation interest.
During the 1960s, however, their interest progressively declined as deposition of silt and blowing
sand gradually led to them drying out completely.
The smaller south loch demonstrates the sequence
of plant colonisation, from open water rushes and
reeds to alder and willow carr.

In 1976 a major programme was carried out to
restore the north and west lochs, which involved
complete drainage and mechanical excavation of
large quantities of silt. Islands and promontories,
designed to increase the areas available for nesting, roosting and feeding, were created from the
excavated material and were sown with grass and
planted with rushes, sedges, willow, birch and
hawthorn. The flourishing growth already provides adequate nesting cover and food for a
variety of birds.

Migrant waders, such as redshank, greenshank
and lapwing, visit this loch to feed and rest on
the exposed mud of the sloping shores. Mallard,
teal and mute swan breed, and several other duck
species, including gadwall, are fairly regularly
recorded in autumn and winter. Willow and sedge
warbler are among the small birds breeding in
the scrub woodland and reedbeds, and heron are
often seen on both north and south lochs. Nine
distinct species of willow and a variety of hybrids
are represented on the reserve.

Tentsmuir Point

NO 5027; 515ha; NCC reserve
Foreshore, dunes and scrub woodland
No access to Abertay Sands
*May–August: flowers and butterflies; September–March:
waders and wildfowl*

The foreshore and the offshore Abertay Sands,
which account for more than 80 per cent of the
reserve area, are of major importance as roosting
and feeding grounds for large numbers of waders
and wildfowl. At times the wader population totals
around 9000 and includes significant numbers of
grey plover, sanderling and bar-tailed godwit as
well as dunlin and oystercatcher. In late summer
the offshore sandbanks are white with roosting
gulls and terns, and during the winter both pink-
footed and greylag geese roost there, the former
in the largest numbers. The sands are also used
regularly by common and grey seals, which haul
out on to the banks and lie there like fat slugs.

The dune section of the reserve has been
expanding in area as a result of lateral accretion;
much of the ground is less than 50 years old. All
stages of plant colonisation, from pioneering lyme-
grass on the fore-dunes, through lichen-rich heath,
to alder, birch and willow scrub, are represented
and the flora is rich and varied. Over 300 flowering
plants have been recorded. Grazing by rabbits
keeps much of the herbage short and in summer
the lawn-like turf carries an astonishing abundance of grass-of-Parnassus. Purple milk-vetch,
common and seaside centaury and coralroot
orchid are also plentiful.

A variety of butterflies and moths frequent the
dune area. Grayling are particularly abundant at
times and there are good numbers of small copper,
dark green fritillary and ringlet. Six-spot burnet
moths are frequently seen and the striking orange
and black caterpillars of cinnabar moth can often
be found on ragwort growing near the woodland
edge of the reserve.

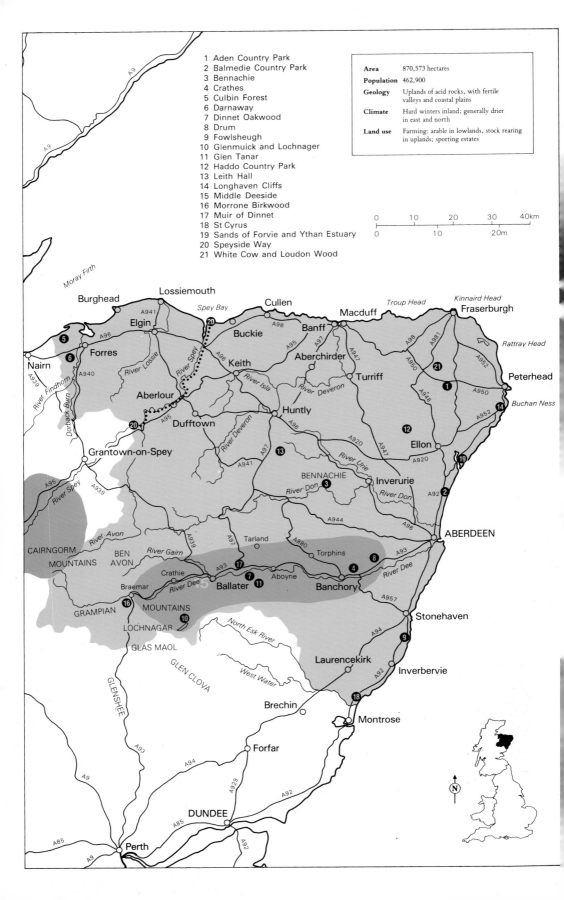

1 Aden Country Park
2 Balmedie Country Park
3 Bennachie
4 Crathes
5 Culbin Forest
6 Darnaway
7 Dinnet Oakwood
8 Drum
9 Fowlsheugh
10 Glenmuick and Lochnager
11 Glen Tanar
12 Haddo Country Park
13 Leith Hall
14 Longhaven Cliffs
15 Middle Deeside
16 Morrone Birkwood
17 Muir of Dinnet
18 St Cyrus
19 Sands of Forvie and Ythan Estuary
20 Speyside Way
21 White Cow and Loudon Wood

Area	870,573 hectares
Population	462,900
Geology	Uplands of acid rocks, with fertile valleys and coastal plains
Climate	Hard winters inland; generally drier in east and north
Land use	Farming: arable in lowlands, stock rearing in uplands; sporting estates

Grampian

Contrast and space are Grampian's features. It is a broad land of sweeping mountains and beaches and wide skies, where the view often includes the distant hills and grey sea together. The Cairngorms (partly in Grampian and partly in Highland South, where they are described) are not sharp, small peaks but a great range of rounded hills and boulder-strewn plateaus, at all seasons providing Britain's only truly arctic–alpine experience. Here you walk in awe, realising that you are in a place where great climatic forces are dominant, and where only a handful of hardy plants and animals can snatch their living in the short summer. These impressive hills are approached by attractive valleys and skirted by an agricultural plain running to Aberdeen, Peterhead, Elgin and the sea. The valleys are Deeside, with its Caledonian pine forests; Donside, wider, more fertile and equally beautiful; and the smaller vales to the north, where the clean springs allow production of the finest whisky anywhere.

Agriculture dominates the lowlands and the great Buchan plain stretches from BENNACHIE to the sea. This treeless, unrelieved area has its own sad charm, and the breadth of view means that its skies are dramatic and immense. A winter storm can be a thrilling event when you can watch it building up from a great distance, but there is no relief from the fierce wind which is so much a part of Buchan life. To the north the Moray coastal strip is relatively dry and warm, and so is pleasant and fertile even though it has light, sandy soil, with many small woods and valleys to make it a varied and interesting place.

Grampian's coast is also impressive. The dramatic cliffs hold huge seabird colonies, as at FOWLSHEUGH, or are natural rock gardens, as at Muchalls; and in other places great dunes and beaches are backed by colourful maritime heaths. There is always space in Grampian and the visitor is often alone with the hills or the sea.

The scenery and wildlife are overwhelmingly influenced by the climate and the presence of the Cairngorms. Most of the rocks are acid and the summers are cool, so man's activities do not reach far up into the hills. The lowland agricultural zone is dominated by barley, beef, turnips and potatoes, but this soon merges into upland farming where cattle and sheep graze hard for their living. On these fairly dry, eastern hills heather grows well and so grouse moors are a feature of the landscape: their pattern of burnt stripes and the purple blossom in August are characteristic, especially on Donside, where the more fertile rocks allow profitable shooting estates to flourish. Finally, above the grouse moor, comes the dwarf shrub vegetation and the sedges and lichens. The Cairngorm tops are the largest remnant of reasonably undisturbed natural vegetation in Britain and are of international importance. In contrast little of the natural lowland vegetation remains in Grampian, except at the coast. Some lowland mosses survive in damp hollows; a few valley woods exist, as at Gight, and there are the birch, juniper and Scots pine woodlands in the middle valleys. Many of these areas are now reserves.

The climate on the high tops is truly arctic with frost and snow likely in any month, and some snow patches are almost permanent. The plants and animals surviving here have a fascination for the naturalist which is increased by the real achievement of climbing to find them in the corries and boulder fields. A snow bunting by the coast in winter is not the same prize as one seen nesting in the hills.

It is not only the hills, however, which have a continental climate. The upper valleys, which can be fiercely cold, as at Braemar where a British record low of $-27°C$ has twice been recorded, can also be very hot in summer. These valleys escape the coastal breeze which keeps lowland Grampian cool, and it can be a revelation to experience stifling days in the hills. The red deer range high in the summer to avoid the heat and flies of the valleys. Generally Grampian is cool but dry and there are many brilliant, cloudless days, though usually accompanied by a breeze or a sea mist.

The acidity of much of the rock is relieved in places. Serpentine rocks, and limestone in a narrow belt from Blair Atholl to the Banff coast at Cullen, allow a richer flora to develop. An energetic and observant botanist can find exciting and unusual plant communities on these rocks, and the extra searching needed for these in the Cairngorms is rewarded by a rarer satisfaction.

A naturalist in Grampian will find the coastline very worthwhile. The seabird colonies at FOWL-SHEUGH, LONGHAVEN and Troup are dramatic, with vast numbers of kittiwake and guillemot and other common species, and, at SANDS OF FORVIE especially, terns and eider duck abound on the sand dunes. Winter brings grey geese to coastal lochs in their thousands, as at LOCH OF STRATHBEG, and waders and ducks to the estuaries. The coastal plants are also exceptional, ranging from the luxuriant dunes at ST CYRUS to the maritime heaths of crowberry and ling, and the cliffs with their banks of roseroot and Scots lovage as at Bullers of Buchan. The varied rock types and microclimate on the coast make it a mosaic of interest at all seasons,

and the base-rich sands near Cullen and Portsoy, with their banks of kidney vetch, contrast attractively with the pines at CULBIN or spring squill at Troup.

Deeside is described elsewhere and deserves its fame, but all Grampian's river valleys are of interest and the clear streams are rightly famous for trout and salmon. The lowlands need a more selective itinerary, but many areas remain of interest and in the spring the bird cherry and blackthorn are especially attractive. Even Buchan has its wooded river valleys and mosses and is worth visiting, but naturalists in Grampian will be inevitably and rewardingly drawn to the varied coastline or to the Cairngorms, one of Britain's last few wildernesses.

MARK YOUNG

Aden Country Park

NJ 984480; 93ha; Banff and Buchan DC
Mixed woodland, river valley and lake
Leaflets from visitor centre
All year

The park contains conifer plantations and ancient broadleaved woodland of ash, cherry and birch. The banks of the River Ugie are rich in flowers. There are a wide variety of resident and migrant birds and the site is especially good for butterflies.

Balmedie Country Park

NJ 976180; 72ha; Grampian RC
Beach, dunes and grassland
Leaflets from visitor centre
All year

The beach is backed by a large system of stable and moving dunes, with the most interesting areas for plants being in the dune slacks and in marshy grassland along the streams. An east wind at migration time can bring a variety of rare birds into the clumps of bushes and trees along the shore. All year a variety of seabirds can be seen off-shore, with large flocks of eiders and scoters in winter; several species of terns, from their breeding colonies on the Sands of Forvie, feed close to the beach in summer.

Bennachie

NJ 6821; 2344ha; FC
Plantations and open moorland
Information centre; forest walks; guide booklet
All year

A good variety of tree species is represented around the fringes of this forest; many of them are labelled near the Don View Centre at NJ 672190. Ferns, mosses, lichens and fungi are abundant along the edges of the tracks. The open heather moorland above the plantation includes the summits of Millstone Hill, the Mither Tap and Craigshannoch, displaying characteristic tor weathering of the granite.

Coulnacraig Meadow

Permit only; 0.5ha; SWT reserve
Marshy meadow
June–August

A small wet meadow grazed by horses but to which no fertilisers have been applied. There is a fine display of early marsh-orchid and early-purple orchids.

Crathes

NO 7396; 241ha; NTS
Woodlands
Trails leaflet on site; guided walks programme; ranger-naturalist
All year

The grounds of Crathes Castle include a variety of habitats, among them mature deciduous woodland, conifer plantations, ponds and an old sand quarry. Many tree species are represented: introduced exotics; birch, rowan and wild cherry colonising the quarry; and Scots pine crowning a rocky outcrop. The ground vegetation is equally varied, with marsh thistle and herb-Robert in the damper areas; heather, tormentil and wood-sorrel along the forest tracks; and mullein, red campion and wild pansy in the quarry. Roe deer are numerous in the woodland and red squirrel quite common. A good range of woodland birds is also present.

Culbin Forest

NH 9861; 2400ha; FC
Afforested sand dunes and adjoining saltmarsh
Access, on foot only, from Wellhill (NH 997614) and Cloddymoss (NH 983599); organised groups wanting guided tours should contact chief forester, Newton Nursery, by Elgin, tel. Elgin 2832
Forest may be closed in periods of acute fire danger
April–August

A large tract of planted forest today clothes and anchors the sands of Culbin, once notorious for their mobility and their tendency to bury both farmland and dwellings. The history of the area is fascinating, and equally interesting to the naturalist is the way in which the relatively recent forest has been colonised by native species.

The planted forest area is largely Scots pine but includes some Corsican pine and lodgepole pine. Birch is widespread and there are willows in the damper hollows. Creeping lady's-tresses, coralroot orchid, chickweed wintergreen and one-flowered wintergreen occur among the heather and sand sedge ground flora. Culbin Forest is notable for its crested tits; first recorded in 1948, this species has steadily increased to a current population of 150–200 pairs. There are also good numbers of capercaillie and goldcrest. Other breeding species include buzzard, sparrowhawk, short-eared and long-eared owl, water rail and great spotted woodpecker, and there is a variety of small passerines associated with the forest edge.

About 200 roe deer inhabit the forest and there is a resident population of around 50 badgers. Red squirrel are fairly common and both pine marten and wild cat have been recorded.

The saltmarsh along the western shore of Findhorn Bay and fringing the unplanted CULBIN SANDS (Highland South) is dominated by sea aster, thrift and sea milkwort; other plants of interest include long-bracted sedge and Baltic rush. Due to the very mild climate of the Moray Firth some 48 plants occur here at their northern limit in Britain.

Darnaway

NH 9951; 2857ha; Moray Estates
Woodland and river gorge
Access restricted to waymarked paths unless accompanied by countryside ranger
Visitor centre at Tearie Farm (NH 989569) open May–September; guided walks in summer; leaflets from Moray Estate Office, Forres
Summer

This large estate includes extensive areas of both deciduous woodland and conifer plantation which support a very varied flora and fauna. Waymarked paths through the woodland start from car parks at NJ 013525 and NH 996514 and both offer views of the spectacular gorge of the River Findhorn.

Dinnet Oakwood

NO 464980; 13ha; NCC reserve
Semi-natural oakwood
Permit only from NCC Aboyne
May–June

Both sessile and pedunculate oak, as well as many hybrids, are present in this small wood, one of the few remaining oakwoods in north east Scotland. Although probably planted, the woodland has much of the character of a natural upland oakwood. The ground flora is varied and includes such northern species as chickweed wintergreen, common wintergreen and stone bramble. A variety of woodland birds is present, among them wood warbler, spotted flycatcher, jay and great spotted woodpecker. Several locally uncommon insects occur in the wood.

Drum

NJ 7900; 166ha; NTS
Woodland
Leaflet from NTS, Crathes and Drum Castle; guided walks in summer; ranger-naturalist
April–July

The old Forest of Drum has been a woodland site for several centuries. Today it carries magnificent mature beech, oak and Scots pine, well spaced and consequently natural in form. Wych elm, juniper, venerable yews and ancient twisted wild cherries are also present. Much of this open woodland has a lush carpet of grasses, ferns and wood anemone. Great clumps of rhododendron add colour and cover and here blackcap and garden warbler sing. Redpoll trill above the more open birch areas, woodcock 'rode' overhead and great spotted woodpecker drum on the dying limbs of ancient oaks. Rooks nest in a group of Scots pine and the woodland holds an important winter roost serving most of lower Deeside. Roe deer, hare and rabbit are common and the old forest holds several species of moths, snails and fungi that are very local in their distribution.

Fowlsheugh

NO 880798; 11ha; RSPB reserve
Coastal cliff
Access by path from Crawton
May–mid-July

Fowlsheugh can aptly be described as a seabird city; a total of around 80,000 pairs of six species breed on this magnificent cliff, which is 1.6km long and up to 65m high. It probably holds over 50,000 guillemots and 22,000 kittiwakes together with 4500 razorbill and smaller numbers of fulmar, shag, herring gull and puffin. This is one of the largest seabird colonies on the eastern mainland of Scotland. There is a ceaseless crying of kittiwake, especially from the non-breeding birds which alternately sit about in groups and then fly off in sudden 'panics', to alight out at sea for a brief spell before returning. Deep indentations in the cliffs make it easy to observe the colony without disturbance to the birds or danger to the observer, although care must, of course, be taken to keep well back from the cliff edge. In May and June the place is alive with the noise and movement – not to mention smell – of its inhabitants. Where trickles of water muddy a gully in the cliff nesting kittiwakes busy themselves gathering mud, and where a stream topples over the edge they bathe in and drink the fresh water.

Many of the guillemot and kittiwake nests, as well as those of razorbill, are sited in individual niches formed where a large stone has worked loose and fallen from the surrounding conglomerate. Only in a few places are there long ledges where the guillemots can pack tightly together. The off-duty guillemots dot the surface of the sea below the cliff; a substantial proportion have the white eye-ring of the bridled form.

Herring gull occupy many of the sites near the clifftop and their nest-building activities leave the coarse grass nearby looking as though it has been raked. Nesting fulmar are scattered fairly thinly among the gulls, and a few puffin are present, though Fowlsheugh is not well provided with terrain suitable for burrow-nesters. Nor is it well suited to shag; those that do nest mostly occupy ledges in caves.

Glenmuick and Lochnagar

NO 2585; 2570ha; Balmoral Estates–SWT reserve
Mountainous area with lochs
Visitor centre; reserve booklet; ranger service; further information from Balmoral Estates Office or ranger
April–September: birds and flowers; All year: deer

The boulder-strewn slopes of 'dark Lochnagar' rise abruptly from the shore of Loch Muick and conceal much of the higher ground, allowing just a glimpse of the knobbly tor of Cac Carn Beag from the visitor centre at the Spittal (NO 307851). This is wild country – especially in winter: the haunt of peregrine, golden eagle and red deer.

Crowberry, bilberry, bearberry and cowberry are scattered among the heather by the shore of Loch Muick. Sundew, butterwort, petty whin and alpine lady's-mantle also occur, and there are a few aspens, rowans and birches near the Black Burn. Adder and lizard bask by the path on sunny days, snipe and redshank frequent the boggy areas in the valley bottom, and common sandpiper bob at the waterside. In early summer large northern eggar and emperor moth are on the wing, while in July and August butterflies and several species of dragonfly are likely to be seen.

Trailing azalea makes vivid splashes of colour among the wind-dwarfed heather around the 700m level, while above 1000m patches of bare granite gravel are interspersed with clumps of stiff sedge, mounds of woolly fringe-moss and prostrate mats of least willow. Three-leaved rush grows in the most exposed situations of all and lichens are unusually abundant for a Scottish summit. Ptarmigan and dunlin breed high up on Lochnagar, red grouse and golden plover at a somewhat lower level. Mountain hare are not uncommon on the moorland and the red deer move freely from high ground to valley bottom, according to the season and weather conditions.

Ledges and gullies on the cliffs, continuously dampened and enriched by trickles of water and inaccessible even to deer, carry a luxuriant growth of flowers, such as red campion, globeflower, roseroot and melancholy thistle, and big tufts of great wood-rush. Saxifrages flourish in the wettest spots, among them starry saxifrage and yellow saxifrage. Alpine speedwell, alpine willowherb and Norwegian cudweed are also present. At the foot of the cliffs alpine lady-fern and parsley fern grow among the scree of granite blocks that litters the ground. Where the snow lies longest on the floor the growth of bilberry is particularly lush and there are scattered plants of dwarf cornel, chickweed wintergreen and bog bilberry.

From the visitor centre the low-level track to Loch Muick is easy going but the route up Lochnagar is steep, rough and very exposed. The old drove road over the Capel Mount to Glen Clova provides an interesting alternative high-level path with a good viewpoint less than 1.5km from the visitor centre. Visitors are asked to keep to the tracks and to avoid disturbing the deer, both during the stalking season and in winter. Stag stalking lasts from 1 July to 21 October and hinds are stalked between 20 October and 16 February.

Loch Kinord is regularly visited by otters, which find good fishing and cover in the marshes.

Natural regeneration of Scots pine is a feature of the old Caledonian forest in Glen Tanar.

Glen Tanar

NO 4891; 4185ha; Glen Tanar Estate–NCC reserve
Caledonian forest
Permit only, from Glen Tanar Estate Office,
off waymarked paths
Visitor centre with wildlife exhibition open
April–September; countryside ranger service in
summer
May–September

This is one of the finest, and the driest and most easterly, remnants of the old Caledonian forest. It contains large areas of fine mature native Scots pine, mainly on the banks of the River Tanar and around the Water of Allachy, and natural regeneration is taking place on an unusually extensive scale, in some places on open moorland adjoining the forest. Juniper is scattered through the forest and there are occasional rowan, aspen and birch.

Many of the plants and animals characteristic of pinewoods occur here. Heather, bilberry, cowberry, hair-grass and mosses dominate much of the ground cover; creeping lady's-tresses and chickweed wintergreen are widespread; and lesser twayblade, twinflower, common wintergreen and intermediate wintergreen are present.

Crossbill, siskin and capercaillie, all birds associated with pinewoods, are present in good numbers, while the more varied woodland along the River Tanar and around the policies attracts a wide range of species. The site is good for birds of prey.

Fencing has kept red deer to the higher hill ground but there are roe deer in the valley woodlands. Red squirrel are occasionally seen and wild cat, otter, fox and mink, though seldom sighted, are known to be present.

Haddo Country Park

NJ 875345; 74ha; Grampian RC
Parkland, grassland, woodland and lake
Leaflets from visitor centre
Spring, summer, autumn

The lake by the abandoned deer park is an excellent area for wildlife; kingfishers and occasionally ospreys can be seen fishing and frogs, toads and newts are all present. The mixed woodlands and parkland are rich areas for fungi; there is a flowery field where butterflies abound.

Leith Hall

NJ 5429; 116ha; NTS
Woodland, moor and farmland
Hide; trail leaflet on site; ranger-naturalist
May–August

Two trails, each 2.5–3km long, lead through this small estate. One climbs through mixed plantation, where the herb layer includes wood-sorrel, leopard's-bane and pink purslane, to a viewpoint on open moorland. Roe deer occur in the woodland and in one grassy glade Scotch argus and ringlet butterflies can be seen in August.

The second trail passes a wide variety of native trees; a side track leads off to the ponds with their observation hide. Mallard, tufted duck, teal and heron are among the birds that visit these pools, which are an important breeding site for common toad.

Loch of Strathbeg

NK 063564; 1024ha; RSPB reserve
Loch, marshes, dunes and woodland
By permit only from RSPB warden, The Lythe,
Crimonmogate, Lonmay, Fraserburgh AB4 4UB

Access limited to reception area and hides; approach is across MOD land and visitors must obtain permit in advance
Reception hut with display; two hides; leaflet from warden or RSPB, Edinburgh
October–March: wildfowl; April–July: breeding birds

This very large, shallow loch, lying only a few hundred metres from the east coast, acts as a magnet to migrating wildfowl. Many thousands of duck, geese and swans rest and feed there, some staying only a few hours or days and others spending the winter on the reserve. At times the number of wildfowl on the loch exceeds 20,000 and the sight and sound of their flights to and from the farmland on which many of them feed is an exhilarating experience.

Mallard are the most abundant of the wintering duck, with tufted duck coming a close second. Several hundred goldeneye are sometimes present and pochard, red-breasted merganser and goosander are all regular visitors. So too are barnacle geese, which often appear at Strathbeg in early October, en route from Spitsbergen to their winter grounds at CAERLAVEROCK on the Solway. However the majority of wintering geese are pink-footed and greylag.

Mallard, tufted duck, eider and shelduck breed on the reserve and water rail nest in the dense vegetation of the marshes. The reedbeds at the north west end of the loch and the willow and alder scrub there hold populations of reed bunting, sedge and willow warbler, and wren.

Sparrowhawk, merlin and short-eared owl can often be seen as they hunt over the reserve, and the cover available draws small birds that have made a landfall on the coast nearby. The 185 or so species recorded since 1973 have included such exciting rarities as pied-billed grebe, little egret, crane, Caspian tern and red-footed falcon.

Roe deer can often be watched as they browse in the surrounding scrub and badger are occasionally seen. Otter are also present but seldom observed and mink have unfortunately become established in the area, presenting a threat to breeding wildfowl.

With habitats ranging from freshwater marsh to lime-rich dunes the reserve has a diverse flora and a good variety of insects. Grass-of-Parnassus, field gentian and Scots lovage occur on the dunes and angelica, early marsh-orchid and greater butterfly-orchid in the marsh. Migrant butterflies such as red admiral, peacock and painted lady occur quite often; resident species include dark green and small pearl-bordered fritillary, common blue and small copper.

Longhaven Cliffs

NK 1239; 50ha; SWT reserve
Coastal cliffs
Access from NK 116393
May–August

The coastline in this part of Buchan is really spectacular; its pinky red granite cliffs are deeply indented and carved into impressive stacks and holes, the best known of which, the Bullers of Buchan, lie just south of the reserve boundary. Nine seabird species breed on this 2.5km stretch of cliffs, the total population numbering somewhere around 23,000 pairs. The distribution of most species is uneven, governed by the form of the weathered rock and the availability of suitable ledges and niches, but every stack and headland has its quota of wailing herring gull. Perhaps 2000 pairs nest in the area, along with a few pairs each of greater black-backed and lesser black-backed gulls. Kittiwake too are numerous but their nests here are widely scattered. Huddles of guillemot pack the lower ledges and crannies, while shag favour the lowest sites of all, sometimes building their untidy seaweed nests only just clear of the hightide mark. There are numbers of puffin to be seen here too, standing outside their burrows or hurtling by on whirring wings.

Not all the Buchan cliffs area is sheer and bird-strewn. Here and there steep slopes lead down to bays and inlets bright with flowers: sheets of red campion tossing in the wind, rounded cushions of thrift, primroses and violets tucked into sheltered nooks, and marsh-marigold and celandine where water seeps down. There are bluebells too, in both blue and white forms. Along the clifftop much of the vegetation is low and stunted by the wind. Patches of heath occur here and Scots lovage and burnet rose are among the more interesting species present, with abundant roseroot.

Middle Deeside

See map; includes 17 sites
Information from tourist offices in Ballater or Banchory
All year

Middle Deeside, with its imposing string of castles – Balmoral, Braemar, CRATHES and DRUM are simply the better-known few among many – has been a tourist haunt since Queen Victoria's day.

The Dee is one of Scotland's most famous salmon rivers, while its banks and hillsides carry woodlands of great attraction and variety; but as farmland Deeside is poor and unproductive in comparison to neighbouring Strathdon.

One of the few large Scottish rivers unaffected by hydroelectric schemes, the Dee is also free of industrial pollution except in its lowermost reaches. It has the additional advantages of a largely granite bed and the greatest altitudinal range of any river in Britain. Pure, well-oxygenated water such as this is ideal for salmon; for the angler there can be few more scenic places in which to pit his wits and strength against those of the king of fish.

Other fishers on the Dee include mink and otter, both of which have been studied from the Institute of Terrestrial Ecology's research station at nearby Hill of Brathens. It was found that mink in this area fed largely on rabbits in summer and duck in winter, while otter took mainly eels in summer and small salmon and trout in winter. Quiet waters with plenty of cover, such as Loch Davan on the MUIR OF DINNET reserve, proved important as 'nursery' areas where the otter cubs could be reared to independence in peace, and thickly wooded stretches of river bank were also valuable in ensuring the necessary seclusion.

A colourful early summer feature is the great swatches of brilliant blue nootka lupin that adorn the riverside shingle banks downstream from Ballater. At this time of year the cascading white blossom of bird cherry is also very evident along the roadsides and in some of the mixed woodlands, while thickets of gorse and broom glow vivid yellow in odd corners. The contrasting forms of silver and downy birch, the one pendulous and the other erect and angular, are both represented. Rowan and wild cherry are also common and aspen occurs more locally. There are oaks on Deeside too, notably at DINNET OAKWOOD, Aboyne and Craigendarroch, on the north side of Ballater, with a few real old worthies still surviving in the ancient forest of Drum. There are also many fine mixed policy woodlands, such as those at Crathes.

Birch and pine are, however, the trees most typical of middle Deeside. Although often forming separate woods they sometimes grow intermixed, as happens near Crathie in a wood where juniper is also present, and both readily regenerate in this area when conditions are right. Young birches are rapidly colonising, and changing the appearance of, the Muir of Dinnet, and in GLEN TANAR pines are becoming established in open moorland. Even in the ancient forest of the Ballochbuie, where little regeneration has taken place for many years due to pressure of deer grazing, a recent fencing programme has already resulted in the appearance of thriving young trees. Deer pressure is heavy in GLENMUICK too, where there are virtually no young trees outside the fenced plantations.

Interesting changes in bird populations have taken place in recent years. Green woodpecker are now well established in the mixed woodland and have even been recorded from pinewoods. Jay have spread widely, breeding in plantations as well as deciduous woods. Buzzard too have increased greatly: scarce on Deeside until about 1945, they have become a regular sight. While Scottish crossbill remain firmly associated with the native pinewoods, the smaller-billed common crossbill appears to be colonising some of the conifer plantations. Perhaps more surprising was an influx of crested tits during the 1970s. Other recent exciting records include wryneck and gos-hawk; the latter, once widespread in Scotland, now shows signs of re-establishing itself in several areas with extensive plantations.

There have also been changes in mammal populations. Since grey squirrel were first reported on Deeside, in Glen Tanar in 1971, they have spread through many of the valley's hardwoods, despite endeavours to exterminate them. A more welcome expansion of range has been that of pine marten, with sightings now being reported well down the valley.

Changes in the distribution of birds and mam-mals cannot always be explained by changes in habitat availability, however. Lochs Davan and Kinord have not undergone any significant change in recent years, but goldeneye are summering there increasingly. Soon, perhaps, the pairs dis-playing there will breed, as they have done on Speyside since 1970. The breeding of red-throated diver on a hill loch in Deeside, after an absence from the area of over 95 years, is not easy to explain; nor is the upsurge in breeding redwing and fieldfare in the Highlands from the late 1960s.

To enjoy middle Deeside's wildlife to the full, explore the minor roads south of the river and up into the Forest of Birse, and to the north around Tarland, Lumphanan and Torphins. Follow the 'high roads' on to the moorlands, from Banchory up to the Cairn o' Mount and from Ballater up the notorious Cockbridge to Tomintoul route.

Morrone Birkwoods

NO 1390; 225ha; NCC reserve
Birch–juniper woodland
Access restricted to waymarked paths, starting from car park at NO 143911
May–July

With many features typical of similar woods in Norway, this is the best example in Britain of a subalpine birchwood on basic soils. The wood is pure downy birch, with a few stands of aspen and an understorey of low, heavily grazed juniper. The combination of lime-rich soils, the protection from grazing provided by the juniper bushes, and many flushes and wet hollows, has resulted in a rich and varied flora; some 280 species of flowering plants and ferns have been recorded.

This is one of the few places in Britain where mountain plants such as alpine cinquefoil, Scottish asphodel, alpine rush, three-flowered rush and hair sedge grow in a woodland setting, and the flora has changed comparatively little since post-glacial times. The limestone schist crags and the scrub above the wood hold an interesting plant life which includes serrated wintergreen, twinflower, small-white orchid and holly fern. The wood is also notably rich in bryophytes and lichens.

Muir of Dinnet

NO 4399; 1428ha; NCC reserve
Moorland, woodland, bog, open water and striking landform features
Landform trail; leaflet at tearoom, NO 429997, or from NCC, Aberdeen; comprehensive reserve report from NCC
May–July: birds and flowers; October–December: wildfowl

Spring, when the birches are just coming into leaf, and late summer, when the heather is in full bloom, are when the Muir of Dinnet is perhaps most visually attractive. But the famous rock cauldron of the Vat, a gigantic pothole, is even more spectacular in wet or frosty weather than on a sunny day; and the twin lochs of Davan and Kinord hold many more birds in autumn and winter.

The reserve is well known for its wealth of features formed towards the end of the ice ages. Mounds and ridges of deposited material are widespread, deep channels cut by streams running under the ice score the hillsides. The Burn O'Vat occupies one of the deepest meltwater channels.

On the lower granite hills and gravel moraines of the western part of the reserve, heather and heather–bearberry heathland cover much of the ground. Rapid colonisation of Scots pine and birch has taken place in the last 20 years since muir-burning ceased. This moorland carries a species-rich heath in which mosses and lichens are abundant and intermediate wintergreen and petty whin quite common. The wet granite walls of the Vat support a rich bryophyte flora and a variety of ferns. Lemon-scented fern, brittle bladder-fern and beech fern are present.

Silver birch dominates the woodland which clothes some 243ha of the reserve. Much of the ground cover is grassy but in the older wood at New Kinord, where aspen, ash, hazel and blackthorn are present, there is a more varied plant life. Fungi grow profusely in the birchwoods in late summer and species represented include fly agaric, chanterelle and woolly milk-cap.

Lochs Davan and Kinord are shallow and have a moderately rich aquatic flora; the display of white and yellow water-lily in places sheltered from wind and waves is particularly impressive. Extensive stands of bog myrtle are also present.

The lochs are an important feeding ground for otter; family parties are regularly seen although there is no evidence of breeding on the reserve. Visitors hoping to see otter should watch from the A97 beside Loch Davan or the north shore of Loch Kinord near the Celtic Cross, but should not enter the surrounding vegetation as this disturbs them. Mink are known to breed here, fox and wild cat visit occasionally, as do red deer, and there is a large resident population of roe deer.

Some 140 bird species have been recorded, 76 of them breeding regularly. Populations of willow warbler, redpoll, great tit and woodcock are notably high. Numbers of breeding wildfowl are not large but the autumn and early winter flocks of duck, geese and whooper swan are often substantial. Peak counts of greylag goose have been nearly 8000 and of pink-footed goose on passage 2000. Moorland birds include wintering merlin and hen harrier and breeding black grouse.

More than 380 species of moth have been noted in the reserve, among them several uncommon and local species such as Kentish glory, scarce prominent, cousin german, and large red-belted clearwing. This site is important for dragonflies; rare beetles and bugs have also been recorded.

St Cyrus

NO 7464; 92ha; NCC reserve
Foreshore, dunes and cliff
Access restricted in tern breeding area,
May–August
Leaflet from NCC, Aberdeen; comprehensive report also available
April–July: flowers and breeding birds; July: butterflies; September–November: migrants

A 4km sweep of golden sand, backed by narrow dunes, and a relict cliff, makes St Cyrus an attractive beach to the casual visitor. To the naturalist this reserve, although nowhere more than 400m wide, offers a surprising diversity of habitats and a remarkable range of wildlife. A bonus is the active salmon fishery, with its traditional netting methods, which also influences the wildlife of the area.

The reserve musters an impressive 350 flowering plants and ferns, including several species at the northern limit of their distribution here. Most of

St Cyrus: the cliffs and dunes support a remarkable variety of flowering plants.

Mottled plumage camouflages the eider ducks that nest along the Grampian coast.

the latter occur on the inland cliffs, which are dry, sheltered and of south eastern aspect. The night-scented Nottingham catchfly grows on the drier ledges, as do the small annual soft clover, with pale pink flowers, and rough clover, with tiny white flowers; all three are very local. Tall yellow spikes of great mullein and vivid blue viper's-bugloss make splashes of colour where there is a slippage of unstable slopes. Marjoram, carline thistle and wild liquorice are among the less common plants of the cliff grassland, and henbane occurs at the northern end of the sea cliffs.

Despite the increasingly rank growth on the dune pastures since myxomatosis decimated the rabbit population, this area is still rich in wild flowers. Cowslip, purple milk-vetch, hairy violet, clustered bellflower and maiden pink are among the most interesting and colourful. Where tracks and rabbit scrapes have disturbed the ground winter annuals such as spring vetch and common cornsalad are found. Since a major sand blow in 1967 the saltmarsh along the coast has almost disappeared and many of the typical saltmarsh species have been replaced by 'weed' and pasture plants.

St Cyrus is important for insects, with 13 species of butterfly and over 200 moths recorded; several of the latter have not been found anywhere else in Scotland. Among the butterflies present are the brightly coloured small copper, small blue and grayling. Moths recorded include the day-flying cinnabar, near its northern limit in Britain, Mother Shipton, six-spot burnet and bordered grey, of particular interest as its only known food plant is heather, which is very scarce here.

Although the land area of the reserve is so limited, 47 bird species have bred there. The little tern colony on the sand and shingle at the south end of the reserve has had varying success, on occasion suffering serious predation from crows, rats, stoats and kestrels. The colony is fenced and wardened during the breeding season. A small population of grasshopper warbler breeds and stonechat, whitethroat and yellowhammer frequent the gorse scrub. Fulmar and herring gull nest on the cliffs and eider throughout the reserve. This area is also good for migrants, with regular autumn passage of skuas and shearwaters, winter records of all three divers, and a total of 29 wader species listed.

Otter tracks are occasionally found on the river bank and common porpoise are sometimes seen offshore. Grey seal occur regularly, but common seal are rare locally.

Sands of Forvie and Ythan Estuary

NK 0227; 973ha; NCC reserve
Estuary, saltmarsh, dunes, moorland, sea cliffs and sandy foreshore
Permit only away from footpaths and foreshore; apply NCC, Aberdeen
Hide overlooking ternery; leaflet and reserve handbook from NCC, Slains, Ellon
April–July: breeding birds; August–December: waders and wildfowl

The largest concentration of eider in Britain breeds here during the summer months, nesting among the dunes and moorland. In June ducklings are everywhere, dark fluffy balls diving in shallow water, bouncing on the waves, and gradually being gathered into large creches. Many eider leave the estuary in autumn to moult but some remain throughout the year, feeding on the mussels that throng the river bed.

Shelduck also breed in the dunes, generally in rabbit burrows where the eggs are safe from marauding crows and gulls. Each pair defends its feeding patch on the snail-rich inter-tidal mud and territorial disputes are common.

Other important summer visitors are terns. Four species nest in the dunes: Sandwich tern in a large, dense colony, common and arctic in smaller numbers and often within the limits of the black-headed gull colony, and little tern, at present making use of an 'inland beach' well away from the hazards of waves and wind-blown sand to which nests on the open beach are exposed. Terns are notoriously temperamental, frequently abandoning apparently suitable sites for no obvious reason, and at Sands of Forvie strict measures are taken to avoid disturbance.

The movements of the dunes themselves, however, can force the birds to change their nesting area. This is the least man-disturbed large dune system in Britain and winter gales regularly alter the shape and location of the Sahara-like mounds of loose sand. All stages in the development of a dune system can be seen here, from marram-covered ridges to dune-heath vegetation of heather, abundant crowberry and many lichens.

In autumn and winter the Ythan Estuary attracts large numbers of waders: sanderling run along the seaward shore, the lower estuary with its mussel beds and pools holds turnstone, ringed plover, redshank, curlew and bar-tailed godwit, and the creeks and flats of the upper estuary are visited by spotted redshank, greenshank, little stint and green sandpiper.

The area is important too for passage and wintering wildfowl. The flocks of pink-footed geese which gather on the estuary and feed on nearby farmland sometimes number as many as 10,000. Wigeon, teal, red-breasted merganser and whooper swan all winter in fair numbers and in rough weather long-tailed duck and goldeneye quite often enter the river mouth. Large flocks of scoter, divers and merganser occur offshore from autumn to spring.

Speyside Way

NJ 349654–167367; 48km; Moray DC
Long-distance walk by River Spey
Leaflets from Moray DC; exhibition in Tugnet Ice
House, Spey Bay; ranger service
All year

From Spey Bay, with its terns, waders and seals, the route follows first a footpath and later the line of the former Strathspey railway, passing through varied landscapes and habitats. Osprey sometimes fish in the Spey below Fochabers, butterflies are plentiful along the tree-sheltered stretches of track, and a wide variety of flowers grows by the path.

White Cow and Loudon Wood

NJ 9550; 270ha; FC
Plantations, and forest walk at NJ 957513
All year

In the largely tree-less Buchan countryside all sizeable stands of trees are important to wildlife. These spruce woods are particularly notable for their badger setts and heronry.

Highland North

The districts of Ross and Cromarty, Sutherland and Caithness together constitute one-sixth of the area of Scotland, yet their joint human population contributes only 1.3 per cent of the total and their burghs would be accorded village status south of the border. This is a land of violent contrasts, from the great Torridonian mountains of Wester Ross towering over 900m straight out of the sea, and the terrible barrens of west Sutherland, to the rich, fertile farmlands of Caithness and the Dornoch Firth. These, together with offshore islands, ancient woodlands, innumerable freshwater lochs, desolate moorland and many kilometres of the finest cliff coastline in Britain complement an equivalent diversity of wildlife with many reserves of national and international importance.

There are no averages, only extremes: rainfall may vary in Ross-shire from 2500mm or more in the Atlantic influence of the south west to a mere 500mm on the east coast of the Black Isle. The effect of wind is reflected in the vegetation: west of the Kyle of Durness trees cannot grow, but there is a 'forest' of juniper heath a few centimetres high. In the same district, in Migdale Wood on the Dornoch Firth, juniper grows as a columnar tree 3m high in the shelter of the old pines.

During the last ice age the thickest and heaviest part of the ice-cap lay over west Sutherland and Ross; it scoured the land bare, leaving a few pockets of soil on the coast only. This effect is seen most vividly on the hard, acid Lewisian gneiss of west Sutherland, where there is literally no soil and little glacial drift, only pockets of peat in the hollows and a magnificent array of 'perched rocks' and glacial erratic boulders unchanged for 10,000 years. Much of the west coast, however, including most of the mountains of Wester Ross, is Torridonian sandstone. This is a more recent, softer and less acid rock which has weathered into spectacular cliffs and stacks like Rudha Reidh, Point of Stoer (with the Old Man) and, notably, the famous bird colonies of HANDA and the Clo Mor where the bedding of the Torridonian forms such admirable ledges for auks and kittiwakes.

The Durness limestone shows its influence in a narrow strip from Kishorn to Faraid Head, in the limestone pavement of RASSAL ASHWOOD, the botanically rich area of INCHNADAMPH, and finally in Durness itself, an oasis of calcareous grassland and lime-rich lochs in a sour and barren landscape. To the east, large tracts of Ross and Sutherland are of Moine schist, much overlain by peat and blanket bog but elsewhere with a rich flora – Ben Dearg and Seana Bhraigh are considered to have the finest montane flora in the north Highlands, surpassed in Scotland only by the CAIRNGORMS (Highland South) and BEN LAWERS (Tayside).

Finally there is the old red sandstone of the east, well known for its spectacular cliff scenery and fossil fish beds. It underlies the high-quality arable farmland covering most of Caithness, east Sutherland and the whole of Easter Ross and the Black Isle, so different from the narrow strip of glacial drift forming the croft lands of the north and west. It is no coincidence that the fertility of these lands is reflected in the rich feeding in the bays, firths and shallow seas of the east for the incredible numbers of wildfowl and waders which frequent these coasts, and are protected there in several reserves of international importance.

Geology apart, however, the north Highlands today are a product of the activities of man. Pastoral people inhabited these lands in pre-Roman times and 2000 years of grazing, burning and felling have reduced the natural woodlands to a few pitiful relics. Sutherland suffered most in this respect, and at an early date lost all the original pine and most of the oak. Ross-shire suffered rather less, and fortunately has retained several fine examples of the old pine forest such as those at BEINN EIGHE, LOCH MAREE and TORRIDON.

Man's influence has not been entirely on the debit side; reafforestation by estates began in the eighteenth century, notably in Sutherland. At LOCH FLEET occurs what is probably the only example in Britain of natural regeneration of pine on sand dunes, seeded from one of the original estate plantations, and on the adjacent reserve are the magnificent MOUND ALDERWOODS, a spontaneous growth on land reclaimed from the sea by the erection of the Mound barrier in 1816.

More recently the Forestry Commission has transformed much of Sutherland's 'wet desert' into coniferous forest. This is a source of much criticism, although welcomed by many, and certainly provides new habitats for birds and mammals. The older plantations are gradually acquiring some of the characteristic plant and animal life of primary forest, for example one-flowered wintergreen at Loch Fleet; and crested tit and Scottish crossbill are now breeding in the Shin Forest.

The diversity of landscape and habitat, mountain, moorland, sea coast and woodland in the northern Highlands is unsurpassed elsewhere in

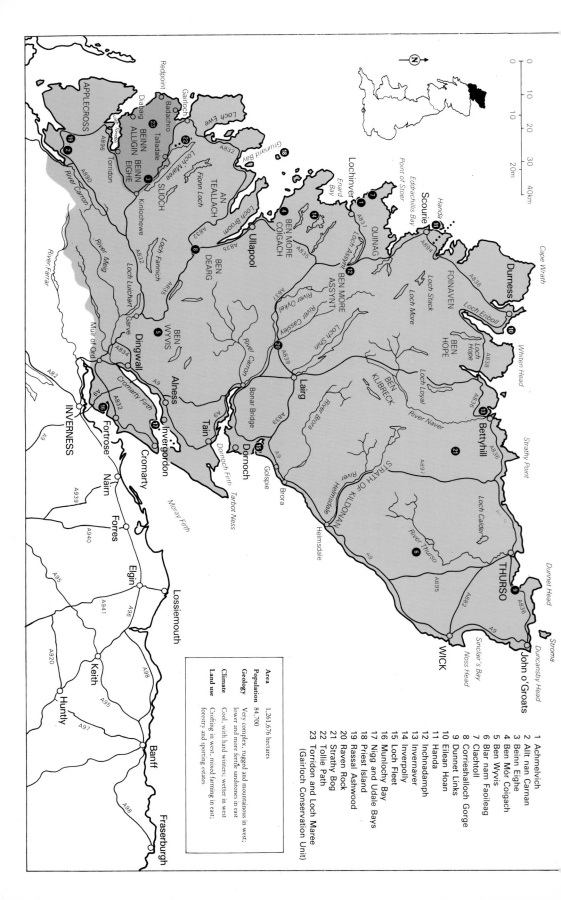

N

0
10
20m
0
10
20
30
40km

APPLECROSS

Redpoint
Diabaig
Badachro
Gairloch
Talladale
Torridon
Kinlochewe
Loch Torridon
River Carron
A896
A890
BEINN
ALLIGIN
BEINN
EIGHE
SLIOCH
Loch Maree
Fionn Loch
AN
TEALLACH
Loch Ewe
Loch Maree
Gruinard Bay
A832
A832
A835
A835
BEN
DEARG
Ullapool
Loch Broom
A835
Enard
Bay
Eddrachillis Bay
Point of Stoer
BEN MORE
COIGACH
QUINAG
Lochinver
BEN MORE
ASSYNT
Loch Assynt
River Oykel
River Cassley
Loch Shin
River Carron
A837
A837
A839
Loch Fannich
Loch Luichart
Garve
A832
A834
A9
BEN
WYVIS
Dingwall
Alness
Invergordon
Cromarty Firth
Tain
Dornoch Firth
Bonar Bridge
Lairg
Dornoch
Golspie
Brora
Helmsdale
STRATH OF KILDONAN
River Helmsdale
River Brora
A9
A897
BEN
KLIBRECK
Loch Loyal
Loch Naver
River Naver
BEN
HOPE
Loch Hope
Loch More
Loch Stack
FOINAVEN
Loch Eriboll
A838
A838
A836
Durness
Scourie
Handa
A894
Whiten Head
Cape Wrath
Strathy Point
Bettyhill
Loch Calder
River Thurso
A836
A882
A9
A882
A836
A895
THURSO
WICK
John o'Groats
Dunnet Head
Duncansby Head
Stroma
Noss Head
Sinclair's Bay
Dunnet Bay
Muir of Ord
INVERNESS
Fortrose
Cromarty
Nairn
Forres
Elgin
Lossiemouth
Keith
Huntly
Banff
Fraserburgh
A82
A9
A832
A835
A9
A9
A9
A939
A940
A96
A95
A96
A941
A98
A920
A98
A95
A97
River Farrar
River Meig
Moray Firth
Tarbot Ness

Area	1,261,676 hectares
Population	84,700
Geology	Very complex, rugged and mountainous in west; lower and more fertile sandstones in east
Climate	Cool, with hard winters; wetter in west
Land use	Crofting in west; mixed farming in east; forestry and sporting estates

1 Achmelvich
2 Allt nan Carnan
3 Beinn Eighe
4 Ben Mór Coigach
5 Ben Wyvis
6 Blar nam Faoileag
7 Clachtoll
8 Corrieshalloch Gorge
9 Dunnet Links
10 Eilean Hoan
11 Handa
12 Inchnadamph
13 Invernaver
14 Inverpolly
15 Loch Fleet
16 Munlochy Bay
17 Nigg and Udale Bays
18 Priest Island
19 Rassal Ashwood
20 Raven Rock
21 Strathy Bog
22 Tollie Path
23 Torridon and Loch Maree
(Gairloch Conservation Unit)

the kingdom. Fortunately the nature reserves carry a fair representation of all these. A few, such as STRATHY BOG and ACHANARRAS QUARRY, are of such specialised interest that they have little to offer the casual visitor. Handa is an island gem even without its famous seabird cliffs, although ornithologists on holiday will probably find much more on the east coast firths. The vast wilderness areas, however, such as Torridon with Beinn Eighe or INVERPOLLY with BEN MÓR COIGACH, may be enjoyed by everyone from bryologists or ecological historians to lovers of fine scenery.

I.D. PENNIE

Achanarras Quarry

Permit only; 44ha; NCC reserve
Disused quarry
Collection restricted and by permit only, from NCC, Golspie
All year

This site is of international importance for the very rich fossil vertebrate fauna preserved in a 5m exposure of Caithness flagstone.

Achmelvich

NC 053243; 8ha; Highland RC
Beach, dunes and machair
Spring, summer

Attractive beach with an interesting dune system and areas of machair grassland with a rich flora. Eider duck, mergansers and occasionally divers can be seen off shore.

Allt nan Carnan

NG 8940; 7ha; NCC reserve
Wooded gorge
April–June

Carved through calcareous schists, this 1.6km long gorge is up to 30m deep, with dangerously slippery, sheer sides. Oak and birch dominate the woodland, with some bird cherry, ash, rowan, holly, aspen and hazel, and a good range of bryophytes on both trees and exposed rocks. The rich and varied ground flora includes stone bramble, yellow saxifrage, opposite-leaved golden-saxifrage and alpine lady's-mantle.

Beinn Eighe

NG 9862; 4758ha; NCC reserve
Mountainous area with remnant Caledonian pine forest
Access restricted 1 September–21 November; contact wardens (Kinlochewe 254 or 244) or Aultroy Visitor Centre (Kinlochewe 257) for advice
Nature trail and reserve leaflets from Aultroy Visitor Centre (open weekdays May–September) or from NCC, Inverness
May–August

The jagged ridge of Beinn Eighe, with its long snow-white skirt of quartzite scree, gives the southern aspect of this reserve a somewhat forbidding look. In contrast, the north east slopes present a more welcoming appearance, with native pinewoods extending from the shores of Loch Maree up to about 400m above sea level. This fragment of Scots pine forest, with its scattering of birch, rowan and holly, carpets of heather, bilberry and cowberry, and colourful mounds of bog mosses, is full of interest for both general and specialist visitors. So too are the slopes above the tree line, where dwarf shrub heath is interspersed with patches of lusher vegetation and outcropping bands of fossil-bearing lime-rich rock. Beinn Eighe has been internationally recognised and designated a Biosphere Reserve under UNESCO's Man and Biosphere Programme.

The shorter (1.5km) of the reserve's two trails, both of which start from the car park at NH 000650, winds through a representative section of the pinewood. Roe deer are fairly common in the woodland, and in winter many red deer come down from the hills to find shelter and food. Pine

Beinn an Eoin rises steeply from the moorlands of Ben Mór Coigach; the distant hill is Stac Pollaidh.

marten and wild cat, although present, are rarely seen. The bird population is rather limited in both variety and numbers but a number of rare invertebrate species, not recorded elsewhere in the area, are found in the woodland.

The second trail (6.5km) climbs to an altitude of 540m and passes through a variety of montane habitats. Immediately above the tree line, dwarf juniper, heather and bearberry sprawl through a dense carpet of mosses and liverworts; slightly higher up, the vegetation is more varied and includes creeping willow, crowberry, trailing azalea, dwarf cornel and moonwort. This is ptarmigan, red deer and mountain hare country, though they are not abundant; their predators are correspondingly scarce, but golden eagle, buzzard, merlin and fox all hunt here occasionally.

A pony path which leaves the road at NH 022628 provides the best approach route to the highest ground. Up on the exposed ridges and summit plateau woolly fringe-moss–mat-grass heath is the most widespread form of vegetation. Where weathering of mineral-rich rocks has produced a more fertile soil, arctic–alpine species such as moss campion, mossy saxifrage, alpine saw-wort, alpine meadow-rue, sibbaldia and northern rock-cress are present while the larger cliff ledges carry mountain sorrel, globeflower, purple saxifrage and the more local Highland saxifrage and pyramidal bugle. Hill walking equipment is essential in these areas.

Belmaduthy Dam

Permit only; 20ha; SWT reserve
Calcareous heath with planted pine on three sides
May–August

Acid and lime-loving plants are growing together and include heather, bell heather and juniper along with alpine bistort, alpine meadow-rue and several species of orchid. The rare narrow-bordered bee hawkmoth which lays its eggs on the devil's-bit scabious is also recorded.

Ben Mór Coigach

NC 0807; 5949ha; SWT–RSNC reserve
Mountain and moorland, coastline and islets
No access to islets
April–October: insects, plants, birds

Shapely Ben Mór Coigach (743m) and the twin peaks of Beinn an Eoin dominate all views of this vast area of rock and wet heath. To the north the steep sandstone slopes of Beinn an Eoin give way to heather–grass moorland streaked with brighter green, mineral-rich flushes. Scrub birch lines the gullies running down to the lowland around the shores of Loch Lurgainn, whose barrenness is relieved by scattered small birchwoods containing some aspen, rowan and holly. Deergrass and cottongrass blanket bog with sundews and bog asphodel covers the undulating western moorland, while the smoother slopes above Achiltibuie are largely heather-clad. Much of the croftland included in the reserve is no longer actively cultivated, but is still used for grazing stock and

should not be entered without permission from the crofters. Barnacle geese graze this ground in winter and eider can frequently be observed on the shoreline and islets.

The botanical interest of the reserve centres largely on the woodland, and on the crags and summits of the hills. Brittle bladder-fern, northern buckler-fern, alpine scurvygrass, three-leaved rush, trailing azalea and dwarf juniper are among the species present.

Breeding birds on the reserve include ptarmigan, raven, ring ouzel, golden plover, greenshank and twite. Large numbers of red deer roam the hills and pine marten, otter, badger and wild cat may be seen. Although the insect life has not yet been studied in detail five species of dragonfly and at least five of butterfly have been recorded.

Ben Wyvis

NH 460680; 5673ha; NCC reserve
Mountain and moorland
Spring, summer

Ben Wyvis is the highest mountain in Easter Ross. The broad summit plateau, coupled with a rainfall that is considerably less than that of the hills in the west, supports an almost continuous carpet of moss heath and is the largest single area of this type of vegetation in Britain. The mountain also contains fine examples of lichen-rich blanket bog, rich in northern species such as dwarf birch, alpine bearberry and mountain crowberry; on the ground where the snow lies late bilberry covers the ground. The two main corries expose pelitic greiss, which supports relatively few arctic–alpine flowers but a wide variety of vegetation characteristic of acid rocks. Parsley fern and Alpine lady-fern are well represented. The block screes carry snow late into the year and these patches also contain a number of rare mosses and liverworts.

Blar nam Faoileag

ND 144450; 2126ha; NCC reserve
Blanket bog
Permit only from NCC, Old Bank Road, Golspie
Spring, summer

One of the best examples of an undisturbed watershed mire in Britain. The vegetation is largely heather, cottongrass and deer sedge growing through a carpet of bog mosses. Other characteristic peat-bog plants are found – bog asphodel, the insectivorous sundews and, in the pools, bogbean. The area is important for breeding moorland birds including several species of waders and wildfowl.

Clachtoll

NC 039273; 4ha; Highland RC/Sutherland DC reserve
Beach, machair and dunes
Leaflet on site
Spring, summer

Superb west coast beach backed by a dune system and machair grassland rich in flowers, fine views to the Outer Isles.

Corrieshalloch Gorge

NH 204777; 14ha; NTS–NCC reserve
Wooded gorge
April–September

This spectacular gorge, a fine example of a box canyon, is 1.6km long and reaches a maximum depth of 60m at the Falls of Measach. A narrow strip of woodland, mainly of mixed native species, fringes the ravine, and a rich variety of mosses and liverworts grows on the sheer walls of the gorge and on the boulders in the stream bed. The bridge offers good views of the falls and of the inaccessible depths of the River Droma below.

Creag Meagaidh

NN 445880; 3948ha; NCC reserve
Birch woodland
Leaflets from NE Scotland Regional Office and Aberarder Farmhouse Information Centre
All year

The vast area of Creag Meagaidh was bought by the NCC in 1985 to save it from the threat of afforestation. The reserve extends north from the shores of Loch Laggan and rises to a summit plateau of about 1100 metres. From here there are outstanding views over some of Scotland's most spectacular scenery.

The area is fascinating in that as one moves from loch side to mountain summit the plants reflect the changes that have taken place since the ice retreated some 9000 years ago at the end of the last Ice Age. The frozen landscape was first taken over by moss and heath plants very like those now found on the top of Creag Meagaidh. But as the weather warmed dwarf birch trees moved in, and, in time, this scrub was replaced by mature birch and Scots pine woodland.

From the shores of Loch Laggan one can see tufted duck, goldeneye, pochard and mallard, which all feed here, and greylag geese breed nearby. In summer the spectacular osprey often takes brown trout, while in winter cormorants and whooper swans use the loch to feed and roost. Dippers and grey wagtails hunt for insects at the edges of the many small streams flowing into the loch, and otters are occasionally seen.

There is a mosaic of heaths, grassland, peat bogs and birch wood back from the loch side to about 450m above sea level, which provides a varied habitat for many plants and animals. There are scattered willows, rowans, alders and occasionally aspens and holly among the birches, while frog, heath-spotted and marsh-orchids add colour along with tormentil, cow-wheat, primrose and marsh cinquefoil.

The woods provide nest-sites for a variety of resident and migrant birds, including redstart and wood warbler. In winter, siskins, redpolls and goldfinches feed on the plentiful supplies of birch seeds, and these are joined by other visitors such as redwings, fieldfares and snow buntings.

Above the tree lines, ptarmigan and red grouse feed on dwarf heather which, along with crowberry and blaeberry, dominate the windswept upper spurs of the mountain. These are the hunting grounds of the majestic golden eagle, which adds to its diet of ptarmigan and grouse by taking mountain hares, water voles and occasionally fox cubs and even red deer calves. Peregrine falcons also breed on the reserve along with buzzards, sparrowhawks and kestrels, and the impressive blackcock.

The mountain top is mainly short heathland with some blanket bog, and once the snows have melted least cinquefoil, mouse-ears and Alpine foxtail flower. This is the favoured haunts of the dotterel and snow bunting, both of which are rare as breeding birds in this country.

Amongst the crags and boulders in the high corries rarities such as Alpine speedwell and highland cudweed can be found, along with downy willow, Scottish asphodel, Alpine saxifrage and an unusually rich community of Alpine hawkweeds. Ring ouzels and wheatears can be seen on the tops of the rocks.

Red deer can be watched grazing at any time of year, but in summer they are inclined to move to the tops away from the biting mosquitoes. Foxes and hare are common, but far rarer are the wildcat and pine marten, which breed here.

Drummondreach Oakwood

Permit only; 19ha; SWT reserve
Deciduous woodland
April–July

The richness of the ground flora under these near-mature oaks suggests that they were planted on an old natural oakwood site. Regeneration of oak, ash, rowan and birch is taking place in the wood, which also contains beech, wild cherry, bird cherry, blackthorn and juniper, over herb-Paris, moschatel, enchanter's-nightshade, meadow cow-wheat and hard shield-fern.

Dunnet Links

ND 2269; 465ha; NCC reserve
Rich dune and links grassland
Permit required for all area other than forest from NCC, Golspie
Spring, summer, autumn

Shell sand blowing inland from Dunnet Bay has caused a lime-rich, sand soil over a large area, which, with the uneven nature of the ground and high-water table, gives a great diversity of soil types. The Scottish primrose and the Baltic rush grow here in their normal habitat, while others, such as hair sedge and mountain everlasting, are montane species growing at sea-level. The forest is a good butterfly locality.

Eilean Hoan

NC 4567; 40ha; RSPB reserve
Uninhabited island
Access very difficult
All year

Although this low grassy island is not far from the mainland, the sea between is rough enough to ensure that the bird population is little disturbed. In winter the most northerly regular flock of barnacle geese grazes here and in summer eider, oystercatcher, ringed plover, lapwing and terns nest among the thrift, sea campion and bird's-foot-trefoil. Great northern diver in breeding plumage gather off Eilean Hoan in spring before migrating to Iceland, and are visible with a telescope from the coast road.

Gairloch Conservation Unit

See TORRIDON AND LOCH MAREE.

Gualin

Permit only; 2522ha; NCC reserve
Mountain, moorland, lochs, bogs and river
Permit from NCC, Golspie
April–July

This vast wilderness includes the quartzite ridges of Foinaven (908m), extensive areas of undulating and rugged gneiss plateau, and the intricately patterned peat bogs of Strath Dionard. It supports an interesting variety of northern montane and bog plant communities.

Handa

NC 1348; 363ha; RSPB reserve
High inshore island
Day visits (not Sundays) April–August
Leaflet from RSPB, Edinburgh; access by small boat, weather permitting, from Tarbet, NC 1648
May–July

Some 140m high on the north side, the near-vertical cliffs which bound Handa on three sides gradually decrease in height southwards, finally giving way to sandy bays. The horizontally layered rock weathers unevenly, forming ideal breeding ledges which attract guillemot, the most numerous species. They are seen most dramatically on the sides of the famous Great Stack of Handa. Numbers of razorbill are also high, with large populations of kittiwake and fulmar, and a few hundred pairs each of puffin and shag.

Six lochans enliven the moorland interior of the island and provide freshwater bathing sites for the birds. A plantation of lodgepole pine and alder near the bothy gives cover for small migrants and for breeding robin, song thrush and dunnock. Deergrass and heather dominate the moorland, with heath spotted-orchid, northern marsh-orchid, bog asphodel and pale butterwort giving colour in the damper areas. Other plants of interest include royal fern, few-flowered spike-rush and Scots lovage. Details of a comprehensive survey of the flora are available from the Summer Warden.

Wheatear, skylark and meadow pipit are the commonest birds on the moorland, which has been colonised since 1964 by both great and arctic skua. Several pairs of each now breed along with shelduck, eider, ringed plover, stonechat and occasionally golden plover and red grouse. Visitors are asked to keep to the marked paths to avoid disturbance to the birds. In winter a small flock of barnacle geese grazes on the island.

Inchnadamph

NC 2719; 1303ha; NCC reserve
Moorland with limestone outcrops
Access restricted late summer; contact Assynt Estate
Office, tel. 05714 203
Leaflet from NCC, Inverness, or Visitor Centre, Inverpolly
May–June

This reserve is best known for the great range of erosive features contained in the limestone plateau, including caves, swallow-holes and underground streams. The Allt nan Uamh caves have yielded relics of human occupation dating back to the late Stone Age and bones of animals now extinct in Scotland. The reserve's rich plant life includes mountain avens, holly fern and serrated wintergreen, and several uncommon willows.

Invernaver

NC 6961; 552ha; NCC reserve
Seashore, dunes, raised beach, and rocky moorland with lochans
Access easiest from Borgie, at NC 681612
May–July

Suilven forms a fine backdrop to Inverpolly's undulating moorland.

A strange combination of physical features and climatic conditions makes this a site of particular ecological interest.

Exposure to frequent northerly gales inhibits tree growth in all but the most sheltered spots, and carries sand from the beach and dunes far up on to the hinterland of acid moorland. This shell-sand enriches the otherwise poor soils and supports an unusual mixture of plants. Montane and oceanic species appear in close proximity with lime-loving plants and those typical of acid moorland.

Dwarf juniper grows at all levels, from the moorland plateau almost down to the shore, and there are great mats of dwarf shrubs like mountain avens, crowberry, bearberry and creeping willow, and abundant thrift, sea campion, moss campion, yellow and purple saxifrage and alpine bistort. Scottish primrose is among the less common species present and the rich bryophyte flora includes one moss not yet recorded from any other British site.

A strip of birchwood along the lower slopes by the Naver adds habitat diversity and attracts bird species like sparrowhawk and woodcock which would not otherwise be found on the reserve; kestrel and buzzard hunt along the hillside and snipe and greenshank breed on the moorland lochans and bogs. Fox, badger, otter and wild cat have all been recorded.

Inverpolly

NC 1312; 10.857ha; NCC reserve
Moorland, mountain, woodland, lochs, bogs, seashore and islands
Access restricted 1 September–21 October: contact Assynt Estate Office, tel. 05714 203
Reserve and trail leaflets available at Knockan Visitor Centre (NC 187094) or from NCC, Inverness
April–May

This vast area of rock hummocks, interspersed with numerous lochs and boggy hollows and dominated by the spectacular peaks of Stac Pollaidh, Cul Mor and Cul Beag, is in many senses a wilderness. The roughness of the terrain, the apparently endless undulating platform of gneiss, and the unreliability of the weather make a venture into the interior of Inverpolly quite an undertaking, but fortunately it is possible to get an impression of the reserve by walking the peripheral roads and the trails of Knockan Cliff on the eastern boundary. Those who do decide to tackle Stac Pollaidh (613m) should note that the summit ridge is crumbling and dangerous.

One hundred and four bird species have been recorded, including golden plover, wheatear, ring ouzel, greenshank and stonechat on the moorland; wood warbler, treecreeper, long-tailed tit, spotted flycatcher and long-eared owl in the woodland; divers, mallard, wigeon, red-breasted merganser and goosander on the lochs; and shag, fulmar and black guillemot on the coast. Barnacle geese visit the islands in winter, ptarmigan and raven breed on the hills, and several birds of prey frequent the reserve.

Around 500 red deer roam freely over Inverpolly, generally moving up the corries and away from the road during the summer months and feeding on the flats near Elphin in winter. Otter fish along the shoreline and in the lochs, which contain char and eels as well as trout and salmon. Wild cat and pine marten are occasionally seen, as are badger, which often live in holes among the rocks rather than in setts.

The many small woods represent all that remains of what were once extensive birch–hazel woodlands. Birch is now the dominant species with some hazel, and rowan, holly, oak and bird cherry are also present. Some of the woodland soils are moderately fertile and support a varied ground cover including such species as selfheal, melancholy thistle, meadowsweet and hay-scented buckler-fern, and a variety of mosses, liverworts and lichens. Lemon-scented fern and Wilson's filmy-fern are abundant in some areas.

Much of the undulating gneiss plateau is covered with wet heath dominated by heather, cottongrass, deergrass and purple moor-grass. Bog myrtle flourishes in the wetter areas, with the pools supporting bogbean and intermediate bladderwort, and great sundew and common butterwort around the margins. Lesser bladderwort and pale butterwort are more localised in their distribution. Altogether some 360 plant species have been recorded.

Although the Inverpolly reserve is of great natural history interest, Knockan Cliff played a major part in the history of geological discovery: from studying this cliff geologists first realised that forces arising deep within the earth can cause great masses of rock to slide up a gently inclined fault line and eventually come to rest on top of much younger rock. The basis for this discovery is clearly demonstrated along the Knockan Cliff Geological Trail.

Loch a' Mhuilinn Wood

Permit only; 67ha; NCC reserve
Woodland, heath, fresh water and coast
Permit from NCC, Golspie
April–July

Set in a characteristically undulating Lewisian gneiss landscape, this reserve is a mosaic of different habitats. Small patches of lichen-rich birch woodland are of special scientific interest as they include oak, near its northern limit in Britain. The heathy areas, marshes and coastline support a variety of flora and fauna typical of the area.

Loch Fleet

NH 7996; 1163ha; SWT reserve
Tidal basin, dunes and pine woodland
Access to woodland restricted to path
May–July: flowers and breeding birds;
October–March: wildfowl; April–September: waders

Only a narrow channel between shingle bars separates Loch Fleet from the sea, and when the tide is out mudflats are exposed over most of the basin. In summer shelduck, redshank and oystercatcher feed on the rich invertebrate life in the mud, and eider on the mussel beds along the course of the river. In autumn many different species of wader appear, some on passage and some to winter in the area. Curlew, golden plover and knot are often present in large numbers. This is also an important resort for wintering duck: mallard, teal and wigeon in and around the basin, goldeneye, red-breasted merganser, common scoter, eider and long-tailed duck commuting between sheltered water and open sea according to weather and tidal conditions. Common seal can often be seen on the sandbanks – the minor road along the south shore provides good viewpoints – and fishing arctic and common tern hover over the shallows in summer.

Although the woodlands are largely planted, natural regeneration of the Scots pine is occurring and the ground flora, typical of old-established pinewood sites, includes one-flowered wintergreen, creeping lady's-tresses, twinflower and lesser twayblade. Capercaillie, siskin and crossbill all breed here, and in one part of the woodland herring gull have established a small colony.

Loch Maree Islands

Permit only; 200ha; NCC reserve
Island group
Permit from NCC, Annancairn Reserve Office,
Kinlochewe
April–June

The reserve consists of about 40 small islands and three large ones which are interesting principally for their native Scots pine and well-grown juniper cover. Most of the species present are also found on BEINN EIGHE.

Mound Alderwoods

Permit only; 267ha; NCC reserve
Wet woodland, fen and open water
Viewing possible from public road at NH 775983
Permit from NCC, Golspie
April–June

This unusual alderwood developed on the estuary of the River Fleet after the construction of the Mound embankment stopped tidal flow into the area. Sluices hold back the waters of LOCH FLEET on the seaward side of the bank at high tide and also prevent adult salmon and their fry from moving upstream and downstream respectively. As the tide drops, there are often fine views from the bridge of the fish waiting for the sluice gates to open. Many wildfowl frequenting Loch Fleet visit the marshes on the downstream edge of the alderwood and terns fish in the open water.

The alderwood itself is of specialist, as distinct from special, interest. It contains no plant rarities but its fascination lies in the way in which the communities vary with changes in the watertable and level of salinity. Drainage cuts and the unevenness of the woodland floor make access very difficult in wet weather.

Munlochy Bay

NH 6753; 443ha; Highland RC reserve
Tidal mudflats and saltmarsh
Open days, advertised locally; otherwise viewing from car park on A832 at NH 657537
September–March

This very sheltered inlet on the northern shore of the Moray Firth attracts up to 1000 wigeon in mid-winter and around 200 shelduck in the first three months of the year. Several hundred teal and smaller numbers of mallard also frequent the bay, and greylag and pink-footed geese roost there fairly regularly in late winter.

Nigg and Udale Bays

NH 7873 and 7367; 640ha; NCC–RSPB reserves
Inter-tidal flats
Access difficult but much of the area can be viewed from the road
August–December

This reserve lies within the larger area of the Cromarty Firth, which is by far the most important site for wintering and passage wildfowl and waders in north east Scotland. Despite nearby industrial developments, the sheltered bays and great stretches of sand and mud are still internationally important for a variety of migratory wildfowl.

A good growth of eelgrass is largely responsible for attracting the thousands of wigeon and hundreds of whooper and mute swans that feed on the two sections of the reserve and elsewhere in the Firth, while an abundant invertebrate population provides food for the several thousand waders generally present in autumn. Oystercatcher, redshank, curlew, knot and dunlin are the most numerous. Fair numbers of goldeneye winter on the Firth, and teal, pintail, shelduck, scaup and pink-footed geese are also regularly recorded. The autumn greylag goose population in Easter Ross often exceeds 10,000; many of these birds roost on the estuary.

Priest Island

NC 9303; 121ha; RSPB reserve
Uninhabited island
Landing is extremely difficult
All year

This grassy sandstone island is notable for its colony of storm petrel, estimated at over 10,000 pairs and the largest known in the United Kingdom. Other breeding species include greylag geese, which nest beside the small freshwater lochs, and a few seabirds. Otter are also present and breed on the island.

Rassal Ashwood

NG 8443; 85ha; NCC reserve
Ashwood on limestone
April–June

The ashwood, which occupies only 13ha of the reserve, is a prominent feature in a landscape of heath and rough grassland and the most northerly true ashwood in Britain. Some of the trees are large and the woodland is open in character with a curious hummocky floor produced by limestone ridges. Although subject to heavy grazing the wood contains abundant hazel and some rowan, blackthorn and hawthorn. Woodland flowers are common only within the fenced enclosures or on the steep sides of the Allt Mor Gorge, part of which lies in the reserve.

On the lime-rich wet ground outside the wood, field gentian is present, broad-leaved cottongrass and black bog-rush flourish and there are drifts of yellow saxifrage around the many small rivulets. Further away from the limestone outcrop the ground cover is of bracken-dominated grassland and heather moor.

The lichens of Rassal Ashwood are of particular interest, with a number of relatively uncommon species growing on either the trees themselves or the rocks on the woodland floor.

Raven Rock

NC 5001; 2km; FC
Plantation and gorge
Leaflet from Lairg tourist office
All year

The steep-sided, damp gorge which lies at the heart of this plantation is particularly rich in mosses and ferns.

Strathy Bog

NC 7955; 281ha; NCC reserve
Blanket bog
Access by foot only; no road suitable for vehicles
Permit from NCC, Golspie
April–June

This reserve represents one of the best remaining examples of low-lying blanket bog in Britain. Its physical features suggest the pattern of its past development and indicate how it may change in the future. Among a large variety of bog species present are dwarf birch, sundews and bearberry.

Under the humid conditions of Torridon, woolly fringe-moss is wrinkled by its own wet weight.

Talich

Permit only; 13.5ha; SWT reserve
Alderwood and grassland
May–June: orchids

Talich includes both dry pasture, believed never to have been ploughed, and wet grassland with boggy flushes where a wide range of orchids can be found, among them fragrant and early-purple orchid, and lesser butterfly-orchid. The alder wood, in which cattle graze in winter, shows signs of previous coppicing.

Tollie Path

NG 889723–859790; 8km; FC
Conifer plantation and open hill
All year

This rough track gives fine views of the LOCH MAREE ISLANDS as it climbs from the loch shores up through rugged open hill country to join the A832 above Poolewe.

Torridon and Loch Maree (Gairloch Conservation Unit)

See map; various bodies
Mountainous country
Visitor centre at NG 905557, open 1 June–
30 September; display and audio-visual programme; deer museum; booklet, from centre or NTS, Edinburgh; guided walk programme; contact ranger-naturalist
Seasonal access restriction: see below
All year

Extending over some 40,500ha of mountainous country, the land between Lochs Torridon and Maree can truly be described as one of Scotland's last great wildernesses. No roads penetrate its interior, nor do any encircle it. In some respects the beauty and grandeur of the area can best be appreciated from a distance: looking across the calm waters of Upper Loch Torridon towards the soaring peaks of Liathach, or down Glen Docherty to Loch Maree, stretching away between its guardian mountains, BEINN EIGHE and Slioch. Those who wish to explore and enjoy its wild beauty to the full must, however, be prepared to do so on foot, adequately shod and equipped to cope with rough terrain, long distances and often unreliable weather.

Before embarking upon any such expedition the visitor should take note of the fact that virtually the whole of this area lies within the Gairloch Conservation Unit, in which the large herds of red deer are managed on a co-operative basis by the various landowners involved. Management of the deer involves cropping the natural population increase, to keep the herd size within the carrying capacity of the ground, and also upgrading the environment for them by draining and burning to improve the grazing and by providing more sheltering woodland. Accurate counting of the stock and selective culling of the surplus stags and hinds both depend on freedom from disturbance; walkers are asked to co-operate by checking with local agents before entering the core of the Gairloch Conservation Unit, where this work is carried out. There is freedom of access at all times to the fringes of the Unit and to the Torridon estate; elsewhere restrictions are most likely to be in force during September, October and November.

Many walkers and climbers use the routes leading into the hills from the car parks on the Torridon estate and Beinn Eighe, but several long paths head southwards from the A832. One of these, up Glen Grudie, offers an 8km walk culminating in a magnificent vista of Coire Mhic Fhearchair, the most north westerly of Beinn Eighe's many corries. Justly regarded as among the finest in the Scottish Highlands, this ice-carved amphitheatre with 400m vertical walls of red sandstone topped with white quartzite rises as a horseshoe around its cold corrie loch.

There is abundant evidence of the action of ice elsewhere in the area at low levels as well as high among the corries and ridges. Just south of Lochan an Iasgair, in Glen Torridon, the mounds of glacial deposit are so thick on the ground that the place is called the 'Corrie of a Hundred Hills'. When this mass of hummocks is lit at just the right angle it looks for all the world like a cardboard egg tray!

That Scots pine once covered the lower slopes of the hills is evident from the many twisted stumps preserved in the peat. Today, apart from plantations and the woodland by Loch Torridon, only scattered pine, birch, rowan and, surprisingly, the occasional oak tree, struggle for survival in this barren country. Heather, cross-leaved heath, deergrass, cottongrass and purple moor-grass dominate the vegetation on the lower ground, with bog myrtle, in some places shoulder-high, in the wetter areas, and crowberry, bearberry and dwarf juniper where it is drier. Woolly fringe-moss and bog mosses are plentiful, the former sometimes growing so luxuriantly on rock surfaces that it sags into wrinkles under its own wet weight. Spotted-orchids, bog asphodel, sundew and butterwort are widespread, and water lobelia and bogbean grow in the peaty lochans.

Higher on the hillsides, where bands of lime-rich rock and absence of grazing animals encourage a more varied and lush vegetation, many of the sandstone ledges are veritable rock gardens. Starry and mossy saxifrage, alpine bistort and alpine willowherb grow around streams and gullies, while on the drier slopes dwarf cornel, parsley fern, alpine lady-fern and bog bilberry occur. The most local plants of these mountains, found at the highest levels among screes and on the exposed ridges, include northern rock-cress, arctic mouse-ear and curved woodrush.

The road along the northern shore of Loch Torridon is well worth exploring – but should not be attempted by those in a hurry. Single-tracked, with steep gradients and hairpin bends, it first skirts the lochside and then climbs above the scattered crofting townships to a fine viewpoint overlooking Loch a Mhullaich. Here clubmosses and lichens grow by the roadside among heather, cottongrass and bog asphodel.

The road starts again at Redpoint, some 13km up the coast. For the energetic the walk from Torridon hostel to Craig and on to Gairloch is not unduly arduous, and Craig certainly offers a fine chance to get away from it all. Most visitors, however, will approach Redpoint from the north, via the narrow road which leaves the A832 near Kerrysdale and winds through knobbly low hills to the attractive little village of Badachro.

Although these bays are not under anything like the recreational pressures experienced by beaches on the Sutherland coast, for example at ACHMELVICH, they nevertheless illustrate clearly just how fragile an environment these 'soft' coastlines are. Wherever the thin *machair* turf of grasses and wild flowers is broken through by wheeled traffic, human trampling or over-grazing, wind-blow soon starts, creating breaches in the vegetated dunes and spreading sand far inland. Once started, such erosion is difficult to stop and it is not long before the appearance of the area is radically altered. Sometimes the level of almost the entire *machair* grassland is lowered, leaving only a few resistant tufts to show how things once were.

This coastline does not attract many seabirds, although a few shag, cormorant and black guillemot may be seen. Eider and red-breasted merganser breed in small numbers, and heron often stand out on the rocks, patiently waiting for an unwary fish to come along. Near the coast, and especially in the woodlands around Loch Shieldaig and Badachro and along Loch Torridon, there is a good variety of small birds; both whinchat and stonechat are fairly common. But this is really a land of moorland and mountain birds. Out in the trackless hinterland you might expect to hear the haunting cry of golden plover and the anxious yelping of a greenshank disturbed on its breeding ground. Both black-throated and red-throated diver find lochs here to suit their respective, and very different, requirements. There are insignificant-looking brown twite here too, with ring ouzel, raven, ptarmigan, peregrine and golden eagle in the hills.

To see something of the area's wildlife the best starting points are undoubtedly the visitor centres at Torridon and BEINN EIGHE.

Highland South

Spanning the breadth of the Highlands from the Moray Firth to the sea of the Hebrides is the massif of the central Grampians and west Highlands. It is a landscape of superlatives and comprises a highly dissected 914m plateau rising to some 1340m at the summit of Ben Nevis, and to nearly 1300m on the Braeriach summit of the CAIRNGORMS, encompassing no fewer than 36 peaks over 914m. This plateau is deeply cleft by the Great Glen fault, plunging over 300m below sea level in a north east to south west gash from Inverness to Fort William.

Glaciers, their meltwaters and the fast, spating rivers have further incised the mountains: the River Spey, for example, separating the Cairngorms from the Monadhliath; and Glen Spean, isolating the southern Nevis and GLENCOE ranges. The water-filled glacial troughs of Loch Ness, Loch Morar and Loch Shiel are the deepest and among the largest freshwater bodies in Britain. Drowned by rising sea levels in the past, other glaciated valleys form a fretted coastline of deepwater sounds and fiord-like sea lochs, penetrating inland 30km or more.

The climate is also one of contrasts. It ranges from the wet and mild Atlantic west coast, through the arctic–alpine summits of the Grampians, to the more continental dry east coast with above-average sunshine.

The ring faults of Ardnamurchan and the cauldron subsidence of Glencoe help to make these places world-famous to volcanic geologists. A hard-rock structure produces a rocky, cliffed coastline with maritime heaths and oak or hazel scrub on promontories and sheltered inlets, with stony or sandy beaches in a few small bays in Ardnamurchan and Morar. In such a geologically young landscape, soils are immature or rudimentary and natural fertility is usually low. In contrast, the soft coast of the north-facing Moray Firth has sandbanks and dunes forming unstable bars and forelands from the CULBIN SANDS to Whiteness Head at the entrance to the shallow, silted Beauly Firth. These softer shores provide nesting sites for terns and ringed plover, wide feeding grounds

for knot and bar-tailed godwit in winter, and for pintail, scoter, goldeneye and long-tailed duck offshore. Inland here is the only arable land where grain and root crops can be grown successfully.

The land is chiefly used for hill sheep farms, conifer forestry and sporting estates, the last varying from grouse moors in the heather-clad eastern Highlands to deer forests on the wetter moor-grass and deergrass-covered western hills, with salmon and trout fisheries throughout. This east–west climatic gradient is quite apparent: the heather moors towards the east become richer in dry heath flowers – bell heather, cowberry, petty whin and wintergreen – while the western moors become upland grasslands with bracken or blanket bogs containing sparse heather, cross-leaved heath, bog asphodel, bog myrtle, sundews, moor-grass and *Sphagnum* moss. There are similar contrasts in woodlands, with juniper and the pendulous silver birch in the eastern woods, and grey and eared sallow and hairy birch in the west, where the tree line is much lower.

The summits of the mountains with their barren crags, stony 'fell-field' and thin cover of lichen, moss and sedge heath are the habitat of arctic birds such as dotterel, ptarmigan and snow bunting, and of mountain hare. Colourful cushion alpines soon come into bloom when the winter snow cover melts. This montane environment covers large areas of country both north and south of the Great Glen. Cliff ledges out of reach of grazing animals support tall herbs including angelica, roseroot, stone bramble, mountain sorrel and holly fern. Golden eagle, peregrine falcon, merlin and raven hunt over wide areas, and red deer also range over large expanses of hill and glen according to weather and season.

Summit areas are far less extensive in the west Highlands; for example, from Kintail through Knoydart, Morar and Moidart to Glencoe the dominant features are generally steep, rugged crags, cliffs and acute ridges and peaks offering sparse roothold to mountain vegetation. Characteristic alpines here are starry saxifrage, parsley fern, Scottish asphodel and alpine lady's-mantle.

Where the foothills flatten out near the west coast, valley bogs and raised bogs form extensive peat mosses, as at the outflow of Loch Shiel and by the River Shiel. Too wet ever to have developed woodland cover, the layers of undecomposed sedge and moss with their preserved pollen grains tell the story of vegetation succession since the last glaciation. These mosses are the habitat and nesting place of greenshank and the wintering ground of white-fronted geese.

All the glens which dissect the Highlands were once clothed by the old Caledonian forest, of Scots pine and birch in inland areas, and oak, ash, elm and hazel lower down near the coast, especially on the warmer, south-facing aspects. The flat riversides of the lower straths were once covered with impenetrable alder and willow thickets.

The bulk of the remaining native Scots pine-woods are found in this central Highland area, and most are now protected within reserves. In these forests survive the predatory pine marten, wild cat and golden eagle, the growing population of osprey, with crossbill and crested tit. Northern pinewood plants of the forest floor include orchids – creeping lady's-tresses, lesser twayblade and coralroot orchid.

The broadleaved woods are equally rich, containing butterflies such as speckled wood, chequered skipper, pearl-bordered fritillary and Scotch argus, mammals such as wild cat, badger and roe deer, and a good variety of woodland birds. Oakwoods with birch hazel, holly and ash cover the steep slopes beside Loch Ness and many of the west coast sea lochs and freshwater lochs. The oak gives place to ash and sometimes wych elm over more calcareous rocks. Of particular interest to botanists are the hundreds of species of epiphytic lichens, mosses and leafy liverworts which luxuriantly clothe all twigs, branches and trunks. They survive here only because of an unbroken history of forest cover, a pristine atmosphere and high humidity. The woodland flora, as well as the ubiquitous bluebells, primroses, wood-sorrel and anemones, has a field layer rich in ferns including mountain fern, hay-scented buckler-fern and the diminutive filmy-fern.

The mixed woodland, farmland and moorland country where Loch Ness opens into the Moray Firth is particularly rich in relatively small, shallow lochs which are a haven for waterfowl such as tufted duck and mallard, and the rare Slavonian grebe which nests in the fringing sedgebeds. The Beauly Firth attracts large numbers of wintering waders and wildfowl including greylag and pink-footed geese, wigeon, tufted duck, mallard and goldeneye, but particularly the sawbills, goosander and merganser, which feed on the herring and sprat shoals. The food resource is also exploited by common seal, dolphin and porpoise which are regular visitors. In summer the firth also holds a flock of moulting Canada geese, and a substantial population of breeding shelduck.

M. E. BALL

Abernethy Forest

NH 998167; 8980ha; NCC–RSPB reserves
Mountain, moorland and native pine forest
Car park at Forest Lodge NJ 018161
All year

Situated on the northern flanks of the Cairngorm mountains, this vast reserve stretches from Caledonian pine forest up through sways of open heather moorland and rocky outcrops to the wild tops of spectacular screes, cliffs and flatter boulder fields crowned by the summit of Cairngorm itself. The valley of the river Nethy forms the central part of the reserve flanked by mountains.

After arriving at Forest Lodge, the visitor can first walk through the native Scots pines – grey-green and covered with lichens. Where they grow close together the trees are relatively uniform, but as one moves up the hill they become more scattered, irregular in shape, ragged-edged and flat-topped. These woods are the nesting place of the magnificent capercaillie which, together with its relative the black grouse, is still plentiful on the reserve. Other special birds of the forest are the crested tit and Scottish crossbill, as well as the more common mistle thrush, chaffinch, coal tit and goldcrest. Along the river there are dippers and common sandpipers, and siskins feed in the stream-side trees. In the more open woodland tree pipits are found and the dead wood of the ancient pines provides feeding places for woodpeckers and nesting holes for redstarts.

The forest floor is clothed with bilberry, cowberry and crowberry as well as heather, and in places juniper creates a thicker understorey suitable for birds such as robins and wrens. Birch, rowan and aspen are scattered among the pines but are held in check by the heavy grazing of red deer which is also affecting the regeneration of pines. Other mammals of the reserves include red squirrel, otter, pine marten, wildcat, fox, badger and roe deer.

Red grouse and meadow pipit are the birds of the open moorland. Golden eagles, peregrines and merlins hunt this area for suitable prey. It is a steep haul to the tops, but the intrepid visitor is rewarded with spectacular sheer cliffs, ice-bound lochans in beautiful corries and dazzling snow-fields. On the high plateau, dotterel and ptarmigan breed and a herd of reindeer feed on the lichen.

Balmacaan Woods

NH 500290; 39ha; WdT reserve
Mixed woodland
Spring, summer

Situated high on the hillside overlooking Urquhart Bay and Loch Ness, the reserve is a mixture of oak and birch woodland and pine plantations. There are fine specimen conifers in and around the former gardens of the now demolished Balmacaan House. The view point at Craig Mony is at the north end of the wood and gives wonderful views of Loch Ness and the surrounding hills.

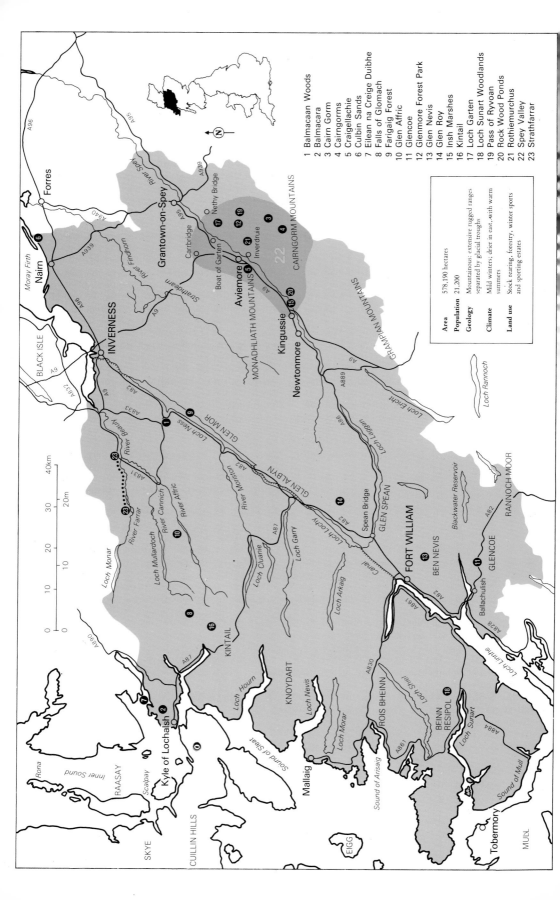

1 Balmacaan Woods
2 Balmacara
3 Cairn Gorm
4 Cairngorms
5 Craigellachie
6 Culbin Sands
7 Eilean na Creige Duibhe
8 Falls of Glomach
9 Farigaig Forest
10 Glen Affric
11 Glencoe
12 Glenmore Forest Park
13 Glen Nevis
14 Glen Roy
15 Insh Marshes
16 Kintail
17 Loch Garten
18 Loch Sunart Woodlands
19 Pass of Ryvoan
20 Rock Wood Ponds
21 Rothiemurchus
22 Spey Valley
23 Strathfarrar

Area	578,190 hectares
Population	21,200
Geology	Mountainous: extensive rugged ranges separated by glacial troughs
Climate	Mild winters, drier in east, with warm summers
Land use	Stock rearing, forestry, winter sports and sporting estates

Craigellachie: the open birchwood is alive with birdsong in early summer.

Balmacara

NG 7930; 2274ha; NTS
Rocky shores and islands, hilly ground, woodland,
lochs and croft ground
Booklet from NTS, Edinburgh and local centre;
visitor centre, open Easter–October, at Lochalsh House;
guided walks programme
All year

This extensive property covers most of the rugged promontory lying between Loch Alsh and Loch Carron. Small rocky islets are scattered thickly along the coastline and the hinterland displays the mosaic of heathery hillocks, bare knobs of rock and small lochans so characteristic of Wester Ross. Much of the land is crofted and visitors are asked to respect this traditional form of land use and not to enter croft land without permission. The policy woodlands of Lochalsh House are open all year.

Cairn Gorm

NJ 0005; 2422ha; HIDB
Mountainous country
All year

Stretching from the limits of afforestation up to the summit of Cairn Gorm, this is the area on which facilities for skiing are concentrated; the roads into Coire Cas and Coire na Ciste provide easy access to the middle slopes, where many species typical of the CAIRNGORMS can be found. Even when low cloud blankets the summits there is much to see, for example on the shoulder of An t-Aonach, between the two car parks. The striking variation in the growth of heather, stunted and low on the exposed face and luxuriant where a hollow gives shelter from wind, is well demonstrated here, while even a short search should soon reveal most of the berry-bearing shrubs, including dwarf cornel and cloudberry. Clubmosses are widespread, several species of fern are tucked away in crannies among the rocks, and there is an abundant growth of lichens. The last are among the food plants of reindeer, once native to Scotland and reintroduced here some years ago. Ptarmigan and red deer can sometimes be seen quite near the roads but a greater variety of birds will be found away from the populous areas, in the eastern corries.

Cairngorms

NJ 0101; 25,949ha; NCC reserve
Mountain, moorland and forest
Access unrestricted, but visitors are asked to avoid
certain areas during deer cull, August–October
Visitor centre, open May–September, nature trail,
publications; further information from Aviemore
tourist office or NCC, Kingussie
April–August

This vast reserve, the largest in Britain, stretches both north and south from the high tops of the Cairngorms down to the pinewoods of the low ground. Only the toughest plants can survive among the pink granite gravel and boulders of the exposed summit plateaus, but the great corries hold a more varied flora and the native pinewoods of the lower slopes have their own special plants and animals. This is a land of red deer and wild cat, of golden eagle and crested tit, and of mountain avens and twinflower.

The reserve lies astride the Lairig Ghru, the rugged and steep-sided pass which links Speyside with Deeside and separates CAIRN GORM and Ben Macdhui – 1310m the highest point in the range – from Braeriach, Cairn Toul and Carn Ban Mor. On the windswept summits moss campion, spiked wood-rush, curved wood-rush and three-leaved rush are among the few flowering plants present with the mosses and lichens. In the corries the flora, which is predominantly one of acid rocks, includes many widespread montane species, such as roseroot, mountain sorrel, purple saxifrage and alpine saw-wort, and a number of rare or very local ones, including mountain hawkweeds, starwort mouse-ear, hare's-foot sedge, arctic mouse-ear and alpine hair-grass. Least willow and sibbaldia flourish where snow regularly lies late, as do parsley fern and alpine lady-fern.

Heather and deergrass dominate the vegetation lower down the mountain slopes, with bell heather in relatively dry areas and cross-leaved heath where the ground is wetter. Bog bilberry, mountain crowberry, bearberry and trailing azalea are widespread, the latter most often on very exposed sites between 750 and 1000m. Dwarf cornel, cloudberry, interrupted clubmoss and chickweed wintergreen are also abundant, and dwarf birch occurs locally.

The most extensive of the pinewood areas lie on the northern and north western edges of the reserve, in ROTHIEMURCHUS Forest and on the slopes above Loch an Eilein, where the trees growing sparsely at 625m above sea level are probably near the upper limit for native Scots pine in Britain. Some of the oldest and finest specimens, around Loch an Eilein, are at least 250 years old; good natural regeneration is now taking place on open moorland nearby. The visual attraction of these woodlands lies largely in their diversity: in some places the trees are densely packed above a mossy carpet, and in others widely spaced among heather, bilberry, cowberry and juniper. The two small pinewood orchids, creeping lady's-tresses and lesser twayblade, are widespread; both lesser and intermediate wintergreen are fairly common but serrated wintergreen is less abundant; one-flowered wintergreen and twinflower are very local in their distribution.

A feature of these native pinewoods is their high population of wood ants. Their big mounded pine needle nests are scattered through the forest and there is constant traffic of ants across the gravelly tracks. Many very local insects – beetles, plant bugs, caddis flies, moths and also spiders – are known only from Rothiemurchus and from the Cairngorms.

Crested tit and crossbill are typical birds of these pinewoods, but though widespread neither species is numerous. Siskin and redstart are quite common, wren and chaffinch abundant, and tree pipit and willow warbler present where birch, rowan and aspen grow in clearings and along the water's edge. Capercaillie and black grouse also breed in moderate numbers, the former deep in the forest and the latter often along its moorland edge. Above the tree line peregrine and ring ouzel haunt the cliffs and screes. On the summits, among the scattered boulders and sparse vegetation, dotterel and ptarmigan rear their young in a situation so exposed that disturbance can all too easily lead to chilling of eggs or chicks. Several pairs of golden eagle nest on the reserve and these magnificent birds can often be seen soaring high above the tops or riding the up-currents along a corrie rim. Their breeding success has, however, fallen in recent years, largely due to disturbance. Other breeding birds of the reserve include greenshank, merlin, buzzard and sparrowhawk.

Large herds of red deer roam the hills, descending into the valleys in winter, and there are fair numbers of roe deer in the woodlands. Pine marten is scarce on Speyside but red squirrel is quite common, though more often found near mixed plantations than in pure pine forest. Badgers have been increasing in recent years and otter tracks are occasionally seen by lochs and streams.

The 5 km nature trail round Loch an Eilein leads through a variety of typical habitats.

Claish Moss

Permit only; 563ha; NCC reserve
Raised peat mire
Permit from NCC, Fort William
May–August

This large, unevenly domed mire area is patterned by a linear series of ridges, pools and streams. Several species of *Sphagnum* moss are present and the ridges carry woolly fringe-moss. A major interest of the site is the fact that its vegetational history since post-glacial times has been traced in the peat.

Craigellachie

NH 8812; 257ha; NCC reserve
Birchwood, cliff and moorland
May–August

Open birchwood clothes the lower slopes of this reserve, which lies on the western edge of Aviemore. Above are sheer cliffs of schistose rock and open heather moorland rising to around 600m. On the upper slopes the jumble of fallen trees and mossy boulders harbours ferns, lichens and fungi and there is a rich ground flora.

Both silver and downy birch are present in the wood, which is one of the largest birchwoods in Speyside. Rowan, aspen, hazel, wych elm, oak, bird cherry and juniper are scattered thinly among the birch and there is a wet area with bog myrtle and *Sphagnum*. Grasses and mosses dominate the ground vegetation, with common rock-rose and alpine bistort in a few localities and local species such as shining crane's-bill, alternate-leaved golden-saxifrage and serrated wintergreen growing on the rocks.

In summer the wood is alive with birdsong; typical birchwood species such as tree pipit, willow warbler, spotted flycatcher, blue tit and long-tailed tit are particularly abundant. Great spotted woodpecker, woodcock, treecreeper and mistle thrush are also among the breeding species. Red grouse nest on the moorland and black grouse at the woodland edge, while kestrel and jackdaw favour the cliffs for their nest sites. But the most notable breeding bird of the reserve is undoubtedly peregrine; for many years, and generally successfully, a pair of these dashing and handsome predators has nested on the sheer cliff overlooking the busy Aviemore Centre.

Craigellachie is well known for its insects, which include several very local moths such as Rannoch sprawler, the delicately patterned Kentish glory and angle-striped sallow. All these moth species are associated with birch trees.

Culbin Sands

NH 9362; 862ha; RSPB reserve
Sandflats, saltmarsh and shingle bars
Access, on foot only, along the shore from Kingsteps (NJ 905575) or through Culbin Forest from Cloddymoss (NH 983599)
September–March: duck and waders;
May–August: flowers and breeding birds

This remote stretch of coastline, backed by CULBIN FOREST (Grampian), is a very important wintering area for wildfowl, especially sea duck and waders.

Two shingle bars lie 1.5km out from the high-water mark; stretching for nearly 8km along the coast, they are constantly changing in size and shape under the action of wind and waves. Greylag geese roost on the bars in winter and several thousand common scoter, long-tailed duck and velvet scoter regularly gather on the seaward side. Ringed plover, oystercatcher, redshank, gulls and a few pairs of common tern breed on the shingle of the reserve's Nairn Bar; in late summer several species of tern rest there in large numbers as they pass through the area on migration.

Between bar and beach lie the flats and saltmarsh, a rich feeding ground for waders and duck. Wigeon, mallard and shelduck can be found here in number thoughout the winter. As many as 1000 bar-tailed godwit and 2000 oystercatcher use these flats in winter, and many knot, dunlin, ringed plover and curlew are generally present. These gatherings of waders draw predators into the area and peregrine, merlin and hen harrier are frequently seen.

Nairn Old Bar, towards the western end of the reserve, is also of physiographical and botanical interest. Its pattern of raised shingle ridges is particularly well marked and it carries an interesting plant succession, from pioneering lichens and stonecrop through to heathland dominated by heather, crowberry and gorse.

Doire Donn

Permit only; 28ha; SWT reserve
Woodland
May–August

By Highland standards this deciduous woodland is unusually rich, with a well-developed shrub layer and varied ground flora. Sessile oak, ash, birch, alder and wych elm all contribute to the canopy and there is an understorey of hazel, rowan, holly, willows and a few guelder-rose and bird cherry, together with seedlings of most of them. The ground vegetation includes both acid-loving plants, such as heather and bilberry, and those typical of richer soils, for example woodruff and sanicle. Many species of woodland birds are present.

Eilean na Creige Duibhe

NG 824335; 1ha; SWT reserve
Wooded island
Access restricted March–June
July–August

The Scots pinewood on this small rocky island holds a flourishing heronry. Eider nest in the dense ground cover of heather, bilberry and bracken and otter frequently visit the island. Drifts of sand-like material along the southern shore are in fact the remains of a lime-covered red seaweed which grows nearby in deep water.

Falls of Glomach

NH 017258; 1134ha; NTS
Waterfall and surrounding valley
Access, on foot only, from Killilan (NG 946302) or Dorusduae (NG 983227)
All year

This spectacular fall is one of the highest in Britain. Confined within a narrow ravine some 180m deep, the mountain torrent drops 100m in a single wild plunge, then jets off a projecting rock to fall a further 20m to the pools below. The falls lie in a remote mountain area and both routes mentioned above are steep and rugged; the wet ground around the falls can be dangerously slippery and visitors should take great care.

Farigaig

Permit only; 5ha; SWT reserve
Scrub woodland
May–September

Situated on steeply sloping ground above the Farigaig River, near Loch Ness, this small area of scrub woodland contains a good variety of species. The wood is open and dominated by birch, with a few relict oak on the drier ground and alder, aspen and willow in the wetter hollows. Juniper, hazel and rose species occur in the shrub layer and common wintergreen is found in the predominantly heather and bilberry ground cover.

Farigaig Forest

NH 523237; 2.5km; FC
Woodland trail
Leaflet at centre or from Inverness tourist office; forest centre with display
All year

The trail climbs steeply, through a mixture of native deciduous woodland and planted conifers, to a mountain viewpoint. An exhibition on the wildlife of the forest is included in the forest centre's display.

Glen Affric

NH 1923; 1265ha; FC reserve
Native pinewood
Trail leaflet from Inverness tourist office or forest office
April–October

Glen Affric is widely acknowledged to be one of the most attractive places in Scotland; hills, lochs, islands, river, waterfalls and woodlands combine to create a remarkable variety of scenery, much of it visible from the road that winds up the glen. The pine forest, lying along the southern side of Lochs Affric and Beneavean (Beinn á Mheadhoin), which contributes so much to the beauty of the area, is managed as a Native Pinewood Reserve. Strict measures have been taken to control deer, in order to allow natural regeneration to take place, and a programme of planting with stock raised from seed gathered in the reserve has been carried out.

Many wetland birds visit the Insh Marshes, now being managed to increase habitat diversity.

The most natural areas of pinewood are those near Dog Fall (NH 2928), and at Pollan Buidhe, between Lochs Affric and Benevean. At both points there are many fine old trees and a good sprinkling of younger ones, with abundant birch and rowan giving spectacular colour contrasts in spring and autumn. The hummocky ground is thickly carpeted with heather, bilberry and a good variety of mosses. Typical ground cover of wet moorland – purple moor-grass, cottongrass and *Sphagnum* – flourish in the damper hollows, and in autumn many different fungi appear along the edges of the sandy forest tracks.

Scottish crossbill, capercaillie and black grouse breed in the pinewoods and there is a varied population of small birds in summer. Goosander and mallard occur regularly on the lochs and dipper and grey wagtail by the river; the chances of seeing one of the larger birds of prey over the glen are quite high. Because deer control is strict there are only a few roe deer in the forest, but red squirrel are fairly common and red deer may be seen on the open hills to the north.

Glencharnoch Wood

NH 900226; 14ha; WdT
Scots pine forest
Summer

This Scots pine woodland may have its origins in the ancient Caledonian pine-forest. Birch, rowan and willow are found here, as well as some juniper. There is access to the wood from the village of Carsbridge.

Glencoe

NN 1556; 5749ha; NTS
Mountainous country
Visitor centre (NN 127565) open Easter mid-October; guided walks programme; ranger-naturalist
All year

The spectacular mountains of Glencoe, where walls of rock rise steeply on either side and great corries are carved from the peaks above, has long made this place famous for its scenery as well as its notorious massacre. This is climbers' country, demanding a high degree of fitness and skill from those who would venture to the tops. The traveller through the glen is unlikely to see anything of particular natural history interest, although both golden eagle and peregrine sometimes pass overhead. Golden plover and ptarmigan breed in small numbers and red deer are present but generally stay well away from the busy floor of the glen. The mountain flora is richest where calcareous rocks outcrop – usually on the most inaccessible cliffs.

Glenmore Forest Park

NH 9810; 2644ha; FC
Coniferous woodland, loch and heather moor
Map-guide and booklet from Glenmore forest office (NH 977097) or Aviemore tourist office
April September

Remnants of the old native pinewoods still survive here in a few places, for example the PASS OF RYVOAN, but most of the plantable land in the

Forest Park now carries commercial woodlands. These are predominantly of Scots pine, Sitka spruce and Norway spruce; natural birch, rowan and willow are widespread along streams and in clearings and many of the pinewood birds and animals have colonised the plantations. Above the economic planting limit of around 500m the heather-dominated moorland supports a good range of plants typical of the lower slopes of the CAIRNGORMS. The hills on the north side of the park rise to around 800m; the higher ground to the south, on which the skiing facilities are located, and the summit ridge itself, are described under CAIRN GORM. The plants of the more open forest and moorland are similar to those found in the CAIRNGORMS reserve. Scenic Loch Morlich, set against a backdrop of the high peaks and corries, lies almost entirely within the park.

Scottish crossbill, crested tit, capercaillie, siskin and goldcrest all breed in the afforested areas, while moorland birds include red grouse and curlew, with black grouse common along the forest fringe. Dipper, grey wagtail, teal, goosander and common sandpiper frequent the streams and loch shore, and the famous Speyside osprey sometimes fish in Loch Morlich.

There are many roe deer and red squirrels in the plantations and both can often be seen along the forest trails. Red·deer are discouraged from entering the forest but they roam the moorland and hills, where mountain hares are also found.

Glen Nevis

NN 1669; 873ha; Highland RC
Mountainous country
All year

The chance of seeing golden eagle from the roadside is as good here as anywhere in Scotland. These majestic birds can often be seen soaring above the crags which rise steeply on either side of the glen. There are also spectacular views around the upper car park (at NN 167692) and along the right-of-way path to Steall and beyond. A countryside ranger is based in the area.

Glen Roy

NN 3090; 1168ha; NCC reserve
Series of ice-age geological features
Booklet from NCC, Inverness; viewpoint
All year

The best-known of the ice-age features visible in Glen Roy are the spectacular 'parallel roads', three distinct horizontal terraces on the hillside, which can be clearly seen from the viewpoint at NN 297854. Scientific investigation has demonstrated that these terraces mark successive shorelines of a large lake formed when ice blocked the entrance to the glen.

Insh Marshes

NN 7799; 852ha; RSPB reserve
Marsh, wet pasture and woodland
Open all days except Tuesday 9a.m. to 9p.m.

or sunset when earlier
Leaflet from RSPB, Edinburgh or RSPB warden, Ivy Cottage, Insh, Kingussie; reception hut; hides
April–July

This vast tract of wetland along the flood plain of the River Spey is important for breeding and wintering wildfowl and also for breeding waders. Although few birds of prey nest here, many hunt over the marshes and along the woodland fringe; hen harrier and osprey are regular visitors.

In the past numerous attempts have been made to drain these marshes for agriculture. Flood banks were constructed along· the riverside and an elaborate network of ditches dug, but the Spey is not an easy river to tame. Severe floods continued to occur, the ditches gradually silted up and eventually all attempts at reclamation were abandoned. Today the reserve is largely fen – marsh, which covers great stretches of the valley floor and is interspersed with willow carr, drainage ditches and areas of open water, and fringed with birch and juniper on the higher ground. In midwinter a metre or more of water or ice often covers the area, but in summer many of the smaller pools dry out. New, deeper pools are being created, and summer grazing by cattle has been reintroduced, to improve conditions for breeding birds.

Good numbers of mallard, wigeon, teal and tufted duck nest on the reserve; shoveler, goosander and red-breasted merganser occasionally breed and pochard did so for the first time in 1978. All the common wetland waders breed in these wetlands, and the much rarer wood sandpiper regularly feeds there. The dense beds of water sedge, a local northern species, and other marsh plants provide ideal cover for water rail and

The striking elephant hawk-moth is regularly recorded on the Insh Marshes.

sometimes also for spotted crake – both more likely to be heard than seen.

The reserve boasts an impressive list of birds of prey observed from the hides. Buzzard, sparrowhawk and hen harrier are the most frequently recorded, while osprey fish the river and pools regularly between April and August. Peregrine, kestrel and merlin occasionally hunt over the marshes and there have been sightings of golden eagle, goshawk and marsh harrier. A sudden panic in the big black-headed gull colony often gives the first hint that a raptor is around.

Seventeen species of butterfly and over 200 moths, including the very local Kentish glory and Rannoch sprawler, have been recorded on the reserve. Both elephant hawk-moth and poplar hawk-moth are seen every year. Other insects of interest include the very locally distributed bee beetle, which looks like a bumble bee, and several species of dragonfly.

A number of roe deer spend most of their time in the marsh, where the tall vegetation gives a good cover for the young kids. Fox and badger are also present and are sometimes seen from the hides.

Kintail

NH 0019; 5182ha; NTS
Mountainous country
Possible seasonal restrictions: see below
Booklet; visitor centre at Morvich (NG 961211)
open June–September; guided walks;
ranger-naturalist
All year

The clustered peaks of the Five Sisters of Kintail form the core of this site. Rising steeply from near sea level at the head of Loch Duich, several of the Sisters just top the 1000m mark. Crowned with a spectacular array of corries, crags and precipices, these are among the sheerest grassy mountains in Scotland. Advice on the best routes into these hills, and on any restrictions because of deer stalking on adjoining properties, can be obtained from the National Trust for Scotland representative at Morvich Visitor Centre.

Although not carrying the wealth of plants found on BEN LAWERS (Tayside), these mountains support a varied and interesting flora. Among the more notable species on the grassy slopes are pale butterwort, fragrant orchid, greater and lesser butterfly-orchid, dwarf cudweed and mountain azalea, while the corries support alpine rue, dwarf willow, three-flowered rush and starry, purple and mossy saxifrage. There are herds of red deer and wild goats in the area and a good variety of moorland birds.

Loch Garten

NH 9718; 1192ha; RSPB reserve
Pine forest, lochs and wet moorland
Access within statutory bird sanctuary strictly confined to marked path leading to osprey observation post; elsewhere on reserve along pinewood paths
Leaflet from hide or RSPB, Edinburgh; observation hide, open 10a.m.–8.30p.m. end April–end August
Mid-April–August

Famous as the site which initiated the osprey's successful recolonisation of the Scottish Highlands, Loch Garten is the only nature reserve in Scotland that can justifiably claim to attract over 90,000 visitors a year, most of whom visit the observation hide. Yet with its old-established pinewoods and variety of other habitats Loch Garten contains a wealth of interest for the botanist and entomologist as well as the ornithologist.

The reserve forms part of Abernethy Forest, a remnant of the ancient Forest of Caledon and now the largest surviving area of semi-natural woodland in Britain. Around Lochs Garten and Mallachie the pines are well grown and mature; elsewhere on the reserve are scattered trees more than 200 years old, and areas of active regeneration. In the wetter stretches of peat bog the stunted growth of the moribund trees belies their age, and a 6m stem may represent a 100-year-long struggle to survive. An important feature of the pine forest is the many dead and decaying stumps, for it is here that the crested tit makes its nest. A thriving population of 40–50 pairs of these delightful little birds breeds on the reserve, along with other birds particularly associated with the pinewoods.

Heather, bilberry and cowberry are abundant and juniper is the dominant shrub. Cow-wheat, wood-sorrel and chickweed wintergreen are widely distributed, and less common species such as creeping lady's-tresses, lesser twayblade, serrated, common and intermediate wintergreen and moonwort also occur. In the peat bogs yellow bog asphodel and the insectivorous sundew and butterwort flourish, while field gentian, rock-rose and goldenrod are found on the drier gravelly ridges. In July white water-lily adorns the rather acid lochs, which also support water lobelia and greater bladderwort.

The lochs hold only small populations of breeding wildfowl but they are important roosting sites, for black-headed gull in spring and for duck, greylag geese and whooper swan in winter. Buzzard, kestrel and sparrowhawk breed on the reserve and other birds of prey, such as hen harrier, merlin and peregrine, are often observed.

Roe deer and red squirrel are common on the reserve and frequently seen; badger, fox and wild cat occasionally visit but are often identified only by tracks left in the snow. Otter too visit regularly and at one time bred on an island in the middle of Loch Mallachie.

About 350 beetle species, some of them rare and very closely associated with old pinewoods, have been identified. The 11 dragonfly species recorded include white-faced dragonfly, here close to its northern limit in Britain. Over 260 moths and 18 butterflies are known to occur, among the latter the very local dingy skipper.

The track leading into the forest a short distance to the west of Loch Garten itself offers a 2km route through a variety of habitats, to Loch Mallachie and back.

Loch Sunart Woodlands

NM 8464 and 6558; 163ha; NCC reserve
Natural woodland
Access to Glencripesdale (NM 6558) by permit
only apply NCC, Fort William
Booklet from Strontian information centre or NCC,
Inverness;
April–August

This reserve comprises two contrasting woodlands on opposite sides of Loch Sunart. Ariundle Wood (70ha), in Strontian Glen on the north side of the loch, is predominantly oak, with scattered birch, hazel and rowan. Much of the oak has been coppiced in the past. There is a walk through the reserve which starts from the car park at NM 823632. Glencripesdale Wood (93ha), situated on steep north-facing slopes and on more fertile soil than Ariundle, is an ashwood, with some alder and hazel and a lot of birch.

The scientific interest of these woodlands lies largely in the luxuriant growth of mosses, leafy liverworts and lichens resulting from the high humidity of the area and the long history of woodland on these sites. Many local and some rare species flourish on the woodland floor, especially on the rock surfaces, and on the trees themselves.

Pass of Ryvoan

NJ 9910; 121ha; SWT–FC reserve
Natural pinewood and scree slopes
April–July

Between the steep sides of this narrow pass, which links GLENMORE and Strathnethy, lies the intriguing Green Loch – in Gaelic Lochan Uaine. Not algal growth but a quirk of reflected light is responsible for its strange olive green colour. The muted shade of the loch contrasts with the vivid greens of bilberry and birch, which in turn stand out against the background of dark Scots pine, heather and grey scree. On the southern wall of the pass a cascade of loose stones falls right to the loch shore. On the northern slope the rock is richer in minerals, giving rise to unusually varied plant life for natural woodland of this type.

Dense stands of juniper, some upright and some sprawling, are scattered through the open pinewood and there are clumps of silvery-grey willows among the birches. Primroses, violets, woodruff and moschatel grow on the reserve, as do petty whin and common wintergreen. The marshy floor of the pass holds butterwort and a variety of mosses and sedges.

Crossbill, goldcrest and crested tit are among the resident bird species, while summer visitors include tree pipit, redstart and grey wagtail. Red deer and red squirrel occur regularly on the reserve, through which the public path to Abernethy passes.

Rahoy Hills

Permit only; 1764ha; RSNC–SWT reserve
Mountainous country

Permit from Estate Office, Ardtornish
Botanical list available with permit
May–July

The basalt-capped peaks of Beinn Iadain and Beinn na h'Uamha, with their arctic–alpine plants, are the focal points of this large reserve. On their unstable crags and screes the mineral-rich soil supports a luxuriant flora including four species of saxifrage, alpine meadow-rue, roseroot, globeflower, moss campion, northern rock-cress, Norwegian sandwort and holly fern.

The northern shore of Loch Arienas carries the largest area of woodland on the reserve. Oak, coppiced in the past, is dominant, with much birch and a shrub layer of hazel, alder, holly, rowan and aspen. Blanket bog and acid grassland covers most of the moorland, with marshy ground fringing the several small lochans.

Red-throated diver and greenshank breed on this ground and golden eagle and peregrine are regularly recorded.

Rock Wood Ponds

NH 8302; 17.5ha; FC
Lochans, bog and plantation
Signed trails (1.6 and 2.1km) from NH 8302; hide
All year

Red squirrel, roe deer, goldcrest and crossbill frequent this forest area and a variety of duck visit the lochans. Many typical bog and moorland plants grow in the open areas and insects include red damselflies.

Rothiemurchus

NH 9110; 8800ha; Rothiemurchus Estate
Native pinewood, lochs and hill ground
Access restricted to waymarked paths through
forest, to specified hill routes and by arrangement
Visitor centre at Inverdruie (NH 903109), with exhibition,
open all year 9a.m.–dusk; visitor guide
leaflet; guided walks programme in summer; for further
information tel. Aviemore 810647
All year

The Rothiemurchus Estate includes 800ha of pine forest and 5000ha of hills, plateau and moorland, all lying within the boundary of the CAIRNGORMS reserve, and 3000ha outside it. Most of the finest stands of native pine in the area are found on the estate and many of the typical pinewood species, such as creeping lady's-tresses and chickweed wintergreen, can be seen along the forest paths. Crested tit, redstart, crossbill and tree pipit are quite numerous and there are many red deer and roe deer on the hills and in the woods.

Spey Valley

See map; includes nine sites
Visitor centre at Carrbridge with display and
audio-visual programme; tree-top trail and
bookshop; exhibition at Aviemore tourist office;
further information and guided walks programme
from Rothiemurchus Estate ranger service,
Inverdruie, and Highland Guides
All year

Scots pine, juniper and birch, typical species of the Caledonian forest, frame a view of Cairn Gorm.

There can be few visitors to the Scottish Highlands who do not at least pass through the Spey Valley, the most visited stretch of countryside in Scotland. Pressures on LOCH LOMOND-side (Central) are heavy in summer, especially at weekends, and Deeside is a busy tourist corridor, but it is only on Speyside that so many people spread over such a wide area during so much of the year.

Between the mighty rampart of the CAIRNGORMS, scalloped by corries and cleft by the deep V of the Lairig Ghru, and the comparatively featureless rolling plateaus of the Monadhliath to the north, the Spey winds its leisurely way along the valley floor. From Kingussie to Kincraig its pace is so slow, and the valley floor so flat, that much of the adjoining land forms one of the largest fens remaining in Britain. Part of this great swamp, INSH MARSHES, is now actively managed to make it even more attractive to wetland birds.

At Loch Insh the pattern changes. Scattered across the valley floor between Kincraig and Boat of Garten lies a jumble of humps and hollows, relics of the last ice age. Most of the hummocks are wooded, with graceful birches or sombre pines above a carpet of heather and bilberry, and many of the hollows hold lochs, some large and windswept like Loch Alvie and some little more than pools. It is this mosaic of different landforms and woodland textures, of contrasting colours and of light and shade, that makes this section of the valley so attractive.

Among the best known and most popular of the lochs in the Spey Valley are LOCH GARTEN, with its famous ospreys, and Loch an Eilein, at the edge of the vast Cairngorms reserve. Few people penetrate beyond the well-beaten tourist track, yet at each of these sites a comparatively short walk will take you away from the coach parties and picnickers into the quiet of the old pine forests, where on a still day you may hear the cracking of crossbills extracting the seeds from cones, the scratching of a squirrel's claws as it scampers along a branch, or the purring calls of a family of dainty little crested tits.

It is to the mountains, however, that the eye inevitably keeps straying. The massive rolling plateaus of the Cairngorms form the most extensive area of land above 1000m anywhere in Britain. If conditions are right the view from the summit can be truly superb. Below lies Loch Morlich, tree-fringed and with a beach of golden sand at its eastern end, and virtually as far as the eye can see, in every direction, are mountains. To the south and west the summits of Ben Macdhui, Cairn Toul and Braeriach all rise above CAIRN GORM itself, while Beinn a Bhuird to the east is only slightly lower. Beyond Aviemore stretches the barrier of the Monadhliath and far away to the north stands Ben Wyvis.

Mountains may seem permanent and indestructible features of the landscape, but changes are taking place, both through natural processes such as weathering and also as a result of man's impact.

Many of the changes resulting from the development of roads bringing tourists and skiers are obvious but there have been other, more insidious, changes too. High on Cairn Gorm, where plant life has a constant struggle to survive and regeneration may take many years, trampling feet have bared the thin gritty soil over an everwidening area. Around the ski slopes the easy pickings provided by discarded picnics have attracted gulls and crows to scavenge in areas where they were formerly seldom seen – and both are potential predators of the eggs of scarce mountain birds. Conservationists are understandably concerned about the long-term effects of such changes in an area of unique and fragile habitats and animal communities.

From the ruins of Ruthven Barracks dominating the marshy flood plain of the Spey below Kingussie, to the picturesque old arch across the River Dulnain at Carrbridge, and from the crags of CRAIGELLACHIE, to the summit of Cairn Gorm, the Spey Valley offers an impressive variety of opportunities to those who wish to discover something of the area's wildflife. Two good starting points are the Aviemore tourist office and Landmark visitor centre, Carrbridge (see above for facilities). Once armed with a map and a little basic information you can go where and when you like – though this may well be influenced by the weather. Highland Guides hire out boots and protective clothing – essential for anyone planning to leave the well-marked lowland paths and venture on to high ground or off the beaten track. For the less adventurous there is the Highland Wildlife Park at Kincraig, where deer, snowy owl, pine marten, wild cat and many other Scottish species can be admired at close quarters. And at GLENMORE visits can be made to the famous herd of reindeer.

Colourful fly agaric is among the fungi that appear in autumn in the Spey Valley.

Strathfarrar

NH 2737; 2189ha; NCC reserve
Native Scots pinewood
Vehicular access is restricted; apply gatekeeper's house,
NH 395406, for permit; organised groups should contact
warden. Eilean Aigas, Hughton, Beauly,
tel. Kiltarlity 310
Leaflet from NCC, Inverness
March-July

The pinewoods of Glen Strathfarrar represent the largest surviving remnants, in this part of Scotland, of the ancient Forest of Caledon. Obstacles such as alder marshes and deep gorges, which presented major problems for early timber extractors, resulted in these woods being left unscathed when more accessible forests were cleared. Little regeneration has taken place here for many years but the Strathfarrar woods still display the mosaic of fine mature pines, clumps of birch, and hummocks of heather and bilberry so characteristic of native pinewoods.

The finest stands of pine are on the south side of the River Farrar at Coille Garbh, the Rough Wood, where the trees, many at least 200 years old, grow on rocky knolls and morainic terraces. Aspen, rowan and holly, as well as birch, are scatttered among the pines and old stands of juniper grow on the flatter ground by the river. Some of the massive pines in this area are especially magnificent and may be up to 300 years old. Crossbill and crested tit, both breeding locally, frequent these pinewoods, and red squirrel and roe deer are plentiful. Pine marten are also present, but less likely to be seen.

Beneath the pines the uneven ground is thickly carpeted with bilberry, cowberry and mosses, among which are many of the wild flowers particularly associated with pinewoods, for example chickweed wintergreen, intermediate wintergreen, lesser twayblade and creeping lady's-tresses.

The woodland on the south-facing slopes of the reserve contains a much higher proportion of birch – mainly the graceful pendulous variety. Aspen, rowan, alder, holly and willow are more abundant here and there are a few sessile oaks. A more varied ground flora is present on the richer soils of the birchwood floor. Woodland flowers such as wood sorrel, wood anemone and lesser celandine are widespread and the wetter hollows hold sundew, heath spotted-orchid and bog asphodel.

To ensure the continued existence of this important pinewood a long-term programme to encourage regeneration is under way. Since the youngest trees currently on the site are at least 100 years old, this programme will have to be carried on for a full century.

Urquhart Bay Wood

NH 522295; 24ha; WdT
Mixed woodland and swamp
All year

This is a beautiful woodland area on the north-western shore of Loch Ness. It is a fine example of swamp alder habitat, and it also includes ash, rowan and wych elm. The wood has a rich population of insects and birds.

Lothian

In many ways a microcosm of Scotland, Lothian Region ranges in its landscapes from the wide sand dunes of the EAST LOTHIAN COAST to the rounded tops of the Pentland Hills, which reach 579m at Scald Law. Despite the high population density centred on Edinburgh, Scotland's capital and second largest city, the region is not highly industrialised. Although man's influence is always evident, some remarkably wild corners remain, their unexpectedness adding to their charm. Watching sea duck dive in the Forth on a crisp winter's day, or a skein of pink-footed geese fly in to a reservoir in the Pentlands while a grouse scolds on the hill behind, one can feel miles away from civilisation.

Each of the four administrative districts has its own character. East Lothian is a fertile coastal plain shaped by increasingly intensive agriculture. West Lothian is predominantly upland acid moor, sweeping up to the Pentlands themselves, although there has been extensive afforestation in recent years. Midlothian is an area of mixed farming and some industry based around several coal mines. Much woodland remains, as ribbons along the various dissecting rivers, as shelter belts, and as policy plantations from the last century. Even Edinburgh has a number of wild areas, centred on its open hills.

The climate is relatively temperate, although winter temperatures as low as −18°C have been recorded, and temperatures on the hottest summer days can be reduced by the coastal fog known as east coast haar. Strong winds are not uncommon, but rainfall is typical for eastern Britain.

The Pentlands, Robert Louis Stevenson's 'old huddle of grey hills', dominate the landscape of the Lothians. Essentially they are an eroded mass of volcanic lavas and old red sandstone, on a base of more ancient rock. The surrounding plains are considerably younger, dating from a time, 340 million years ago, when Scotland lay close to the Equator and the plains were lush tropical forests of fernlike plants interspersed with freshwater swamps. The vestiges of this plant life remain today as the extensive Midlothian coalfield, mined for at least 750 years, while the hard shells of the animals of the swamp and encroaching sea form the fossil-rich limestones found north west of Edinburgh.

The active vulcanism of this period has also left a dramatic impression on the region. The 251m high Arthur's Seat in the centre of Edinburgh is the remnants of a complex volcano, while Edinburgh's Castle Rock, North Berwick Law in East Lothian, and the gannet-populated BASS ROCK in the Forth Estuary are all old volcanic plugs. Later, glaciation scooped away all but the hardest rock, isolating the rounded tops of the Pentlands and sculpting the volcanic cores into distinctive crag-and-tail features, most clearly seen at the Castle Rock, where the tail forms Edinburgh's Royal Mile. This whole intricate landform can be seen impressively displayed from Soutra Hill on the A68 road south of Edinburgh.

The glacial plains left in East Lothian and Midlothian were probably once covered largely in oak woodland, but only remnants remain at ROSLIN GLEN and near Dalkeith. The rest were cleared to make way for agriculture, but in the late eighteenth and nineteenth centuries the local lairds planted new policy woodlands to provide cover for game and shelter for their houses, and as an investment. Many of these remain, together with a well-established alien flora including leopard's-bane, white butterbur, pink purslane, and even, in places, patches of the giant *Gunnera*. These woods provide refuge for a large roe deer population and small numbers of red squirrel. Tits and other woodland species abound, and woodcock can still be seen roding in the spring twilight.

West Lothian, too, must have been partially wooded, recorded in the name of towns like East Calder ('calder' being an oak wood). In much of the area, however, the soils were so poor and water-logged that large boggy mosses developed, with their characteristic plants and insects and only scattered trees of birch or alder. Extensive draining and fertilisation have largely converted these to upland sheep pastures, but to this day farmers have to battle against the invasion of these pastures by rushes and other poor acid vegetation. Remnants of the mosses can still be found at TAILEND MOSS and the RED MOSS OF BALERNO, while small bogs in the Pentlands are still the home for rare plants like hairy stonecrop and the yellow marsh saxifrage.

The natural vegetation of the high Pentlands was the more typically northern forest of birch and Scots pine, and fragments of juniper scrub remain. Today, however, this has largely been converted to sheep run and grouse moors which are still burnt to maintain the heather. Red grouse are common, along with mountain hare which were introduced to the area from 1834. Peregrine are occasional visitors.

Several reservoirs in the Pentlands, including Cobbinshaw and Threipmuir, as well as GLAD-HOUSE in the Moorfoot Hills, provide winter roosts for large numbers of greylag and pink-footed geese, whooper swan, wigeon, teal and other duck. The only large natural bodies of water in the area are DUDDINGSTON and Linlithgow Lochs, where duck winter in large numbers and great crested grebe nest in summer. Several medium-sized rivers flow through the area, providing fishing for dipper and heron, but some are polluted and, partly as a result, the otter is close to extinction in the region. Ponds are scarce.

Edinburgh's volcanic hills provide refuge for much wildlife. Among the rough grassland and gorse of Holyrood Park, dominated by Arthur's Seat, snow bunting can be seen in winter, while short-eared owl and, occasionally, sparrowhawk hunt in summer. Rare plants like maiden pink and forked spleenwort grow amongst the crags, and fulmar have recently begun nesting. Craig-lockhart and Corstorphine Hill have badger and fox, and grey squirrel abound in the city parks, successors of a group that escaped from Edinburgh Zoo in 1913.

The Forth shoreline of Edinburgh is famous for its wintering sea duck. In the past up to 30,000 scaup could be seen near the sewage outfalls. Improved sewage treatment has drastically reduced these numbers, but quantities of long-tailed duck, scoter, eider, great crested grebe and merganser can still be seen from Seafield or by the ash lagoons at Musselburgh.

Certainly the most important and impressive natural feature of the region is the long coastline of cliffs, dunes and saltmarsh, together with the FORTH ISLANDS, including the Bass Rock with its gannetry and kittiwakes, Fidra and Inchmickery with terns, and Craigleith with puffins and guillemots. The increasing use of the Forth by oil tankers is an ever-present threat to these birds.

MICHAEL M. SCOTT

Aberlady Bay

NT 4681; 582ha; East Lothian DC reserve
Open bay with sand and mudflats, saltings, dunes and grassland
Access points at NT 472806 (car parking for permit holders only) and Gullane Dunes (NT 465831)
Access restricted from time to time; organised groups should contact warden, Dairy Cottage, Craigielaw, Longniddry, tel. Aberlady 588, in advance
April–July; breeding birds and flowers;
September–March; wildfowl and waders

Aberlady Bay is best known for its birds. The area also has considerable botanical interest, since its communities represent the full plant succession from mudflat through saltmarsh and dune to dune scrub and grassland. Most of the reserve lies below the high-water mark.

The list of some 228 bird species recorded reflects the importance of the site for migrants as well as regular visitors, and the thoroughness with which it has been observed for many years. Fifty-five species breed, among them ringed plover, over 100 pairs of eider and a good number of shelduck.

In winter several thousand scoter gather in the open Firth off Gullane Bay, and grebes and divers are regularly seen there. Several hundred mallard and wigeon feed on the mudflats, the latter generally concentrated where glasswort is most abundant. The bay is used as a roost by up to 3000 pink-footed geese which flight to and from the rich East Lothian farmland to feed. Waders are present in large numbers in autumn and winter, especially bar-tailed godwit, knot and grey plover; dunlin are also numerous.

All three species of eelgrass grow in the bay and some unusual saltmarsh mosses are present. The grey-hummocky fixed dunes carry abundant mosses and lichens and in some areas autumn gentian, grass-of-Parnassus, burnet rose and moonwort. Bog pimpernel, early marsh-orchid, northern marsh-orchid and 15 species of sedge occur in the dune slacks, and the Marl Loch holds bogbean, amphibious bistort and intermediate bladderwort. Both grey and common seal are frequently seen off Hummel Rocks, near the eastern boundary of the reserve in Gullane Bay. This area is also of geological interest.

Addiewell Bing

NT 003631; 21ha; SWT reserve
Reclaimed spoil heap
Spring, summer, autumn

Once an industrial wasteland of oil-shale spoil bings Addiewell is now woodland scrub, moor, marsh and grassland with a rich variety of plants and birds making it an important refuge for wildlife in an agricultural area.

Bass Rock

NT 602873; 10ha; privately owned
Cliff-girt island
Permission to land obtainable through local boatman
Regular daily sailings, weather permitting, in summer:
contact Fred Marr, 24 Victoria Road,
North Berwick, tel. 2838
May–July

This volcanic neck, rising to over 90m, is famous for its gannets, an association recognised in the bird's scientific name, Sula Bassana. Some 9000 pairs nest on the island; the colony has outgrown the cliff sites and spread on to the sloping summit. Other breeding seabirds include kittiwake, puffin, guillemot, razorbill, shag and fulmar. A stand of tree mallow is of botanical interest.

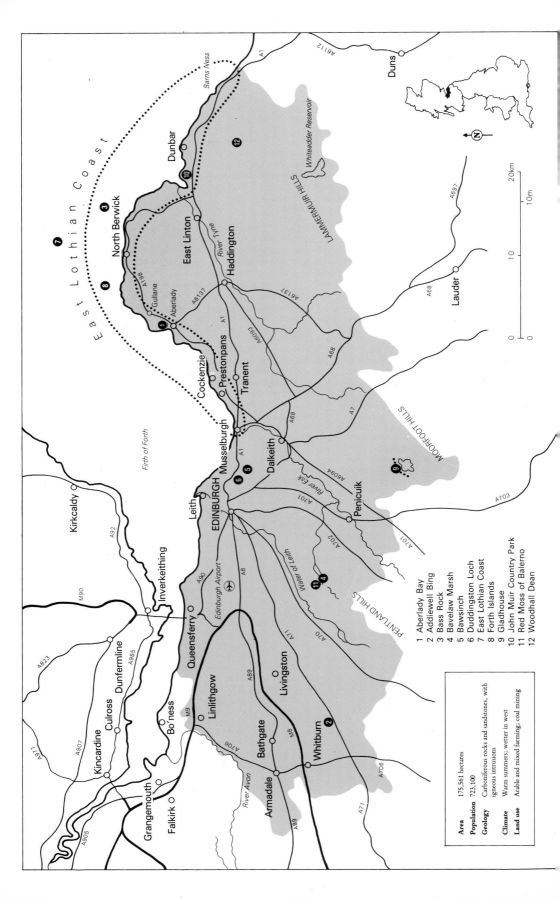

Area 175,561 hectares

Population 723,100

Geology Carboniferous rocks and sandstones, with igneous intrusions

Climate Warm summers; wetter in west

Land use Arable and mixed farming; coal mining

1 Aberlady Bay
2 Addiewell Bing
3 Bass Rock
4 Bavelaw Marsh
5 Bawsinch
6 Duddingston Loch
7 East Lothian Coast
8 Forth Islands
9 Gladhouse
10 John Muir Country Park
11 Red Moss of Balerno
12 Woodhall Dean

East Lothian Coast

Firth of Forth

Barns Ness

Whiteadder Reservoir

LAMMERMUIR HILLS

MOORFOOT HILLS

PENTLAND HILLS

River Tyne

River Esk

Water of Leith

River Avon

Duns
Dunbar
North Berwick
Gullane
Aberlady
East Linton
Haddington
Lauder
Cockenzie
Prestonpans
Tranent
Musselburgh
Leith
EDINBURGH
Dalkeith
Penicuik
Edinburgh Airport
Queensferry
Bo'ness
Linlithgow
Livingston
Bathgate
Armadale
Whitburn
Inverkeithing
Kirkcaldy
Dunfermline
Culross
Kincardine
Grangemouth
Falkirk

20km
10m
10
0

A1
A6112
A697
A68
A698
A6137
A199
A1
A6093
A6137
A7
A703
A701
A702
A70
A71
A89
A8
A90
M9
A706
A985
M90
A823
A907
A917
A905
A92
M8
A71
A68

Bavelaw Marsh

NT 162635; 38ha; Lothian RC reserve
Open water, carr, scrub and grassland
No access except to bird hide, prior booking essential.
Reserve can be viewed from road.
Leaflet and booking from Pentland Hills Ranger Service,
Hillend Country Park, Biggar Road, Edinburgh, EH10 7DU.
Spring, early summer, winter

Situated at the shallow western end of Threipmoor reservoir, the reserve is excellent for both breeding and wintering water fowl. Little and great crested grebe, teal, tufted duck all nest and there is a colony of black-headed gulls. During the winter the main species are teal, wigeon and whooper swans.

Bawsinch

NT 284725; 18ha; SWT reserve
Variety of habitats on former waste ground
Open Wednesday and Saturday by appointment
with SWT
Some restrictions on access 1 March–30 June
Hide with bird and plant list
June–July: flowers and insects

This small reserve is a fine example of habitat creation to benefit wildlife. Acquired to form a buffer zone along the southern edge of DUDDINGS-TON LOCH, the once derelict ground now supports thriving trees and shrubs. Nearly all the native Scottish and British species are represented and most specimens are of known origin. Among the trees grow various flowering plants: some garden escapes, presumably dumped in the past, some self-seeded, and some introduced. The last include teasel to attract goldfinches – which it has done; buddleia for butterflies; and species such as cowslip, increasingly rare in natural habitats.

 Five small ponds of varying size and depth have been excavated; each now holds its own distinctive flora and fauna. Water-starwort, broad-leaved pondweed and common duckweed arrived by natural means; water-milfoil, water-crowfoot and white water-lily were introduced. The pond snails too were 'imported' but water fleas, pond skaters and whirligig beetles just appeared.

 About 66 bird species have been recorded on the reserve, and many more seen from the hide which overlooks Duddingston Loch. The resident Duddingston greylag geese regularly move across to graze on the 'goose green' established for them. Foxes occasionally visit and grey squirrel, water vole and pipistrelle have all been seen.

Blawhorn Moss

Permit only; 69ha; NCC reserve
Peat moss
Permit from NCC Galashiels
April–July

This peatland is one of the few in central Scotland still relatively unaffected by peat-cutting, drainage or afforestation. Both raised and blanket mire are represented and the predominant vegetation is heather, hare's-tail cottongrass and cross-leaved heath, with crowberry, common cottongrass and *Sphagnum* moss in the damper hollows.

Duddingston Loch

NT 2872; 8ha; Scottish Dev. Dept (Ancient
Monuments)–SWT
Loch with reedbeds
Access restricted to north shore near car park
All year round

Duddingston is best known for its wintering pochard. Numbering up to 8000 at its peak in the late 1970s, the flock spends the day bathing and resting on the loch, and flights at dusk to feed on the Firth of Forth. Recent years have seen a drop in numbers, probably associated with the reduction in sewage pollution of the Forth. Pochard and feral greylag geese breed near the loch and the geese also visit other lochs in Holyrood Park. In winter the reedbeds are an important roosting area for small birds such as pied wagtail and yellowhammer. Heron are frequent visitors and water rail are occasionally heard calling in the reeds. The BAWSINCH hide gives good views over the loch.

East Lammermuir Deans

NT 703700; 22ha; SWT reserve
Four narrow, deep valleys
May–August

Valleys cut out of the soft, poorly consolidated conglomerate by meltwater streams during the last Ice Age: in some places the vertical walls rise over 15ft. Amongst over 170 plants are mountain melick, wood vetch, hairy stonecrop and stone bramble whilst butterflies include small heath, common blue and dark green fritillary.

East Lothian Coast

See map; includes 11 sites
Information and nature trail booklets from tourist offices
in North Berwick and Dunbar, or from East
Lothian DC; countryside ranger service
All year

A quite remarkable range of land uses and habitats is displayed along the East Lothian coast. There are power stations at Cockenzie and Torness, at either end of the district. Between them, the land immediately behind the foreshore supports industry, a nature reserve, world-famous golf courses, public open space, private woodlands, holiday resorts, intensive farming and a large cement works. The foreshore itself includes mud-flats, fine sandy beaches, low rocky coastline and steep cliffs, with a scatter of small islands offshore.

 In the built-up section of the coast the Mussel-burgh lagoons are one of the local birdwatchers' most popular haunts and a good illustration of how industrial development may sometimes benefit wildlife. These lagoons are used for the disposal of waste ash from the Cockenzie power station; originally flooded, they now offer an extensive flat area with a mud-like surface. Almost concurrently with the construction of the lagoons reclamation was taking place on the shore nearby, where waders roosted at high tide. As the birds were driven from their traditional sites they started to roost on the lagoons, choosing areas where the ash had not dried out and become compacted. Secure from human disturbance, this roost rapidly increased until the former Musselburgh population of around 800 birds had reached a winter average of about 7000. Knot (sometimes numbering 10,000), oystercatcher and curlew particularly favour this site, which is also used by many golden plover, turnstone, redshank, bartailed godwit and ringed plover.

Some 10km further east lies Gosford Bay, so exposed to westerly winds that the woodlands of Gosford House are trimmed to an even slope above the level of the boundary wall. With a largely stony shore and scattered scrub on the strip of ground between the A198 and the high-tide line, Gosford Bay looks unprepossessing, but it is probably the best place in Scotland for wintering grebes. Over 100 Slavonian grebe are regularly present in midwinter, often with 20–30 red-necked grebe and a few great crested; the bulk of the 500 or so great crested grebe that winter on the Firth of Forth tend, like some of the diving ducks, to be found further west, between Musselburgh and Leith.

Gullane Point is good for observing the large flocks of sea duck on this section of the Firth. Common scoter are present for much of the year: counts of 1500 in August and 1000 in May are not uncommon; autumn counts of velvet scoter are usually in the region of 300, and over 200 long-tailed duck are often in the area in February–March.

Gullane Bay is the finest and most popular beach within easy reach of Edinburgh. Not many years ago erosion was a serious problem: the foredune was virtually destroyed and major blow-outs of sand took place. Fortunately a restoration programme was initiated by the local authority.

At Yellowcraig a nature trail has been laid out along the rocky shore, where rock pools and shells provide varied interest. There are good views from here of the FORTH ISLANDS.

North Berwick, a popular holiday resort, has both sandy and rocky shores and a small harbour busy in summer with sailing craft and boat trips to the BASS ROCK. Gannets from the Bass often dive quite close inshore; the rocks beyond the swimming pool provide a good vantage point. Tantallon Castle, another good viewpoint, is notable for nesting fulmar.

The next stretch of coast is much less frequented, being backed by farmland and accessible on foot only over considerable distances. At JOHN MUIR COUNTRY PARK however, better known as the Tyninghame Estuary, there is much of interest to botanists and ornithologists, as well as a magnificent beach.

Dunbar's rich red cliffs and busy little harbour add to its attractions. Kittiwake nest on the old castle ruin and on many of the harbour buildings, while the cliffs have considerable botanical inter-est. They also provide good viewpoints for sea-watching and the passage migrants seen along this stretch of coast are many and varied.

Slightly further down the coast, at Barns Ness, a lighthouse, patches of scrub and freshwater pools attract small migrants off the sea. Many species have been recorded, their arrival often coinciding with similar arrivals on the ISLE OF MAY (Fife), which is usually visible from Barns Ness. Among the less common ones are woodchat shrike, lesser whitethroat, red-breasted flycatcher, and hoopoe.

The stretch of coastline from just north of Barns Ness south to Torness displays a succession of lower carboniferous limestones and calciferous sandstones along the foreshore. At low tide these rocks, many of them fossil-bearing, can be clearly seen. One of the most spectacular sections, not far from an old lime kiln, is a creamy white wave-cut platform of nodular limestone, the surface dimpled with basin-shaped hollows. The lime-rich grassland here carries purple milk-vetch and bird's-foot-trefoil; autumn gentian grows on some of the limestone outcrops.

Erraid Wood

Permit only; 4ha; SWT reserve
Mixed woodland
Information booklet for primary school teachers from SWT
Spring, early summer

A mixed woodland situated on the edge of Edinburgh and used for educational purposes. The land is steeply sloping and the woodland contains beech, oak, elm, ash and sycamore. There are good views of the Pentland Hills and regular sightings of roe deer and foxes.

Forth Islands

Fidra NO 513867; Eyebroughty NO 495863; The Lamb NO 535866; 2ha; RSPB reserve
Small inshore islands
No landing on The Lamb; access to Fidra by boat from North Berwick; several boat hirers run round trips; Eyebroughty can be reached by foot at low tide
May–July

Although small, these islands are important seabird breeding sites. Eyebroughty is also a moulting ground for large numbers of eider.

Rapid colonisation by several species has occurred in recent years. Cormorant bred first on The Lamb in 1967, built up rapidly to 250 pairs, and then spread to Eyebroughty and the nearby small island of Craigleith. Razorbill and guillemot colonised The Lamb in the 1960s and Fidra about ten years later; over 1000 pairs of guillemot now breed on the reserve. Kittiwake first bred in the 1960s and have increased steadily: over 450 pairs now nest on Fidra. Until 1967 the only regularly used puffin colony was on Craigleith but a small group has recently settled on Fidra.

Other regular breeders include shag, eider, lesser black-backed and herring gull. Common and arctic tern have bred occasionally.

Gladhouse Reservoir

NT 3054; 162ha; Lothian RC reserve
Reservoir with islands and woodland fringe
No access at present but good views from public road
All year

Up to 13,000 pink-footed geese roost here in autumn. Other wildfowl include up to 700 mallard, several hundred teal, wigeon and tufted duck, and smaller numbers of goldeneye and goosander. Mallard, teal and a few shoveler breed. A recent decrease in duck is possibly attributable to feral mink, but numbers should rise now that the mink are actively controlled. The exposed mud around the shores has attracted more than 20 species of migrant waders.

Hermand Birchwood

Permit only; 10ha; SWT reserve
Birch wood
Spring, summer

Small areas of planted Scots pine and beech, together with marsh and rough grassland, bring diversity to this reserve on a remnant of raised bog. Great spotted woodpecker, redstart, tree-creeper and tree pipit all breed. The meadow supports adder's-tongue and greater butterfly-orchid.

John Muir Country Park

NT 6480; 675ha; East Lothian DC
Estuary, dunes, beach and cliffs
Leaflets from Dunbar tourist office or ELDC;
guided walks programme in summer
May–June: flowers and breeding birds;
September–March: waders and duck

The park is named after the naturalist and explorer John Muir, born in nearby Dunbar; as a boy he emigrated to America, where he became much involved in the national parks movement.

Better known to many naturalists as Tyningh-ame, this estuary, with its prominent headland to the north, surrounding woodland, and sheer cliffs to the south east, attracts a wide variety of migrant birds. Two long sand spits, Sandy Hirst and Spike Island, shelter the inner part of the Tyne Estuary and provide nesting sites for ringed plover; an extensive growth of sea-buckthorn on the spits gives good cover for small migrants. The invert-ebrate-rich mud of the estuary attracts shelduck and wintering waders.

Eelgrass and glasswort on the mudflats are succeeded first by sea-blite, sea plantain and common saltmarsh-grass and then, on ground that is seldom inundated, by saltmarsh rush, sea-milkwort and red fescue. Around the volcanic rocks of Whitberry Point wild thyme, bloody crane's-bill and buck's-horn plantain occur and there is a patch of heather and cross-leaved heath, with green-ribbed sedge and sneezewort. The near-vertical cliffs at Dunbar carry meadow saxi-frage, cowslips and primrose.

More than 30 wader species have been recorded on the estuary, most of them during peak migration periods. Numbers are largest in winter,

with big populations of oystercatcher, dunlin, knot, ringed plover and redshank; grey plover, bar-tailed godwit and turnstone are also generally present. Several hundred mallard, teal and wigeon use the area in winter and small groups of greylag and pink-footed geese occasionally roost on the estuary. There is a wintering mute and whooper swan flock of up to 80 birds. Divers are frequently seen offshore in winter, and great, arctic and pomarine skua are recorded regularly in autumn.

A good variety of lichens, including several locally uncommon species, is present on the dune areas. The marine invertebrate fauna includes seven species of crab, soft coral and several sponges, with shells of many different molluscs.

Linn Dean

NT 468594; 24ha; SWT reserve
Moorland and juniper scrub
May–July

The presence on south facing slopes of the largest rock-rose population in the Lothian Region is due to the seepage of base-rich water along the slopes of the dean; the higher slopes are more acid and covered in heather-bilberry heath whilst the north facing slopes carry several stands of juniper along with brittle bladder-fern and Wilson's filmy-fern. Roe deer and brown hare frequent the area: pygmy shrew has been seen whilst the northern brown argus flies here.

Milkhall Pond

Permit only; 2ha; SWT reserve
Disused reservoir and associated marsh
April–October

A variety of aquatic invertebrates inhabits this shallow pond 350m above sea level. Frog, toad and newt all breed and sedge warbler and reed bunting nest in the surrounding rosebay willow-herb, bramble and meadowsweet.

Pepper Wood

Permit only; 1ha; SWT reserve
Semi-natural woodland
April–August

This tiny wood holds most common native wood-land plants and a large number of other species introduced over 150 years ago. It is now notable for lily-of-the-valley, leopard's-bane, butterbur and heart-leaved valerian.

Red Moss of Balerno

NT 165638; 23ha; SWT reserve
Peat moss
Public access only on advertised open days
or by permit from SWT
June–September

Formerly a peat 'common' regularly cut for fuel, the Red Moss is one of the finest peatlands left in the Edinburgh area. Reaching a maximum depth of around 6m, the heather-covered peat rises to a perceptible dome in the centre. Wet

The fossil-rich rocks at Barns Ness are pitted with shallow pools.

woodland, predominantly birch, willow and rowan, fringes the moss, and scattered birch and Scots pine dot its surface.

The boggy areas hold the most varied vegetation. At least six species of *Sphagnum* moss are known to be present, as are bog asphodel and round-leaved sundew, both uncommon in the Lothians. In summer the marshy margins of the reserve are colourful with ragged-Robin, marsh ragwort, lesser spearwort and heath spotted-orchid.

Red Moss is rich in insects. Swarms of small moths flit over the heather and marsh; these and the water beetles have been the subject of special study. Frog and toad frequent the area and common lizard sun themselves on the drier hummocks. A good variety of moorland and scrub woodland birds use the reserve; among the more interesting are redpoll, tree pipit, short-eared owl and, occasionally, hen harrier.

Roslin Glen

Permit only, 19.2ha; SWT reserve
Mixed woodland in steep-sided valley
April–September

Steep slopes and luxuriant ground cover give this woodland an air of impenetrability that will help safeguard its wildlife interest. Oak, ash and wych elm are dominant, with 14 other broad-leaved species and a few Scots pine and yew. Honeysuckle is everywhere – sprawling over the ground, twining up tree trunks and hanging in great festoons from branches – and provides admirable nesting cover for woodland birds. The more open areas, where oak predominates, hold a good population of wood warbler; redstart and pied flycatcher have been recorded and no fewer than 60 bird species are known to breed.

Much of the wood is carpeted with a typical oak–ash flora including dog's mercury, wood anemone, woodruff and ramsons. Hairy wood-rush abounds and there are clumps of pendulous sedge where the slope steepens and falls away abruptly to the River North Esk below. Beech fern and hard fern are among the six or more fern species, and the woodland is rich in bryophytes. Garden escapes are not infrequent and include several patches of leopard's-bane.

Both red and grey squirrel are found on the reserve, the latter having appeared first in 1968. Roe deer, badger and fox also visit, probably sometimes spending long periods in the wood and at other times passing through it on their way to or from the Roslin Glen Country Park further upstream.

Tailend Moss

Permit only, 29ha; SWT reserve
Peat bog with open pools
Leaflet from SWT
April–July: flowers and insects;
November–February: wildfowl

Cranberry, sundew and bog asphodel grow on the wetter sections of this heather-dominated moss. Mallard, teal, snipe, curlew and redshank breed and wintering wilfowl include whooper swan, wigeon, shoveler, tufted duck, pochard and goldeneye. Six of the seven species of dragonfly and damselfly found in the Lothians have been recorded, as have oak eggar and emperor moths.

Thornton Glen

Permit only, 6ha; SWT reserve
Natural woodland in steep glen
April–June

Apparently virtually untouched for several hundred years, this woodland is predominantly ash, elm, holly and hazel. Various escapes, such as privet and gooseberry, have become naturalised and field maple is present, here at the northern end of its range in Britain. The glen is cut through calciferous sandstone and the resultant soil fertility is reflected in very varied ground cover. Seven species of fern, including hart's-tongue, are present, with abundant bryophytes.

Woodhall Dean

Permit only, 37ha; SWT reserve
Deciduous woodland
Spring, summer, autumn

This large deciduous wood is dominated by sessile oak which has been coppiced in the past. The absence of pedunculate oak, or any hybrids, indicates that there has been relatively little disturbance by man – pedunculate oak is more popular for timber and is therefore frequently planted, making pure sessile oak woods uncommon and thus more interesting.

Orkney

Orkney is a crossroads where north and south, Atlantic and North Sea, sea and land, man and wildlife meet. Its landscape is a mosaic of sea and softly curved landforms. Especially when viewed from the air, the well-stocked, dyke-crossed farms and the moorlands form a smooth patchwork with nothing harsh or angular. Even where sea and land meet the transition is mostly gentle; only when some angle of view profiles the higher cliffs does the skeleton of old red sandstone give any indication of the forces of wind and wave which have exposed it there.

Nearer to the Arctic Circle than to London, the islands are in the track of the Atlantic depressions, making them vulnerable to wind and cloud; gales are frequent, yet the annual rainfall is well under 1000mm. The Gulf Stream brings warmth, and winter temperatures compare well with those of English south coast resorts. Snow rarely lies long, and severe frosts are virtually unknown. Summers are mild and fairly dry, although the coasts and higher land may experience cool onshore winds; this is the season when the sun seems reluctant to set and eager to rise again in the early dawn.

Land that has bent under the ice sheets of the Pleistocene and bowed to wind and sea has also proved amazingly docile under the hand of man, who has cultivated its fertile soil for more than 4000 years. As elsewhere, wildlife is under pressure; compared with the islands of the Hebrides, Orkney carries a higher density of human population, which, after a long decline to the early 1970s, is now rising. Luckily the impact of North Sea oil is hardly discernible to the visitor, but farming is expanding.

Although modern Orkney appears predominantly agricultural, so cunningly are the fields spaced out by lochs and moorland, and so surrounded are they by vast areas of coastal features, that abundant wildlife still manages to exist cheek-by-jowl with the human presence. Even though drainage proceeds at an alarming rate, there are still many small fens dominated by shrubby willows and bright with orchids. There are dune slacks where great clumps of grass-of-Parnassus open 50 or more green-veined white cups at a time, and there are beds of reeds beloved by waterfowl. A glorious jumble of meadow, bog and alpine plants grows together in roadside flushes, and the great eutrophic lochs of the west mainland, with their unique range of water from fresh to salt, are still important for wintering duck and for trout.

The prehistoric mixed birch, hazel and rowan scrub, with its understorey of ferns and flowers, manages to maintain itself in tiny remnants on the cliffs of Scapa Flow and in the gullies of Hoy, and a place name including 'dale' indicates a moorland valley rich with plants of a woodland character. On the higher, exposed hills of Westray, Rousay, and especially Hoy, dwarf shrubs lie flattened among slabby pavement and lime-loving alpines cling to the crumbling outcrops and wet screes.

On the coast, several rare northern plants are relatively abundant. Dunes and sunny, grassy sea banks are good for insects, including butterflies. Most of Orkney's land mammals are probably introductions, but Orkney vole is found elsewhere in the British Isles only on Guernsey; it forms a prey species for several raptors. The absence of ground-based animal predators, apart from the domestic cat, makes low-nesting birds comparatively safe, even though woodland is so scarce.

What Orkney lacks in land mammals is more than balanced by its breeding colonies of grey seals and by the fewer but less timid common seals, which often haul out on reefs quite close to public roads. Out to sea the observant watcher may spot schools of whales and occasionally other cetaceans, while at the opposite end of the scale a moist climate and the Gulf Stream combine to ensure a rich and varied shore life.

If the open Orkney landscape is now almost treeless, the towns and gardens are overshadowed by more big sycamores than many a southern centre. The rooks cawing among Kirkwall trees could be those of any English cathedral close.

ELAINE R. BULLARD

Birsay Moors and Cottasgarth

HY 3719; 2340ha; RSPB reserve
Moorland
Access from Lower Cottasgarth (HY 370194),
where cars can be parked, along track to the Dale
May–August

This large area of rough moorland is typical of
the habitats that are progressively disappearing
in Orkney as heather and deergrass are replaced
with cultivated grasses and clovers. The gently
rolling moorland, with its mosaic of shortish
heather, worked-out peat banks, small lochans
and sheltered dales, is home to an unusually high
population of hen harriers and short-eared owls.
Both need large territories for hunting, ground
cover to nest in, and freedom from disturbance
for successful breeding. There are also unique
ground-nesting kestrels which are largely dependent for their food on the Orkney vole. This
distinct species of vole replaces the short-tailed
vole, and in Britain only occurs on Orkney and
Guernsey.

Other species breeding on the reserve include
golden plover, curlew, snipe, redshank, meadow
pipit, skylark and wheatear. Merlin occasionally
nest – on the ground among the heather – and
both great and arctic skua are sometimes present
too. Most of the breeding species can usually be
seen from the ruined farm buildings at Dale or
the small hide nearby.

The Dee of Durkadale, the western block of the
reserve, is rich in orchids and sedges.

Copinsay

HY 6001; 152ha; RSPB reserve
Island and nearby holms
Access by boat (30 mins) from Newark Bay
lighthouse pier (HY 568042) or Skaill; booking
necessary; S. Foubister, tel. Deerness 252;
landing only possible in calm weather
Visitors should go first to information room
in farmhouse
May-July

Sheer cliffs, rising to 60m along the south east
coast of the grassy island of Copinsay, hold
breeding populations of some 30,000 pairs of
guillemot and 10,000 pairs of kittiwake. Several
hundred pairs of fulmar, razorbill and great black-
backed gull also nest on the island, along with
smaller numbers of puffin, black guillemot, shag,
and lesser black-backed, herring and common
gulls. The little island of Corn Holm, which is
connected to Copinsay by a storm beach exposed
at low water, usually has a small colony of arctic
tern, and cormorant nest on the Horse of Copinsay,
1 km off the main island.

Along the north coast of Copinsay, where the
old red sandstone has been eroded to form a
medley of stacks, geos and promontories, the cliff
vegetation is luxuriant. Sea aster is particularly
abundant, sea pearlwort and sea-spurrey are
plentiful, and sea spleenwort and northern
saltmarsh-grass are also present. Oysterplant
grows abundantly on Corn Holm.

Hill of White Hamars

Permit only; 40ha; SWT reserve
Cliffs and coastal grassland
May–August

A reserve set up to protect the endemic Scottish
primrose which grows only exposed to wind
on salt-blasted cliff-top swards. There are also
colonies of black guillemots, shags and rock doves.
Scots lovage flourishes on the cliff ledges while
spring squill, thyme and bird's-foot-trefoil are
abundant in the cliff-top grassland.

Hobbister

HY 3806; 759ha; RSPB reserve
Moorland with loch
Access restricted to area between A964 and sea;
approached via minor road on east side of
Waulkmill Bay (HY 381067) with car park; the
houses there and surrounding ground are private
property
May–August

Bounded to the south by Scapa Flow and to the
west by tidal flats in Waulkmill Bay, this reserve
has a greater diversity of habitat than the purely
moorland BIRSAY AND COTTASGARTH MOORS, and
consequently a greater variety of breeding birds.
As Scapa Flow is encircled by islands its shoreline
cliffs are not occupied by seabirds, but its sheltered
waters attract large numbers of wintering duck
including long-tailed duck and velvet scoter. On
the more sheltered stretches of cliff the luxuriant
vegetation includes shrubby species which provide cover for small migrants. Raven, jackdaw and
rock dove breed on the cliffs, generally choosing
sites tucked in below an overhang. Eider and
shelduck also nest on the reserve, often quite far
inland, later leading their newly hatched broods
over the cliff edge to the safety of the sea below.

The moorland area, still actively worked for
peat, is largely heather-covered, with cottongrass,
deergrass and sedges in the wetter areas. Four
predators, hen harrier, kestrel, merlin and short-
eared owl, breed regularly on the moor which
also supports a few pairs of red grouse. Curlew,
snipe and redshank are among the breeding
waders, while the freshwater loch holds teal,
tufted duck and red-throated diver. A small
area of saltmarsh behind the shingle bar across
Waulkmill Bay provides additional feeding ground
for waders, but the tidal flats of the bay itself,
though visually attractive, are not rich enough in
invertebrate life to attract many birds.

The Loons

HY 245242; 66ha; RSPB reserve
Marsh
Access to hide only from the road on the north side
Spring, summer

This reserve lies in a shallow basin surrounded
on three sides by low hills and by the Loch of
Isbister on the fourth. Peat cutting has resulted
in many water-filled holes, and the variation in
ground conditions has led to a rich flora with

species such as bog pimpernel, knotted pearlwort, grass-of-Parnassus and small bladderwort. The marsh is most noteworthy for its high density of breeding ducks and waders. Of the ducks, wigeon and pintail are most interesting, while among the waders, lapwing, redshank, curlew, snipe, oystercatcher, ringed plover and dunlin all nest. In addition there is a gull colony with both common and black-headed gulls, and by the loch 250 pairs of arctic terns are found.

The bizarre name indicates the antiquity of this area: it derives from the Norse word *lon* which means a flat meadow beside water.

Marwick Head

HY 2224; 19ha; RSPB reserve
Sea cliffs
For car parking and viewpoints see below
May–July

Like NOUP CLIFFS, WESTRAY, those around Marwick Head have abundant flat nesting ledges which are packed with seabirds during the summer months. Guillemot and kittiwake are the most numerous species, with some 22,000 and 3700 pairs respectively in the colony; smaller numbers of razorbill and fulmar and a few puffin are also present. Great and arctic skua often fly past offshore, ready to give chase whenever they spot a fish-laden kittiwake coming in from the sea. Other birds likely to be seen along this stretch of cliff include raven, jackdaw and the unobtrusive little twite.

Part of the bay of Mar Wick is included in the reserve. Eider, oystercatcher, ringed plover and redshank can be seen there and occasionally seals come well inshore. Sloping slabs of rock form the shoreline at the north end, where the cliff starts to rise. It is at this point (HY 228243) that visitors should park their cars; a path leads along the cliff top to the grey stone memorial to Lord Kitchener which stands on the summit of Marwick Head. A substantial part of this seabird colony is not visible from the land and in some places the cliffs are dangerous. Visitors can obtain a close view of the birds from a point roughly halfway up the path, just below a rock face bearing the painted number 129.

North Hill, Papa Westray

HY 4953; 206ha; RSPB reserve
Maritime heathland
All visitors must contact RSPB warden, Gowrie,
Papa Westray, preferably in advance by letter,
before entering the reserve
Mid-May–July

In the breeding season this rather barren-looking stretch of heath is literally seething with birds. The 2000 pairs of arctic tern breeding in one vast colony, one of the largest in the UK, are constantly in motion; successive 'panics' send waves of screaming birds up into the air to circle for a few minutes before returning to their nests. On the fringes of this throng 100 pairs of arctic skua harry the terns coming in from the sea with fish. Great skua nest in the area too, as well as a sizeable

population of great black-backed, lesser black-backed, herring and common gull. Breeding on the heathland are eider, ringed plover and dunlin, and there are notably high numbers of oyster-catcher.

North Hill represents the best example of maritime sedge heath in northern Scotland; exposure, salt spray and grazing have combined to produce a ground cover which gradually changes from a sward dominated by thrift, spring squill and sea plantain near the cliff top, to heather, crowberry and creeping willow further inland. Sizeable patches of tiny Scottish primrose add to the attractions of the site.

The colony of cliff-nesting seabirds on Papa Westray is particularly easy to observe. Situated on Fowl Craig, at the south east corner of the reserve, the colony holds several thousand pairs of kittiwake and guillemot and small numbers of razorbill, puffin and black guillemot.

North Hoy

HY 223034; 3925ha; RSPB reserve
Moorland, sea cliffs and hill lochs
Daily boat service from Stromness to Moness Pier,
or ferry from Houton to Lyness
Spring, summer

The island of Hoy differs from the rest of Orkney in that it consists almost entirely of Upper Old Red sandstone. The weathering by sea, wind and rain has produced the spectacular coastal scenery of this reserve. Jutting out from the cliffs is the famous Old Man of Hoy, 140m high, the highest sea stack in Great Britain. While the sheer cliffs of St John's Head over 300m high provide ideal nesting sites for a large colony of kittiwakes, guillemots and fulmars, puffins, razorbills, shags and Manx shearwaters nest along the coast in smaller numbers.

On the moors there are large colonies of great black-backed gulls and great skuas, and smaller numbers of arctic skuas. Red-throated divers breed on the hill lochans. Of the waders, golden plover, dunlin, curlew and snipe breed, as do smaller species such as wheatear, stonechat and twite. Merlin, peregrine, sparrowhawk and kestrel nest while short-eared owls and hen harriers are less often seen. There is a large population of mountain hares and otters are occasionally seen.

The reserve has a rich flora of alpine plants such as alpine meadow-rue and purple and yellow mountain saxifrage. The small area of birch, aspen and rowan forms the most northern remnant of native woodland in Britain. Butterflies of 19 species have been recorded, including a good population of large heath. A Neolithic tomb called 'dwarfie stones', formed from a hollowed out boulder, can be seen on the reserve.

Noup Cliffs, Westray

HY 3950; 14ha; RSPB reserve
Sea cliffs
Access from road to Noup Head lighthouse
(HY 391503)
No dogs allowed
May–July

Area	97,591 hectares
Population	18,400
Geology	Mainly sandstones yielding fertile soils
Climate	Windy; winters less harsh than on mainland
Land use	Agriculture, largely pastoral

1 Birsay Moor and Cottesgarth
2 Copinsay
3 Hobbister
4 The Loons
5 Marwick Head
6 North Hill, Papa Westray
7 North Hoy
8 Noup Cliffs, Westray
9 Trumland

Mull Head

NORTH RONALDSAY

Dennis Head

PAPA WESTRAY

Hollandstoun

Noup Head

North Ronaldsay Firth

Pierowall

WESTRAY

The North Sound

Northwall

Broughtown

SANDAY

Westray Firth

Sanday Sound

ROUSAY

Wasbister

EDAY

Egilsay

Whitehall

Eynhallow Sound

Brinyan

STRONSAY

Brough Head

Redland

A966

Stronsay Firth

MAINLAND

A967

A968

A966

Ness of Ork

SHAPINSAY

Auskerry

Loch of Harray

Balfour

Finstown

Loch of Stenness

STROMNESS

KIRKWALL

A965

Deer Sound

Mull Head

Deerness

A964

A960

Graemsay

A961

Copinsay

Linksness

Whaness

Rora Head

Rackwick

Scapa Flow

BURRAY

HOY

Flotta

St Margaret's Hope

Lyness

SOUTH RONALDSAY

Hurliness

A961

Swona

Burwick

Pentland Firth

Dunnet Head

Stroma

Duncansby Head

John o'Groats

A836

A9

N

0   10   20   30

0   10   20m

This 2km stretch of cliffs running south from Noup Head (HY 391503) is arguably the most densely populated seabird city in Britain. Indeed, so closely are the 40,000 pairs of guillemot packed that slum conditions might be said to prevail, with chicks being roughly jostled, dead birds trampled underfoot, and many of the inhabitants liberally bespattered with guano from the floors above. The scene is one of perpetual motion as continuous streams of birds leave for the fishing grounds and return with sand eels for their young. Below, rafts of guillemot are scattered far out over the sea, many of the birds bathing with such energy and enthusiasm that the pattering of their wings on the water is audible even through the background chorus of raucous 'aaarghs'. The smell is equally impressive.

It is the combination of rich, readily accessible feeding grounds and the generous supply of suitable nesting ledges that has made Noup Cliffs such an important seabird colony. Fulmar, razorbill and shag occupy the smallest, detached, residences; kittiwake, of which there are 40,000 pairs on the reserve, favour the longer and shallower shelves. Puffin are present in small numbers.

On the heathland behind the cliffs arctic skua nest. Both they and the great skuas that gather to bathe at the small lochans and to stand around on prominent – and well fertilised – green knolls, can have little difficulty in obtaining food with a kittiwake colony as big as this one so close at hand. Arctic tern and several wader species also breed in the area.

Although the moorland is not part of the reserve visitors are allowed to walk across the unenclosed land, but are asked to be careful to close all gates.

Trumland

HY 427276; 433ha; RSPB reserve
Moorland
Contact warden at Trumland Mill Cottage (HY 431276)
Summer

The dry heather moorland is interspersed with wetter areas of rushes and ferns where meadow-sweet and water avens grow. These areas are perfect breeding places for hen harriers and golden plover. Red-throated diver breed on a small lochan, and there is a large mixed colony of herring and lesser black-backed gulls nesting on the moors. Short-eared owls, merlin, and great and Arctic skuas are regularly seen. Orkney voles are found and otters occasionally visit the reserve.

Inland, fields are taking over Orkney's moors.

Outer Hebrides

From North Rona and Sula Sgeir to Barra Head, and from the Shiant Isles to Rockall, the Outer Hebrides embrace some 120 named islands used for agriculture, of which only 14 are now permanently inhabited: Lewis, Harris, Great Bernera, Scalpay, Berneray, North Uist, Grimsay, Baleshare, Benbecula, South Uist, Eriskay, Barra, Vatersay and ST KILDA. Breached only by the shallow, reef-strewn sounds of Harris and Barra, the Long Island itself (Butt of Lewis to Barra Head) stretches 210km across the prevailing westerly winds and Atlantic surges, and has long been the home of a proud and hardy race with a distinctive culture and ethos, derived from an ancient language, strongly held religious beliefs and an age-long struggle with elemental forces.

The origins of Hebridean man are obscure. It has been suggested that the post-neolithic colonisers were Iberian, but were sparsely distributed when the Viking occupation took place in the ninth century. This may account for the predominance of Norse place names, especially in Lewis, where the Scandinavian element in the population is also more evident than in Harris and the Southern Isles.

The land itself is all that remains of an ancient eroded platform of Lewisian gneiss, 3000 million years old, and mostly under 90m above sea level. Raised and convoluted by subsequent earth movements, its hills have been shaped by glacial action and its surface overlain by glacial deposits, and by peat to a depth of 4.5m in some places.

Along the low-lying western seaboard, lime-rich shell sand has been blown inland by the prevailing westerlies and has transformed the peat into fertile grassland or *machair*, which plays a vital part in the economy and landscape of the islands and which is studded with shallow lochs rich in vegetation, invertebrates and fish. The east coast, on the other hand, is fragmented and intersected by deep, labyrinthine sea lochs, rendering communications difficult and modern roads tortuous. The freshwater lochs here and inland are acidic and, with a few exceptions, support little life.

Blessed with an equable, oceanic climate, yet one which to visitors may seem excessively wet and windy, the islands never suffer the climatic extremes which affect less fortunate parts of the British Isles. Certainly gales occur, on average, on 50 days of the year, but in this respect familiarity breeds tolerance and self-preservation; tolerance, too, of the 1270mm of annual rainfall which ensures that gardens can always be watered, cars washed and salmon, sea trout and brown trout fished for in most of the 6000 lochs.

Wind and rain, often salt-laden, have played a great part in the vegetation of the Outer Hebrides, restricting the number of species and often their shape and structure too. The impervious, underlying gneiss has weathered to produce a topsoil of peaty podsol overlain by blanket bog on which sedges and heather flourish. In accessible areas, beside main roads and unsurfaced side roads, this peat is cut for fuel in spring and carted home after drying to form conspicuous and familiar stacks at each homestead. Within the last 30 years convenient parts of the moor have been reclaimed, by fencing, drainage and liming, to provide pasture for stock, and are now green oases among the heather. Away from the fertile *machair*, the thin soil has been cultivated and gathered into lazybeds to supply subsistence crops of oats and potatoes, and ancient corrugations may still be made out near the sites of former dwellings, abandoned for an easier life in the townships.

The moorland flora of acid-tolerant plants comprises, for example, heathers, butterwort, milkwort, tormentil, bird's-foot-trefoil, sundews, royal fern, lesser spearwort, bogbean, water-lily and water lobelia. The post-glacial scanty cover of trees and shrubs was mostly destroyed by fire, sheep and the growth of peat, but some vestiges may still be found on freshwater islets and sheltered cliffs. Lately, shelter belts of conifers have been planted near townships, and the

Forestry Commission and the North of Scotland College of Agriculture have established woodlands in Lewis and the Uists which are already contributing to a diversity of landscape and fauna. However the most substantial wood in the Outer Hebrides is that surrounding Lews Castle at Stornoway. Planted by Sir James Matheson in the mid-nineteenth century, it is now a mature and diverse mixture of exotic and native coniferous and deciduous trees and shrubs which has attracted some bird and insect species elsewhere absent from the islands; it includes the Outer Hebrides' only rookery.

Some 296 species of birds have occurred in these islands: corncrake, wintering waders and the native mute swan and greylag goose populations are of national significance. The importance of the off-lying island populations of gannet, Leach's petrel, puffin and grey seal are mentioned under the relevant reserves.

Grey seals are a common sight offshore of the main islands, and a few have become almost tame in Stornoway harbour where they scavenge on the waste products of the fishing fleet. In the Sound of Harris and off the Southern Isles common seal is a feature of the shallow western littoral and reefs. Otters are more common than is generally supposed, but are more marine than their mainland counterparts. Mink, the descend-

ants of escapees from Lewis farms, and feral ferrets have over-run Lewis and Harris, and the former may soon gain a foothold in the Uists. Red deer are to be found in Lewis, Harris, Pabbay and North and South Uist. Mountain hares have survived in very small numbers on Lewis and Harris but the rabbit, introduced in the nineteenth century, infests all the main islands. A more recent introduction to Lewis is the hedgehog, which has become established since 1970 around Stornoway. The only bat is pipistrelle, confined to Stornoway. Apart from a recent discovery of palmate newts in South Uist and intermittent introductions of frogs and toads there are no amphibians and only one reptile, slow-worm. Pygmy shrew, long-tailed fieldmouse, house mouse and brown rat are widespread, but short-tailed vole is confined to the Uists and Benbecula.

Perhaps the main attractions of the Outer Hebrides to the birdwatcher are the seabirds and the possibility of encountering Arctic migrants and transatlantic vagrants; to the botanist, the treasures of the *machair* and the vestigial woodlands; to the angler, the wealth of sequestered trout lochs; to the entomologist, a world as yet largely undocumented; and to the visitor wide, unpolluted spaces where time seems to stand still.

PETER CUNNINGHAM

Balranald, North Uist

NF 7070; 658ha; RSPB reserve
Machair, marshes and coastline
Visitors are requested to call at reception cottage on arrival
Display and reserve leaflet at cottage, Goular, Hougharry
April–September

The core of this varied reserve is the shallow Loch nam Feithean and its extensive surrounding marshland. A rich invertebrate fauna, together with the cover provided by great sweeps of emergent fen vegetation – sedges, amphibious bistort, bogbean, marsh-marigold, mare's-tail, yellow iris and grey club-rush – make this an important breeding site for duck and waders. Gadwall, wigeon, shoveler, tufted duck, snipe and redshank are among the regular breeders, while red-breasted merganser and red-necked phalarope nest occasionally. Crofting land surrounds the marshes and in summer the rasping calls of corncrake sound on all sides.

Machair ground lies between the loch and the coastal dunes. Strip-cultivated to varying degrees of intensity, the summer *machair* is a patchwork of contrasting colours: here the dominant rusty-red of sorrel, there the red and orange of poppy and corn marigold, the vivid blue and strong purple of green alkanet and tufted vetch, or the bright pink of stork's-bill. This rich flora and associated insect life supports many pairs of twite, skylark and corn bunting, the latter often singing from clumps of umbels in the absence of more substantial song-posts. Most spectacular of all are

the nesting waders: an astonishing density of lapwing, oystercatcher, redshank, ringed plover and dunlin, all thriving on the cultivated *machair* and wet grassland. Arctic tern and little tern breed on the silver-grey sandy beaches and dunes, with shag and black guillemot on the rocky headlands. Altogether, some 50 species nest annually on the reserve.

Balranald is also important for migrant and wintering birds. The marshes and the tidal strand of Loch Paible between them attract a wide variety of waders. Offshore all three species of diver occur regularly, as do sooty shearwater, and great, pomarine and arctic skua. The passage and wintering wildfowl include pintail, scaup, common scoter, five species of goose and whooper swan. Hen harrier, merlin and peregrine are among the recorded visiting predators, sometimes visible at close range hunting over the marshes.

Like other western isles North Uist has a flourishing population of otter and these delightful animals are frequently seen on Balranald's shores and lochs. A colony of grey seal breeds on the small rocky island of Causamul and porpoises, dolphins and whales have been observed during sea-watches.

Although the northerly latitude limits the likely range of butterflies, eight species have been recorded to date, together with 56 kinds of moth. Green-veined white, common blue and meadow brown – an especially bright Hebridean form, are the most frequent butterflies; moth species include garden tiger, yellow underwing, dark arches and the much less common Portland moth and brindled beauty.

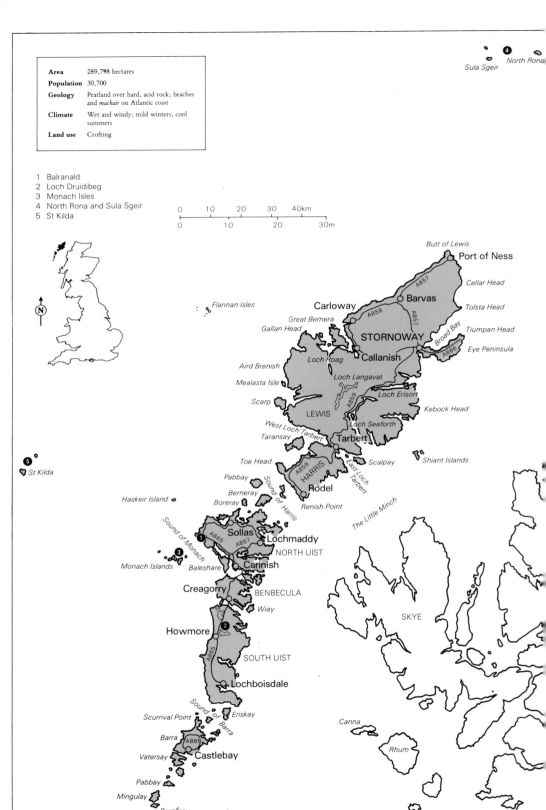

Area	289,798 hectares
Population	30,700
Geology	Peatland over hard, acid rock; beaches and *machair* on Atlantic coast
Climate	Wet and windy; mild winters, cool summers
Land use	Crofting

1 Balranald
2 Loch Druidibeg
3 Monach Isles
4 North Rona and Sula Sgeir
5 St Kilda

0   10   20   30   40km
0   10   20   30m

Sula Sgeir   North Rona

Butt of Lewis
Port of Ness
Cellar Head
Carloway   Barvas
Tolsta Head
Flannan Isles   Great Bernera   STORNOWAY
Gallan Head   Broad Bay   Tiumpan Head
Aird Brenish   Loch Roag   Callanish   Eye Peninsula
Mealasta Isle   Loch Langavat
Scarp   LEWIS   Loch Erisort
Loch Seaforth   Kebock Head
West Loch Tarbert   Taransay   Loch Seaforth
Toe Head   Tarbert   Scalpay   Shiant Islands
Pabbay   HARRIS   East Loch Tarbert
St Kilda   Berneray   Rodel
Haskeir Island   Boreray   Renish Point
Sound of Harris   The Little Minch
Sollas   Lochmaddy
Sound of Monach   NORTH UIST
Monach Islands   Baleshare   Carinish
Creagorry   BENBECULA
Wiay   SKYE
Howmore
SOUTH UIST
Lochboisdale
Sound of Barra   Eriskay   Canna
Scurrival Point
Barra   Rhum
Vatersay   Castlebay
Pabbay
Mingulay
Berneray

Loch Druidibeg, South Uist

NF 7937; 1677ha; NCC reserve
Lochs, moorland, croftland, *machair* and seashore
Permit only during bird breeding season; apply
NCC, Inverness
May–July

The two widely contrasting sections of this large reserve are neatly separated by the road that bisects it. To the east lies Loch Druidibeg, home of the largest surviving British colony of native greylag geese. Its shallow waters are dotted with islands large and small, many of them fringed with tawny royal fern and crowned with scrub woodland of Scots pine, rowan, willow and juniper, often draped with honeysuckle. Undulating peat moorland backs most of the loch's convoluted stony shoreline. Grazing, peat cutting and heather burning have helped to create a wide variety of microhabitats within this superficially monotonous looking area. Floating club-rush and delicate water lobelia grow in the pools; clumps of vivid yellow bog asphodel and silvery tufts of cottongrass stand out against the dark peaty background; and wind-pruned willows, only a quarter of a metre high but with stems several centimetres thick, sprawl over the exposed rocks at the loch's edge.

In addition to the geese the breeding birds of this eastern part of the reserve include a varied assortment of species such as buzzard, red-breasted merganser, mute swan, heron, red grouse, common gull and wren; golden eagle, hen harrier, merlin and short-eared owl are also regularly seen.

Within the western section lie two crofting townships, a series of shallow lochs, lagoons and marshes, and a stretch of dunes with their associated *machair*. The shell–sand *machair* is carpeted with flowers in summer, the predominant colours and species varying from one place to the next according to the way the land is managed. Lesser meadow-rue, wild thyme, daisy, and self-heal are among the constants: red and white clovers dominate the more intensively farmed areas, and yellow seaside pansies and bright pink stork's-bill star the barer sandy patches. Orchids abound, in every shade from nearly white to wine red; many of them are hybrids between heath spotted-orchid and northern marsh-orchid.

Loch Druidibeg is rich in bird life, with important breeding populations of waders such as snipe, redshank, dunlin and lapwing. Corncrake, corn bunting and twite frequent the fields of meadow hay and barley – the latter colourful with poppies, small bugloss and corn marigold. Arctic tern and ringed plover nest where the sand is bare of vegetation, and several species of duck breed in the wetland areas.

Monach Isles

NF 6462; 577ha; NCC reserve
Island group with associated reefs
Access restricted; landing permit from NCC warden,
South Uist

Shrinish, Ceann Iar and Ceann Ear, the three main islands of the group, are low-lying and largely *machair*-covered, with a few marshy areas and pools. Arctic tern breed here, and small numbers of seabirds live on the rockier outlying islets. The islands support an important grey seal colony and are a wintering ground for barnacle and white-fronted geese.

North Rona and Sula Sgeir

HW 8132 and 6230; 130ha; NCC reserve
Isolated islands
Landing permit from NCC, Inverness

In summer the great barren rock of Sula Sgeir, a few hectares in area and rising to 100m, is white with gannets. This is the only place in Britain where fat young gannets can legally be harvested for food, and the men of Ness in Lewis still take their traditional crop of *gugas* despite the danger and privation involved.

The isolated islands and stacks of St Kilda are home to vast numbers of seabirds.

North Rona, 20km away and also 100m high, is a much larger green island which still shows the pattern of the lazybed cultivation of the past; it is now grazed by sheep. The island's importance is as a breeding place for grey seal; several thousand gather from September to December and each year about 2000 pups are born. By the peak of the breeding season the peninsula of Fianuis, the seals' nursery-ground, has become a sea of mud, churned up by their comings and goings.

There are also important colonies of Leach's and storm petrel on the island and large numbers of guillemot, razorbill, kittiwake, puffin and fulmar nesting on the cliffs.

St Kilda

NA 1000; 853ha; NTS–NCC reserve
Isolated island group
Permission to stay on the island must be obtained from NTS
May–July

Everything about St Kilda, the premier seabird breeding station in Britain, demands superlatives. Hirta, the principal island, is the remotest inhabited island in British waters and has the highest sea cliff, almost 430m of precipice on the north face of Conachair. The walls of the smaller islands of Boreray and Soay rise absolutely sheer to over 360m. Stac an Armin, where Britain's last great auk was killed in 1840, and Stac Lee, at 191m and 165m respectively, are the two highest rock stacks in the country. St Kilda holds the oldest, and by far the largest, colony of fulmar in Britain. The gannetry, on Boreray and the adjacent stacks, is the largest in the world, with over 50,000 pairs. This combination of spectacular scenery and vast seabird populations ensures that a visit to these islands is a truly memorable experience.

Approaching St Kilda by sea, as most visitors must, the first impressions are of the scale and ruggedness of the islands and of the great throngs of seabirds: a snowstorm of gannets, circling and plunging off Boreray; a continuous procession of puffins, whirring to and from the steep grassy slopes of Dun; crowds of guillemot, scattered over the surface of the water as far as the eye can see. These are immediately obvious even when low cloud screens the summit of Conachair and the stacks. The important populations of Leach's and storm petrel and of Manx shearwater are much less readily appreciated, since these species are active only at night and tend to favour rather inaccessible spots for their nesting burrows. Few of today's visitors to these islands would care to tackle the cliffs that the old St Kildans climbed as a matter of course when gathering the birds and eggs that provided them with both food and fuel.

The St Kilda wren, a distinct sub-species which is larger and greyer than the mainland version, lives mostly around the old village street and among the dry stone *cleitean*, little turf-roofed chambers in which the islanders stored their crops, fuel and dried birds for winter food. The St Kilda field mouse, here often occupying the house mouse niche left vacant when that species failed to survive the island's uninhabited period, 1930–57, is another local speciality. Flocks of the primitive Soay sheep, left behind when the island was evacuated, run wild on Soay and Hirta, and there are feral blackface sheep on Boreray. More recent arrivals are grey seal, now breeding in considerable numbers on Hirta and Dun, and great skua that have colonised the grassy moorland.

Despite the fact that drenching with salty spray is a frequent occurrence, the cliff vegetation is strikingly rich. Roseroot, primrose, honeysuckle, moss campion and purple saxifrage are among the flowers blooming on the ledges and in the gullies. Over 130 species of flowering plants have been recorded from the island group, while the bryophyte population includes at least one liverwort with Mediterranean affinities – though wet, St Kilda's climate is also relatively mild.

Shetland

People are always attracted to extremes: the highest mountains, the widest plains, the furthest corners of the Arctic, the Antarctic and the tropics have been visited by intrepid explorers. But most people have neither the means nor the opportunity to follow in their footsteps, and must be satisfied with exploring the more remote parts of their own country. A map of Britain may or may not show that the most northerly point of the United Kingdom is Shetland. Lying some 160km north of John o' Groats, it does not fit comfortably into the format of such maps; as often as not the islands are fitted into a box frame in some convenient corner of the page.

The true situation of Shetland is about 320km north of Aberdeen and 290km west of Bergen, the largest town in western Norway. Physically it comprises a group of about 100 islands totalling 142,450ha in area. Only 15 of the islands are now populated; the rest are made up of stacks, skerries and holms inhabited by sheep, seals, otters, rabbits and seabirds. Shetland gives the impression of rolling, heather-clad, treeless hills, spangled with peaty lochs and pools, its coastline bitten into by arms of sea, locally called 'voes', some steep-sided like a tiny Norwegian fiord.

On the largest island, Mainland, lies the only town, Lerwick, which boasts a fine natural harbour visited by ships of all nations and summer yachtsmen. Farther north is the gigantic oil terminal at Sullom Voe. Although physically the huge industrial complex has been absorbed remarkably well into the landscape, the social and economic effects reach into every corner of the islands.

Outside these two centres the rest of the 22,000-odd population lives in small villages in the larger of the islands. These are usually near the shores of some sheltered voe, witness to former depen-

dence on the sea for a livelihood, and dwellings tend to be scattered because originally each family's house or croft was built on its own patch of land which provided basic food.

Ever since the first naturalists visited and wrote about Shetland over 200 years ago, the islands have been acknowledged to contain flora and fauna unique in Britain. The reasons lie in Shetland's geological and physical development, as well as in its geographical situation.

It would seem that, as the climate became warmer, Shetland emerged from the last great ice age as a set of barren mountain tops, cut off by the rising waters and so barred from natural colonisation by any land-based animals. Today Shetland has no deer, foxes, badgers, voles or shrews, nor any evidence that they have ever existed in the islands. However hares, rabbits, stoats, hedgehogs, house and field mice are there in plenty, but have been introduced by man since his colonisation 5000 or 6000 years ago. The field mice are interesting in that, although recognisably different forms occur on different islands, all show genetic affinities to the mice of western Norway, suggesting that Viking colonisation took many forms.

Species that swim had no problems, and there are considerable numbers of both grey and common seal, but Shetland's large and healthy population of otters gives rise to doubts about whether they arrived spontaneously or were escapees from captivity. Wherever otters came from originally, the absence of rivers in Shetland has forced them to adapt to a lifestyle which, like that of seals, is almost wholly dependent on the sea.

There is little doubt that man and his domestic animals have had a profound effect on the landscape. Abundant evidence exists in the peat deposits that Shetland was once extensively

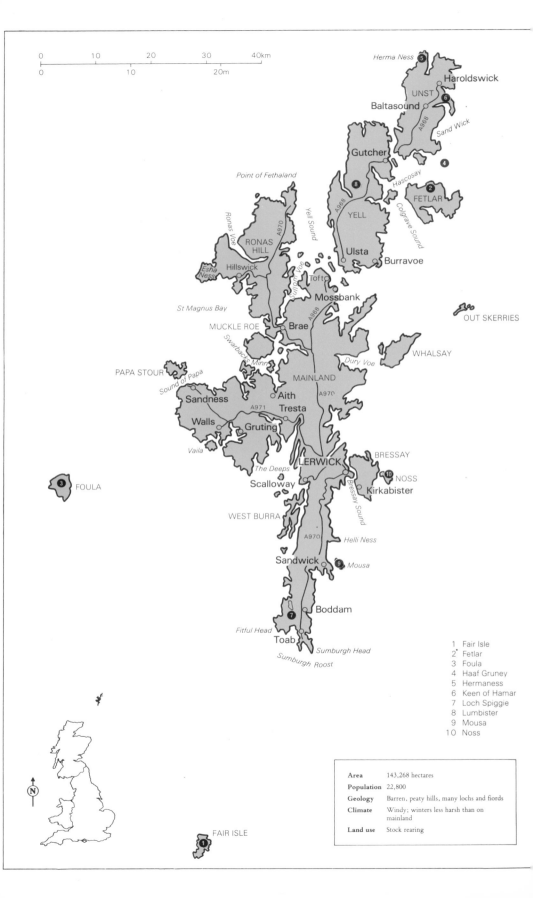

0   10   20   30   40km
0   10   20m

Herma Ness ⑤
Haroldswick
UNST
Baltasound ⑥
A968
Sand Wick

Gutcher ○
⑧
Hascosay
⑨ ④
FETLAR
A968
YELL
Colgrave Sound
Ulsta ○
Burravoe

Point of Fethaland

Ronas Voe
A970
RONAS
HILL
Hillswick ○
Esha Ness
Yell Sound
A968
Sullom Voe
Toft ○
Mossbank
St Magnus Bay
MUCKLE ROE   Brae ○
A968
OUT SKERRIES

Swarbacks Minn
Dury Voe
WHALSAY

PAPA STOUR
Sound of Papa
MAINLAND
Sandness ○   Aith ○
A970
Walls ○   Tresta
A971
Gruting ○
Vaila

BRESSAY
The Deeps
LERWICK   NOSS ⑩
③ FOULA
Scalloway   Kirkabister
Bressay Sound
WEST BURRA
A970   *Helli Ness*
Sandwick ○
⑨ *Mousa*

⑦   Boddam
Fitful Head
Toab
Sumburgh Head
Sumburgh Roost

1   Fair Isle
2   Fetlar
3   Foula
4   Haaf Gruney
5   Hermaness
6   Keen of Hamar
7   Loch Spiggie
8   Lumbister
9   Mousa
10 Noss

N

Area	143,268 hectares
Population	22,800
Geology	Barren, peaty hills, many lochs and fiords
Climate	Windy; winters less harsh than on mainland
Land use	Stock rearing

FAIR ISLE ①

covered in scrub woodland, and in the few places inaccessible to sheep there still remain examples of native birch, rowan and aspen. The attentions of grazing animals are the main factor inhibiting the regeneration of any trees or bushes. However there is plenty of herb vegetation, with currently some 600 varieties of flowering plant.

Spring comes late at this latitude, and it is May before splashes of yellow marsh-marigold and primrose herald an explosion of colour as successive waves of wild flowers make recompense for the drabness of winter. Along the cliff edge swards, the purple haze of spring squill is replaced by pink carpets of thrift, while many of the grassy cliff slopes are a blaze of scarlet as Shetland red campion takes over.

The heather hills change only slowly to subtle shades of purple in late summer, but crofting areas and 'improved' pasture share in the rush of summer colour. In places some of the several species of orchids are abundant enough to provide the dominant colour. On higher hills and screes alpines can be found, and azaleas, saxifrages, mountain rock-cress and arctic sandwort all occur, while a variety of arctic chickweed found nowhere else in the world can be seen on the island of Unst.

Shetland is particularly rich in bird life, which can be placed in three overlapping categories, all tied in with climate and geography. First, Shetland lies in a sea full of fish, for the relatively shallow North Sea basin is constantly enriched by nutrients carried by the warm Gulf Stream. The food attracts huge numbers of seabirds, and since the long coastline, over 1500km, contains a variety of nesting habitats, Shetland has a seabird population of international importance.

Second, the northerly situation of Shetland encourages a number of species whose main distribution is towards the sub-Arctic: breeding seabirds like black guillemot, great and arctic skua and red-throated diver, waders such as whimbrel and red-necked phalarope, and other occasionals like snowy owl and glaucous gull. In the winter Shetland is regularly visited by other birds from the Arctic: long-tailed duck and whooper swan, great northern diver and little auk can all be seen, and rarer species like ivory and Ross's gull, king and Steller's eider turn up from time to time.

Third, there is the excitement of the great seasonal bird migrations. Regular passage birds such as vast flocks of fieldfare, redwing and song thrush pass through in spring and autumn on their way to and from northern breeding grounds. With them appear a bewildering variety of small birds – warblers, chats, flycatchers, shrikes, finches, buntings and many others. The more remote an island – providing it is on or near a bird migration route – the better chance it has of 'collecting' migrants in suitable weather, and FAIR ISLE is justly famous among birdwatchers on this account.

BOBBY TULLOCH

Long inlets cut deeply into Shetland's north mainland.

Fair Isle

HZ 2172; 830ha; NTS
Cliff-girt inhabited island
Bird observatory with hostel, open March–October
Booklet on birds and brochure from FIBOT or NTS
May, September–October: migration;
May–July: breeding birds

Long famous as a migration station, Fair Isle boasts an impressive list of rare bird visitors. First records – for Scotland, Britain and even Europe – are a regular occurrence, with birds arriving from as far afield as Siberia and North America.

Red sandstone cliffs edge most of the shoreline, rising to 200m on the west coast and on Sheep Craig. The rock is soft, weathering readily into caves, arches and stacks, and demands extreme caution. Grey seal breed in the caves and lie out on the rocks singing their sad songs, and colonies of around 25,000 pairs of fulmar, 20,000 pairs of guillemot, 12,000 pairs of kittiwake and 2500 pairs of razorbill occupy the cliff ledges. Gannet first bred successfully in 1975 and this new colony has now grown to over 150 pairs. Some 30,000 puffin and 100 pairs of storm petrel nest in burrows among loose stones and earth where the cliffs and gullies are steep rather than sheer, and Leach's petrel have been caught on the island though not yet proved to breed there.

Much of the rough hill ground is skua territory; the colony, now numbering about 120 pairs of arctic skua and 40 of great skua, has been studied intensively over many years. During the summer months visitors need walk only a few hundred metres from the observatory hostel to experience the realistic injury-feigning distraction display and the aggressive dive-bombing of skuas safeguarding their nests and young.

The Fair Isle Bird Observatory is best known for its work in recording and ringing migrants. Well over 300 species have been recorded, more than at any other British locality.

Fair Isle's flora is varied, with well over 200 recorded species, many associated with the cultivated croft ground. Spring squill is widespread along the cliff tops and field gentian has been recorded at the south end of the island; both species occur in the white form as well as the usual blue one. Lesser twayblade and frog orchid are among the five orchids present, and ferns include Wilson's filmy-fern, moonwort and adder's-tongue. With so much rough grassland and heath with boggy areas, the list of sedges, rushes and grasses is a long one. A full list of plant species is given in *Fair Isle Bird Observatory Report*, 1971.

The tidal rock pools, regularly flushed with the unpolluted waters of the North Sea and Atlantic, hold a rich variety of seaweeds and other marine life. Porpoises, sharks and whales are frequently sighted offshore.

For many visitors it is the island as a whole, rather than any one facet, that arouses enthusiasm, since it is rare these days to find a thriving community on an island as isolated as Fair Isle, separated from the nearest land by 40km of sea.

Fetlar

HU 6091; 699ha; RSPB reserve
Island moorland with lochans and marshes
Island accessible April–August
Access restricted mid-May–end July; contact warden on arrival
Information sheet from RSPB warden,
Bealance, Fetlar
May–July: breeding birds; September: migrants

Although Fetlar, one of Shetland's greenest islands, is probably best known for the snowy owls which bred there between 1967 and 1975 and are still often present, it also has a regular breeding bird community of national importance. None of the species nests solely on the reserve and all may be seen elsewhere on the island when access to the bird sanctuary is restricted.

Much of northern Fetlar, in which the reserve lies, is bare grassy moorland over serpentine rock. Here golden plover, dunlin, curlew and many whimbrel breed, filling the air with plaintive and wilderness-evoking courtship songs. In the wetter areas snipe and redshank nest, and there are many lapwing, oystercatcher and ringed plover. Red-throated diver occur on many of the lochs and red-necked phalarope are best seen at one of their feeding areas, such as Loch Funzie, rather than risking disturbance of the breeding marshes. A large, though fluctuating, population of arctic tern is scattered over 20 or more colonies, while the main concentration of arctic and great skua is on the heather moorland of Lambhoga, outside the reserve.

Fetlar supports populations of both storm petrel and Manx shearwater; a night out along the cliffs of Lambhoga, listening for the purring calls of the incubating petrels and the wild shrieks of shearwaters flighting in from Tresta Bay, can be an exciting and rewarding experience. Compared to other Shetland islands Fetlar's cliff-nesting seabird population is small. Puffin are the most numerous with around 2500 pairs; black guillemot are widely distributed around the island, as are the 300 or so pairs of shag.

Both common and grey seal breed, the population of the latter among the largest on any Shetland island. Otter also occur, and the marine life is rich. Among the more interesting plants are northern rock-cress, northern marsh-orchid, field gentian and creeping willow.

Foula

HT 9639; 1380ha
Isolated inhabited island with high cliffs
Access by boat from Walls (HU 243495);
details from Lerwick tourist office
May–July

Spectacular scenery and vast colonies of seabirds make this one of the most impressive islands in Shetland. To the west precipitous cliffs of old red sandstone rise sheer from the Atlantic, reaching 370m at the Kame, the second highest cliff in the British Isles. Much of the island is, or once was, peat-covered and carries a range of heath and bog vegetation. The high humidity is reflected in widespread Wilson's filmy-fern and varied mosses and liverworts.

At 3000 pairs Foula's great skua colony accounts for half of Shetland's total and nearly 30 per cent of those breeding in the northern hemisphere. Numbers have increased threefold in the last 20 years but now show signs of levelling off. The arctic skua population of about 270 pairs is small in comparison and has grown only slowly since the turn of the century.

It was on Foula that the first Shetland breeding of fulmar occurred in 1878; the cliffs now hold some 40,000 pairs. Auk numbers are also the highest, in total, in Shetland, with around 35,000 pairs of puffin, 30,000 of guillemot, 5000 of razorbill and 60 of black guillemot. Important colonies of shag (3000 pairs), kittiwake (6000 pairs) and arctic tern (3000 pairs) are present and the storm petrel population of over 1000 pairs is by far the largest in Shetland. Foula is as yet the only proven breeding site for Leach's petrel in Shetland and is one of the two known locations for Manx shearwater (the other is FETLAR). With 16 species of nesting seabirds and a total population of over 125,000 pairs, Foula is an internationally important seabird station.

Haaf Gruney

HU 6398; 18ha; NCC reserve
Low uninhabited offshore island
May–July

This small island, accessible only in calm weather, is low and fertile with a plant life reflecting the underlying serpentine rock and the influence of salt spray. Spring squill and the very local northern saltmarsh-grass are present. The boulder beach holds breeding storm petrel and black guillemot and the island is a favourite resting place for common and grey seal.

Hermaness

HP 6016; 964ha; NCC reserve
Cliff-girt moorland peninsula and associated skerries
Visitors are asked to keep to marked path and cliff top during breeding season, to minimise disturbance
May–July

The skuas on Hermaness have been protected for nearly 100 years, in which time great skua have increased from only a few pairs to over 800, but arctic skua have declined. Walking across the skua ground in June means constant dodging of dive-bombing territory defenders! Gannet too have shown a spectacular increase; nesting first around 1920, they now number well over 5000 pairs. Those nesting on some of the stacks can be watched in comfort from the 200m high cliff as they come and go, often harried by great skuas. Since 1972 a black-browed albatross, a wanderer from south of the Equator, has returned annually.

Puffin are the most numerous species present, breeding in tens of thousands on the steep grassy and scree slopes. Some 16,000 pairs of guillemot jostle in tightly packed scrums on the lower ledges of the cliffs; 2000 pairs each of razorbill and shag and a few black guillemot occupy the boulder-strewn shore; 5000 pairs of kittiwake and 10,000 pairs of fulmar ceaselessly call and patrol.

A few red-throated diver nest beside the small lochans scattered over the moorland area. Whimbrel, golden plover and dunlin also breed on the heather-, grass- and Sphagnum-dominated moor, and there are twite and Shetland wren around the cliffs. The plant life of the rather acid cliffs is quite varied and includes such northern species as Scots lovage and roseroot. Moss campion occurs right down to sea level and the Shetland race of red campion is present. Otter and common seal frequent the rocky shores and the grey seals that breed in the caves often haul out on the rocks.

Dark local forms of certain moths occur in Shetland, and many have been recorded on Hermaness, including northern rustic, autumnal rustic, square-spot rustic and the less common arctic northern arches.

Keen of Hamar

HP 6409; 30ha; NCC reserve
Stony hillside
May–June

Montane and maritime plants grow side by side on this Icelandic-type fellfield. As low as 50m above sea level the frost-shattered debris lying around on the serpentine bedrock displays the characteristic striped patterning more frequently encountered at higher altitudes. An imbalance in the essential soil minerals, combined with unusually high concentrations of toxic metals, has resulted in distinct races of thrift and mouse-ear chickweed. Norwegian sandwort, northern rock-cress, moss campion and stone bramble are among the arctic–alpine species present.

Loch of Spiggie

HU 3716; 115ha; RSPB reserve
Loch and associated marshland
October–November: swans and ducks;
March–April: long-tailed duck

Sheltered from the west by the headlands of Foraness and Fitful and from the north by a narrow ridge of sand dunes, shallow Loch Spiggie and its neighbouring Loch Brow are the most important freshwater site for wintering wildfowl in Shetland. This is a regular stopping-off place for migrant duck and geese and early-winter home for a sizeable herd of whooper swan. Tufted duck, pochard and goldeneye are present for much of the winter and in spring as many as 50 long-tailed duck come in off the sea to undergo their pre-migration moult on the sheltered loch.

The two lochs are separated by a floating marsh with varied vegetation. This and the boggy areas around the loch shores hold breeding waders in summer, and the surrounding farmland is often alive with birds during peak migration periods.

Until facilities are provided on the reserve the loch is best viewed from the public road along its north and west sides.

Fetlar is the only site in Britain where snowy owls have bred.

Lumbister

HU 5097; 1600ha; RSPB reserve
Peat moorland with lochans and cliff
May–mid-July

The peat-blanketed island of Yell, on which this reserve is situated, is not visually attractive but its moorlands and lochs hold important breeding populations of several birds that are of limited distribution. Whimbrel occasionally nest on the higher heather moorland, which reaches no more than 150m, and red-throated diver by many of the 20 or so lochs and smaller pools.

Great and arctic skua also breed on the moor, dive-bombing intruders and threatening the survival of the eggs and young of divers and other birds. The wader population is large and varied: golden plover, curlew, oystercatcher, ringed plover, lapwing, snipe and dunlin breed. One or two pairs of merlin prey on twite, meadow pipit and wheatear, while cliff-nesting raven and hooded crow are efficient scavengers. Few seabirds nest on Yell, but there are arctic and common tern by the Lumbister lochs and a colony of great black-backed gull on the moorland.

In the Daal of Lumbister, a steep gorge cut by the stream that drains Lumbister Loch with its sandy bays of sparkling mica crystals, juniper, honeysuckle and roseroot grow, protected from wind and grazing animals. And along the cliff tops, where the peat gives way to grassland, there are wild thyme, moss campion and sundew.

As elsewhere in Shetland, otter are not uncommon, and the reserve supports a flourishing population of them.

Mousa

HU 4624; 180ha Sumburgh Co. Ltd
Low uninhabited inshore island
Access by small boat from Sand Lodge, Sandwick
(HU 438248): details from Lerwick tourist office
May–July

Famous for its extraordinarily well-preserved Pictish broch, this is one of the most interesting, attractive and accessible of the smaller Shetland islands, with a range of animals and plants typical of the lower grassy islands around the coast. Great and arctic skua nest on the rough grassland and there is a colony of several hundred arctic tern. Other breeding birds include fulmar, black guillemot, shag and eider, while the purring of incubating storm petrels enlivens the dry stone walls of the broch in summer. A large rock-bound tidal pool forms a narrow neck linking the wider ends of the island and is a regular hauling-out place for the large local population of common seal. Grey seal also frequent the island's shores.

Noss

HU 5540; 313ha; NCC reserve
Uninhabitated island
Access from Lerwick via the island of Bressay;
summer ferry service across Noss Sound operated by
NCC: details from Lerwick tourist office
Visitors are asked to stay on the clifftop path while on
the reserve
Small visitor centre open in summer
Leaflet from tourist office, Lerwick and NCC.
Lerwick or Aberdeen
May–July

One of Europe's most spectacular seabird colonies occupies this easily accessible island, a site of international importance. Cliffs nearly 200m high fringe the eastern and southern shores, their sandstone layers weathered and eroded to form shelves ideal as nesting sites. Birds throng every shelf, with over 5000 pairs of gannet dominating the headland of the Noup and the area around Rumble Wick. Some 63,000 guillemot shoulder one another on the lower ledges, while many of the 10,000 pairs of kittiwake nest below overhangs and in cave mouths where their cries are drowned by the booming sea.

Gannet and kittiwake are relentlessly pursued by the skuas that nest on Noss's moorland interior. With over 200 pairs of great skua and around 40 of arctic skua present in summer there is always some luckless victim being forced to disgorge its freshly caught fish for a skua to catch in mid-air. The great skuas also threaten eider ducklings hatched on the skua grounds, and indeed any unprotected eggs and young. The great black-backed gull colony on the flat summit of Cradle Holm is one of the largest in Shetland, with over 200 pairs.

Noss is a 'green' island with sedges and grasses dominant among the moorland vegetation. Chickweed wintergreen occurs on the moor and in early summer the cliff tops are bright with spring squill and thrift. Sea and red campion, roseroot and scurvygrass flourish on the cliffs around the nesting fulmars; in contrast the concentrated guano on Cradle Holm has resulted in a lush growth of sorrels.

Yell Sound Islands

Permit only; 162ha; RSPB reserve
Uninhabited islands
May–July

These six small islands represent a wide variety of habitats and the seas around them are an important wintering area for eider, long-tailed duck and divers. The activities at nearby Sullom Voe have already caused some wildlife losses through oil pollution of sea and beaches.

The steep cliffs of Ramna Stacks and Gruney hold big seabird populations: guillemot and kitti-wake on both, with puffin as well on Gruney. Barnacle geese sometimes visit in winter. Unyarey and Fish Holm are flatter and grassier; shag, eider, puffin and black guillemot breed here. On Muckle Holm the cliffs are high enough to attract fulmar and gulls, though not other cliff-nesting seabirds, and small colonies of arctic tern and puffin breed. The largest island, Samphrey, has great and arctic skua, dunlin, snipe and skylark on the hill ground; a large colony of arctic tern on the once-cultivated fields; and storm petrel, black guillemot and starling in the ruined crofts.

A colony of grey seal breeds on Gruney, hauling out well above sea level, the only place they do so in Shetland. Common seal breed on Muckle Holm and Samphrey, while otter, which are seen regularly, breed on Samphrey and may do so on other islands also.

Haaf Gruney: common seals haul out to rest.

Skye and the Small Isles

The late Seton Gordon, a notable naturalist of the Inner Hebrides, called Skye 'The Winged Isle' because of its shape, with its great peninsulas and deep inlets of sea lochs. The 'wings' are overlooked by the ragged ridge of the Cuillins, towering up to almost 1000m, and surrounding hill ranges such as the Red Hills and Lord Macdonald's Forest. The Small Isles – RHUM, EIGG, Canna and Muck in descending order of size – lie south of Skye. The contrasts between them are striking: Rhum is almost entirely mountainous, reaching over 800m on Askival; Eigg's An Sgurr rises to nearly 400m; Canna and Muck are low-lying by comparison.

Some of the complex and diverse geological features have special significance for the vegetation: for instance the tertiary basalt and Jurassic limestone of north Skye, the ultrabasic rocks of central Rhum and the Cambrian limestone in south Skye. Plant communities dominated by mountain avens occur in Raasay and Rhum, but are best seen on the Durness limestone pavement near Ben Suardal in Skye, where herb-Paris, dark-red helleborine and mountain melick are also present.

The climate is oceanic, dominated by westerly winds from the Atlantic. Weather conditions are varied locally by the higher hills, which give rise to higher rainfall and frequent low cloud. Though the winds are less severe than in the Outer Hebrides, they still contribute to lower summer daytime temperatures than those on the mainland. On the other hand, the winds ensure that winter snow does not normally lie long, and the islands escape the severe winters of central Scotland.

About 1 per cent of the islands' surface is standing water, much less than in the Outer Hebrides; most lochs are small, with relatively little plant and bird life. Rivers and streams are short and weather-sensitive, being often either torrential floods or a mere trickle. The moist climate has given rise to widespread and extensive peatland and blanket bog. On the highest hills, the development of plant communities like those on the mainland has been restricted by the limited ground area.

Crofting is a major activity, along with hill and upland farming; though good land for cultivation is scarce, the climate is well suited to pasture and stock rearing. Most native woods have been felled or burned in the last few hundred years; only fragments survive. Little moorland has not been burnt to its detriment, and 'muirburn' is still a major threat to the surviving natural vegetation.

The influence of the sea is felt throughout the islands. Rocky shores make up the entire coastline, with coastal cliffs, stacks and islets providing a major habitat for plant and bird life; the whole range of maritime habitats may be seen in the Rhum reserve. *Machair* is virtually absent from Skye and the Small Isles, but there are a few sand dunes in scattered places such as Glen Brittle in Skye, Kilmory in Rhum and Laig in Eigg. The best saltmarshes are at the heads of Skye's many sea lochs. As a result of the strong winds, coastal influences can extend well inland, giving rise to maritime heaths and grasslands and accounting for sea plantain on moorland. In contrast some mountain flowers grow near sea level, including purple and mossy saxifrage, roseroot, hoary whitlowgrass and moss campion.

Despite the sea cliffs seabird colonies are small; guillemot, razorbill, kittiwake and fulmar are the main species. A few puffin occur at isolated sites such as the Ascrib Islands, and terns nest on a few islets, but it is the huge Manx shearwater colonies of the hills of Rhum which are outstanding, while storm petrel also nest in north Skye and Canna. A few wildfowl and waders winter along the coasts, with large numbers of eider in the Inner Sound of Raasay, and small groups of wigeon round the Skye coast at Broadford, Portree and Dunvegan. Divers and auks winter in the Inner Sound. Mallard, merganser, eider, shelduck, oystercatcher and ringed plover are among the summer nesting birds.

Freshwater lochs, such as Loch Suardal near Dunvegan, in Skye, hold limited numbers of wintering birds including whooper swan, goldeneye, tufted duck and pochard. In summer, common sandpiper nest by lochs and streams, while here and there may be found pied and grey wagtail and dipper. Red-breasted merganser nest in this habitat, and on Skye there are a few pairs of little grebe. Many of the lochs carry fine clumps of white water-lily, bogbean or bottle sedge, and a few near Sligachan in Skye have the rare pipewort. Royal fern grows on islands in some lochs, and here trees and scrub survive in the absence of grazing and burning. Salmon, brown trout and arctic char are among the freshwater fish present.

The native woodland which survives is mainly birch, seen in Raasay, Skye and Eigg, but there are also good examples of oak, ash, hazel and alder. The best ashwood is at TOKAVAIG WOOD where ash grows on Durness limestone with birch and rowan, in contrast to oak which chooses the adjacent Torridonian sandstone. Mixed deciduous woodland occurs in Skye in the shelter of narrow ravines such as the Geary Ravine and Allt Grillan, and fine coastal woodlands may be seen in Strathaird. Hazel scrub clothes some of the slopes below the sea cliffs of Skye and Eigg, and where muirburning has not been too severe willow carr grows strongly, especially on the reserve at Blàr Dubh, in Eigg. Rich moss and lichen communities are associated with the older woods, and include a fine range of oceanic bryophytes. Birds are at their best in the mixed woodlands, and include woodcock, tawny owl, great, blue and coal tit, redstart, willow and wood warbler, treecreeper and tree pipit.

Peatland and bog are represented in oceanic type, with distinctive plants which include great sundew, pale butterwort, lesser skullcap and white beak-sedge. Moorland provides nesting habitats for small birds like meadow pipit, skylark and wheatear, and for waders including curlew, green-shank and golden plover, while the moorland lochs may have breeding red-throated and occasionally black-throated diver. Moorland and hillside provide territories for birds of prey, especially buz-

zard which also frequent woodland. Golden eagle may be seen soaring high on wind currents, particularly on Skye, and peregrine falcon still occupies a few eyries. Kestrel are present on Skye, Eigg and Rhum, as are sparrowhawk and merlin, and on occasion short-eared owl can be seen quartering the ground.

It is the high hills that are the finest attribute of these isles, often obscured by impenetrable cloud, but at other times sparkling in bright sunshine. On Rhum alpine plants such as Scottish asphodel and two-flowered rush can be found. The famous Cuillins of Skye support a range of alpines on their limited surfaces, and Blaven has richly vegetated limestone cliffs with tall-herb communities. The best place to see mountain vegetation in Skye is on the basalt escarpment of Trotternish Ridge, with its banks of yellow saxifrage and lawns of alpine lady's-mantle, as well as the recently discovered Iceland purslane. Birds include ring ouzel, ptarmigan and raven, while over all may soar the golden eagle.

ANDREW CURRIE

Canna

NG 2705; 1515ha; NTS
Large island
Access by Caledonian MacBrayne ferry from Mallaig
Leaflet from NTS or Canna Post Office
Late spring, summer

Canna (the most westerly of the small isles of the Inner Hebrides) and the smaller island of Sanday are designated SSSIs for biological and geological reasons. The cliffs shelter breeding seabirds such as puffins, razorbills and Manx shearwaters, and several species of birds of prey may be seen, including the sea eagle, which has been reintroduced to Rhum. Snipe, curlew and other waders are abundant, and the number of woodland bird species has increased with the establishment and growth of the plantations. Raised beaches of coarse shingle occur at Tarbert and An Coroghon. It is possible to walk along the cliffs or the shore but access between is precipitous and dangerous. Visitors are reminded that the whole island is farmed and disturbance must be minimal.

Clan Donald Centre, Skye

NG 6105; 8000 ha Clan Donald Lands Trust
Woodlands, hill and lochs
Access restricted to waymarked walks unless
accompanied by countryside ranger
Visitor centre at Armadale Castle, Sleat, open
April–October; leaflets
All year

The planted woodlands around the castle include an extensive and long-established arboretum with some fine specimen trees. From their seaward edge otters and seals can sometimes be seen in the Sound of Sleat. The main interest of the area, however, lies in the natural woodlands, which are predominantly birch and hazel with a scattering

of rowan, willow, ash and oak. They occur on mineral-rich soils which support a varied ground flora, including herb-Robert, lesser twayblade, stone bramble and melancholy thistle. These woods also hold roe deer and a wide variety of woodland birds.

Conon Woods, Uig

NG 400637; 12ha; WdT
Wooded glen
Summer

A steep-sided wooded glen, with ash, wych elm, rowan, alder, hawthorn, sycamore and hazel. The Conon river cascades in a series of waterfalls through the glen. There are opportunities for walking along the foreshore, but access to the glen above the weir is not possible owing to the steepness of the slopes.

Corry Walk, Skye

NG 625255; 1.9km; FC
Coast and young conifer plantation
All year

This walk follows the shore for much of its route, providing opportunities to watch seabirds, for instance gannet fishing in Scalpay Sound, and sometimes waders in the muddy bays, as well as woodland species such as siskin and redpoll. Many typical moorland plants can still be seen along the edge of the plantation.

Eigg

NM 474875; 1518ha; SWT reserve
Lime-rich upland area, mixed woodland and small
lochans
May–July

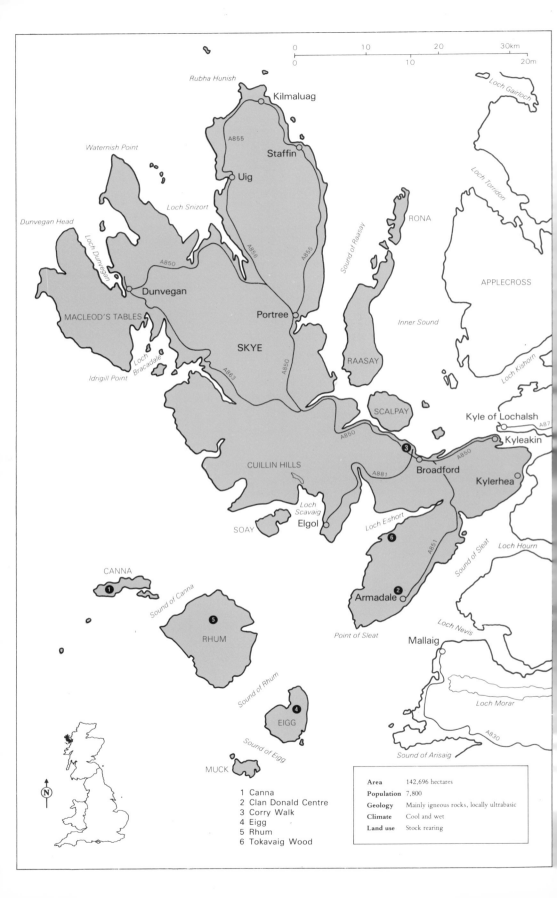

Scale: 0 10 20 30km / 0 10 20m

Rubha Hunish
Kilmaluag
A855
Staffin
Waternish Point
Uig
Loch Snizort
A856
A855
Sound of Raasay
RONA
Loch Gairloch
Loch Torridon
Dunvegan Head
Loch Dunvegan
A850
APPLECROSS
Dunvegan
MACLEOD'S TABLES
Portree
Inner Sound
SKYE
Loch Bracadale
A850
Loch Kishorn
Idrigill Point
A863
RAASAY
SCALPAY
Kyle of Lochalsh
A87
A850
Kyleakin
CUILLIN HILLS
A850
Broadford
Kylerhea
A881
Loch Scavaig
Elgol
Loch Eishort
SOAY
6
A851
Loch Hourn
Sound of Sleat
CANNA
1
Sound of Canna
2
Armadale
RHUM
5
Point of Sleat
Loch Nevis
Mallaig
Sound of Rhum
EIGG
4
Sound of Eigg
MUCK
Loch Morar
N
Sound of Arisaig
A830

1 Canna
2 Clan Donald Centre
3 Corry Walk
4 Eigg
5 Rhum
6 Tokavaig Wood

Area	142,696 hectares
Population	7,800
Geology	Mainly igneous rocks, locally ultrabasic
Climate	Cool and wet
Land use	Stock rearing

Visually most striking of the three separate sections comprising this reserve is that including the Sgurr, a narrow pitchstone lava ridge rising steeply above a hinterland of heather moor and dominating the island landscape. On the bare slopes surrounding the base of the hexagonally columned pitchstone least willow – with its tiny round leaves – sprawls close to the ground, and the moisture-loving Wilson's filmy-fern flourishes among the grass in the damp conditions created by the high rainfall and frequent low cloud. A lime-rich dyke provides one area of markedly more varied vegetation than elsewhere in the section. Here, cushions of pink moss campion, clumps of white-flowered mountain avens and the woolly yellow heads of kidney vetch brighten the scene; moonwort is also found.

At the opposite end of the island the Beinn Bhuide plateau falls away in steep craggy cliffs to both east and west. Here, buzzard and raven ride the up-currents, and golden eagle are not infrequently seen. Below the plateau rim moss campion and the uncommon Norwegian sandwort occur, with roseroot on the cliff ledges beneath. Steep scree slopes, some unstable and bare and others grassed over, form a 'skirt' below the cliffs, and it is here that Eigg's Manx shearwater colony is located.

Scrub woodland clothes the lower slopes, its canopy wind-smoothed to give a bank-like effect. Hazel predominates in the woodland but willow, rowan, hawthorn and blackthorn are also present. Ferns flourish among the jumble of mossy boulders concealed by the trees; those found include lemon-scented fern, broad and narrow buckler-fern, and scaly male-fern. Typical woodland flowers such as wood-sorrel, wood anemone, ramsons, wood sage and wild strawberry grow here, along with yellow pimpernel and great patches of bluebell which extend beyond the woodland to the surrounding bracken-covered slopes. Burnet rose is abundant, too, often in dense clumps.

The third section of the reserve lies above Laig Farm, where two wooded ravines cut through a low stepped basalt escarpment. On the acid moorland above, several species of stunted willow are scattered among the heather, sometimes as isolated specimens and sometimes forming miniature woods in the shallow valleys. At the foot of the escarpment a deceptively deep pool, known as the Giant's Footprint, exhibits a classic pattern of colonisation, with quantities of horsetail, bog-bean and cottongrass, as well as floating *Sphagnum* islands, on the largest of which grow heather and two or three small willows.

Towards the eastern end of Laig Bay a band of lime-rich rock forms outcrops on the shore, and just beyond lie the 'Singing Sands' – an area of rounded quartz grains. The croft land is dotted with orchids, while primrose and speedwell are massed on the Laig dunes and the areas of low marshy ground are bright with yellow iris. There are snipe in the marshes, corncrake in the meadows, eider and shelduck along the tideline, and porpoises and sharks offshore. The 68 bird species known to breed on the island include red-throated diver, long-eared owl, short-eared owl and golden eagle.

Kylerhea

NG 7822; 3km; FC reserve
Rocky shore with otters
May–October

Designed for otter watching: there are suitable places for their holts among the rocks and a plentiful supply of fish in the channel which separates Skye from the mainland. Birds to be seen include red-breasted merganser, black guillemot, osprey, golden eagle, peregrine, buzzard, stonechat and whinchat.

Natural woodland, predominantly hazel, is wind-pressed against this basalt cliff on Eigg.

Rha Glen

NG 397645; 6ha; WdT reserve
Damp woodland and river

This ash and wych elm woodland also contains alder, willow, sycamore and a type of rowan which is unusual in north Skye. The Rha river cascades through the wood in a spectacular two-stage waterfall.

Rhum

NM 3798; 10,684ha; NCC reserve
Large and mountainous island
Access from Mallaig and Arisaig: day trips, but accommodation also available (apply to Hebridean Holidays, tel: 0687 2026)
Permit required to visit parts of the island away from the Loch Scresort area: apply NCC, Inverness
Nature trail and reserve leaflets at Kinloch Castle and Rhum post office, or from NCC, Inverness
May–September

When seen from afar, whether from EIGG, Skye or the mainland, Rhum is dominated by the cluster of spectacular peaks and ridges towards its southern end – all relics of volcanic activity in the distant past. A great variety of rock types, some of them unique to Rhum, are represented in these uplands; only at closer quarters, however, can the full natural diversity of the island be appreciated.

Although the area of lime-rich rock is not extensive it has an interesting plant life including mountain avens, alpine saxifrage, alpine meadow-grass and alpine penny-cress. Scottish asphodel, stone bramble and mountain everlasting flourish on volcanic soils high in the hills, with arctic sandwort, purple saxifrage, cyphel and abundant northern rock-cress growing right up to summit level. Wood bitter-vetch and pyramidal bugle occur on the low-lying Torridonian sandstone soils, while the sandy bays of the north coast are made colourful by gentians, trefoils, pansies and a variety of orchids, including fragrant, frog and marsh-orchid.

Rhum's vast breeding colony of Manx shear-water is one of its ornithological specialities; over 130,000 pairs have their nesting burrows in the deep, loose soil high on the slopes of Askival and Hallival. The heavy manuring of the soil outside the burrows produces lush grass which attracts the intensively studied deer herds in summer. The other bird of particular interest is sea eagle. Once regular breeding birds on Rhum and else-where in Scotland, sea eagles were persecuted until they became extinct early this century. Now, in a project started in 1975, young sea eagles from Norway are being reintroduced and successfully released to the wild. Some are now sufficiently mature to breed, and in 1981 a pair occupied a nest site for the first time.

The bird life of the island has been significantly affected by the extensive afforestation with native species carried out during the last 15 years. Policy plantings around Kinloch Castle initially provided the only suitable habitat for woodland birds such as robin, blackbird, song thrush and dunnock, all relatively scarce in semi-natural woodlands in north west Scotland. These four species, together with chaffinch, willow warbler, wren and gold-crest, have now effectively colonised the new woodlands. Other breeding birds on Rhum include peregrine, merlin, raven, red-throated diver and corncrake, and there are modest seabird colonies along the southern cliffs.

Rhum is notably rich in insects, including the more vividly coloured Hebridean forms of species such as dark green fritillary butterfly. Small pearl-bordered fritillary, green hairstreak, common blue and large heath butterflies are all abundant. Among the larger and more obvious moths are emperor, fox, drinker and northern eggar, and three species strongly associated with aspens: puss moth, poplar hawkmoth and pebble prominent moth.

This wealth of interest, together with the fact that for more than 20 years the NCC has managed the reserve so as to minimise disturbance, explains the great value of Rhum for ecological research – a value recognised by the reserve's designation by UNESCO as a Biosphere Reserve.

Tokavaig Wood (Coille Thocabhaig)

NG 6112; 81ha; NCC reserve
Relict semi-natural woodland
May–June

The sheltered and very humid location of this mixed woodland, together with the variety of the underlying rocks, are responsible for its botanical richness. Ash is the dominant species on the limestone outcrops, with some hazel and bird cherry; the Torridonian sandstone areas support oak. The wood has a varied ground vegetation, and of notable interest are its bryophytes, lichens and ferns.

Strathclyde North

From the Clyde Estuary north into the mountains and islands of Argyll lies a countryside of ceaseless change in mood and endless variety in landform. Peninsulas reach out into the island-studded sea of the Hebrides. From the vast peatlands of Rannoch Moor to the unspoiled beaches of Tiree, and from the Mull of Kintyre to Loch Linnhe, Argyll probably contains a greater variety of natural formations and richer assemblages of plants and animals than any other part of Scotland. There are mountains supporting tundra and alpine flowers; raised bog and valley peatlands; open waters ranging from small peat pools to lime-rich lochs fringed with reed and fen communities; rolling dunes; steep, herb-rich coastline; and native deciduous woodlands. It all starts some 30km from the centre of Glasgow by LOCH LOMOND (described under Central), studded with tree-covered islands and fringed with fine, mixed woodlands.

Sea lochs cut deep into the hinterland, providing shelter from Atlantic rollers. Unpolluted lagoons contain myriads of inshore marine organisms. Clear rivers run down to the head of these long fiords, and in some the great volume of fresh water affects the salinity of the loch, resulting in a gradation of animal and plant communities from near-freshwater to full salinity.

Wet days can be expected at any time of year, but rainfall is usually heaviest in late summer, autumn and winter. In early summer it is possible to experience the weather of all four seasons in one day. The climate varies within and between islands. Tiree and Coll enjoy longer periods of sunshine than most of Scotland, while the mountain mass of central Mull, only 32km east, is very wet. The islands usually escape heavy snow, but inland it can lie deep in the hills for long periods. The influence of the Gulf Stream is felt along Argyll's deeply indented coastline and around the offshore islands, which usually escape extreme frosts.

The action of weather on complex geological formations has led to a wide range of soil conditions. Granite hills produce generally infertile soils around upper Loch Etive, while black, base-rich schists to the east of Dalmally support some of the richest upland plant communities in the Highlands. Nearer the coast a north east to south west configuration of the terrain is created by the bedding of metamorphic Dalradian rocks; and there are limestone bands within these formations. Around Oban, the underlying rock is mostly igneous andesite and the vegetation is influenced by intrusions of basalts.

The geology of the Inner Hebrides is even more complex. Lismore is entirely limestone and the landscape is verdant; three lime-rich lochs support aquatic and fen communities very rare in Scotland. Jura is mainly quartzite, whereas Islay has the full range of Dalradian rocks. The underlying rock of Tiree and Coll is Lewisian gneiss, but Coll has rocky hillocks, and low-lying Tiree is largely raised beach. Both contain dune and *machair* formations, but blown shell sands influence the soil all over Tiree. On Colonsay and Oronsay the underlying rocks are Torridonian sandstones, phyllites, grits, mudstones and flags. Some of the finest raised beaches in Britain are found on Jura, Islay and Colonsay.

The Isle of Mull with its smaller satellites is geologically outstanding. Mull was the centre of violent volcanic activity in the tertiary period. There are granite exposures on the Ross of Mull, but over the rest of the island layers of lava flow have resulted in a terraced landscape with columnar formations along the coast, the most spectacular forming the pillars of Fingal's Cave on Staffa. The great plateau lavas of the central Mull complex contain an almost perfect ring dyke. Formations such as this, the coastal exposures where the plateau lavas cover sedimentary rocks, and sites such as the Ardtun leafbeds, where fossilised ancient forest debris is sandwiched between lava flows, make Mull a petrologist's paradise.

Some islands in the Inner Hebrides support plant communities dependent on sands derived from seashells. The air is seldom still here and the fine, calcium- and phosphate-rich sand is taken up by the wind and deposited over the islands, which bear a *machair* turf studded with wild flowers. This in turn supports distinctive insect and bird communities. *Machair* is most

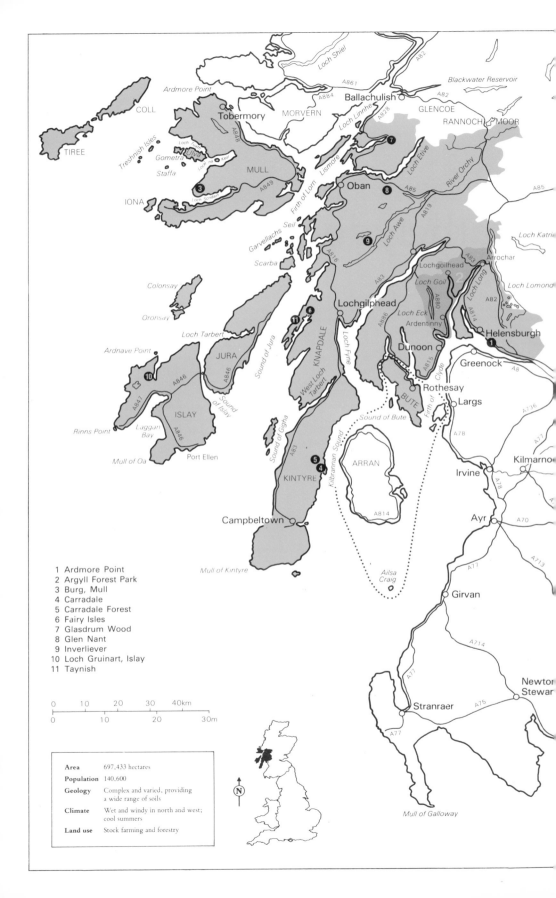

COLL

TIRE

Ardmore Point

Treshnish Isles

Gometra

Staffa

IONA

MULL

Tobermory

MORVERN

Ballachulish

GLENCOE

RANNOCH MOOR

Blackwater Reservoir

Loch Shiel

Loch Linnhe

Lismore

Firth of Lorn

Oban

Loch Etive

River Orchy

Loch Awe

Loch Katrine

Arrochar

Lochgoilhead

Loch Goil

Loch Long

Loch Lomond

Lochgilphead

Loch Eck

Ardentinny

Dunoon

Colonsay

Oronsay

Loch Tarbert

Ardnave Point

JURA

Sound of Jura

KNAPDALE

West Loch Tarbert

Loch Fyne

Firth of Clyde

Rothesay

Largs

Sound of Islay

ISLAY

Rinns Point

Laggan Bay

Mull of Oa

Port Ellen

Sound of Gigha

BUTE

Sound of Bute

Kilbrannan Sound

ARRAN

Irvine

Kilmarnock

Ayr

KINTYRE

Campbeltown

Mull of Kintyre

Ailsa Craig

Girvan

Greenock

Helensburgh

Scarba

Seil

Garvellachs

1 Ardmore Point
2 Argyll Forest Park
3 Burg, Mull
4 Carradale
5 Carradale Forest
6 Fairy Isles
7 Glasdrum Wood
8 Glen Nant
9 Inverliever
10 Loch Gruinart, Islay
11 Taynish

0   10   20   30   40km

0   10   20   30m

Newton Stewart

Stranraer

Mull of Galloway

N

Area	697,433 hectares
Population	140,600
Geology	Complex and varied, providing a wide range of soils
Climate	Wet and windy in north and west; cool summers
Land use	Stock farming and forestry

extensive on Tiree, probably the biggest blown sand formation in Britain unaffected by rabbit grazing: although brown hare are present, rabbits were never introduced to Tiree.

Argyll contains more relict native woodlands than other parts of Scotland. Fragments of fine old native pinewoods survive by Loch Tulla, near Bridge of Orchy and along Glen Orchy. Nearer the coast and on many islands the original forest cover consisted mainly of deciduous species – oak, ash, wych elm, wild cherry, birch, alder, rowan, hazel, with sallows, holly, bird cherry and guelder-rose sometimes present in the shrub layer. It is not surprising that three of Argyll's National Nature Reserves, GLASDRUM, TAYNISH and GLEN NANT were designated primarily as examples of native deciduous forest. These woods have been exploited by man over the centuries, first for fuel, tools and building timber, and later also to supply charcoal for the iron smelting industry centred on Loch Fyne and Loch Etive, and oak bark for tanning. Had it not been for the management of woods by coppicing, for a sustained yield, all these ancient forests would perhaps have long since been destroyed.

An interesting feature of the oceanic deciduous woodlands of western Scotland is the profusion of lichens, mosses and liverworts, which cover tree trunks as well as the forest floor. Over 200 species of lichens may occur in a single wood, with a similar number of mosses and liverworts, while some of the oceanic species existing here are found nowhere else in Europe. Many of the oceanic lichens are sensitive even to low levels of atmospheric pollution and their survival here is evidence of clean air.

Man's past use of the land has been mainly pastoral. Until the nineteenth century cattle were herded in the hills in summer and brought down to the glens in winter. Later sheep were introduced in enormous numbers and muirburning became a regular practice, aimed at encouraging young growth of the moorland vegetation in early spring. At the same time deer stalking developed as a popular sport on the large estates. The coppicing system came to an end and the woods were exposed to browsing by sheep and deer and the effects of fire. For over 100 years natural regeneration has only been possible where grazing has been relaxed for periods.

Today dramatic changes are taking place. In the past 40 years extensive areas have been commercially afforested, and conifers now grow on hillsides where native woodlands have long since vanished. Dense, dark spruce woods blanket the hills, suppressing the natural vegetation, but the potential threats to wildlife have been recognised. Streamsides and river courses are left unplanted or planted with alder and willow, and native woodland relics are protected as wildlife refuges within areas of afforestation. In the ARGYLL FOREST PARK care is being taken to achieve a greater diversity of species in second-generation forests, and woodlands developing by Loch Goil and Loch Eck have an uneven canopy structure and contain a wide range of conifers as well as substantial areas of native deciduous species.

The larger animals and birds are all well represented in this corner of Scotland. Golden eagles soar around coastal cliffs as well as the high corries. Peregrine, merlin, hen harrier, sparrowhawk, kestrel and buzzard are abundant. Fox and badger are widespread on the mainland and otter occur around the coastline and on most of the islands. Red and roe deer play an increasingly important part in currrent land use.

PETER WORMELL

Spikes of mare's-tail in a moorland pool on Jura.

Argyll Forest Park

See map; c.240sq.km; FC and others
Information from forest offices at Ardgartan
(NN 272034), Glenbranter (NS 112977) or Kilmun
(NS 160825); guide from FC, or HMSO bookshops
All year

This forest park is unique in that roughly half its perimeter is bounded by sea water. The narrow, fiord-like fingers of Loch Long and Loch Goil thrust far into the forested hills, the former reaching, at Arrochar, to within 2.5km of LOCH LOMOND, (Central) and the latter almost bisecting the park. This was the first forest park to be set up in Great Britain, in 1935, and it has demonstrated with ever-increasing success how commercial forestry can be combined with a wide variety of recreational facilities and still maintain great natural history interest.

Much less than half of the land within the park has been afforested, the upper limit of planting being around 350–400m, depending upon exposure. Above this fringing band of conifers lies open hill ground, mostly grassy moorland, with heath rush, cottongrasses, bog mosses and sedges on the peaty wetter areas, and bracken, heather and bilberry where the drainage is freer. Arctic–alpines such as alpine lady's-mantle, mountain everlasting, alpine meadow-rue and moss campion are not uncommon from 700m, with dwarf willow and three-leaved rush on the summits, and holly fern, alpine lady-fern and alpine saw-wort also occurring. Where glacial action has carved out corries, or water has worn through the rock to form gorges, one can often find good displays of globeflower, goldenrod, purple saxifrage and roseroot.

This high ground is used for sheep grazing, and also supports several hundred red deer; in autumn the hills ring with the roars of rutting stags. A few ptarmigan are present on the summits, and the birds of the lower moorlands include red grouse, curlew, skylark, twite and stonechat. Hen harrier breed in some areas, buzzard and raven are fairly common, and one may see a golden eagle. There are many good walking routes over the high ground as well as the more challenging hills of the 'Arrochar Alps' which rise to just over 1000m.

The forests offer a maze of tracks, some way-marked as circular routes and others simply working forestry roads. Crossbill, capercaillie, sparrowhawk, goldcrest and siskin breed in the plantations, with black grouse along the forest fringe, where trees give way to moorland. Both red and grey squirrel live in these woods, but neither is very numerous.

Semi-natural woodlands still survive in many parts of the park. Oak dominates the woods along the shore of Loch Lomond, north of Tarbet, and in Glen Loin there is a virtually untouched stand of mixed ash, hazel, birch, alder and oak. In Glen Branter natural woodland lines the hillside gullies, and along the east shore of Loch Eck are mixed woods with much beech and oak. Many of these woods produce masses of primroses, bluebells,

wood anemones and violets in spring. The fact that no part of the park is more than 6.5km from sea water means that the climate is relatively mild and this, together with the high rainfall, results in an exceptionally rich growth of ferns, mosses, liverworts and lichens.

These areas of mixed woodland support a more varied bird population than do the plantations. Long-tailed tit occur in them, as well as blue, great and coal tit; willow warbler are numerous in summer and jay are most abundant where there are oak trees. Magpie are very local – often the case in Scotland – and are most likely to be seen around Strachur. The best prospect of hearing the delightful shivering trill of wood warbler is in the predominantly oak woodland, while blackcap, garden warbler and chiffchaff are most likely to be found in the exotic surroundings of the Younger Botanic Gardens at Benmore, or in the Kilmun Arboretum.

Although in no way resembling natural woodland, these two sites are well worth a visit. Both owe their success to the temperate climate which enables many non-hardy exotics to be grown. At Kilmun there is an interesting and varied collection of trees from all over the world; trails have been set out and a guide book is available. In the Younger Botanic Gardens the unrivalled collection of rhododendrons takes pride of place, but there are also many magnificent specimen trees of such species as noble fir and redwood. In the soft west-coast climate rhododendron naturalises readily and spreads rapidly; along the eastern shore of Loch Goil young plants are plentiful. A more unexpected exotic, also abundant in this area, is flowering nutmeg, rampant on some of the rocky slopes beside the forest track.

Sandy areas along the shoreline are few and far between, occurring only at the heads of Loch Goil and the Holy Loch, and near Ardentinny. Elsewhere the shores are mostly composed of stones set in sand and gravel, but there are interesting and easily accessible rock pools around Strone Point on the southern tip of Kilmun. Because the narrowness of the sea-lochs restricts tidal scour, dense beds of seaweeds flourish in the inter-tidal zone. Among the seaweeds and stones beadlet sea-anemones and the grey sea-slugs that feed on them, sea-lemons and starfish, sea-urchins and well-camouflaged, armadillo-like chitons all flourish. Mussels – both the common variety and the larger horse-mussel – are abundant on the gravelly shores, providing food for the eider that frequent the coasts, and there are many other 'shellfish' such as periwinkles, limpets and whelks. In the rock pools shore crabs, shrimps, sea-scorpions and the almost transparent aesop prawns hide among the fronds of seaweed, while bread-crumb and purse sponges, star sea-squirts and jellyfish occur in the deeper water. Grey seal frequently visit the sea-lochs and basking shark have been seen both in Loch Goil and as far up Loch Long as Arrochar.

There is much more that is equally worthy of mention in the Argyll Forest Park – otter in the rivers and sea-lochs, for example, golden-ringed dragonflies hawking over the track-side ditches, hart's-tongue fern on a shady wall, or powan and char in Loch Eck. Within the park are four outdoor education centres, offering many facilities to the general visitor: hill walking and climbing, fishing, orienteering, sailing and pony trekking can all be enjoyed.

Ballachuan Hazelwood

Permit only; 49ha; SWT reserve
Hazel wood, marsh, rocky shore
Spring, summer

Ballachuan Wood lies in the south-west corner of Seil Island, south of Oban. From early spring the ground is carpeted with flowers and the narrow-leaved helleborine is worth looking out for. As with many hazel woods, Ballachuan was once coppiced but the 'trees' have now run wild and some are over 8m high. The hazel and bird cherry are draped in lichens, for which the wood is a site of international importance with over 250 species. The local heronry and nesting buzzards add ornithological interest, and marsh fritillary butterflies are abundant in the wet, marshy grassland.

Burg, Mull

NM 426266; 617ha; NTS
Cliff, grassland and shoreline
Access by foot only, from Tiroran (NM 478278)
Further information at Burg Farm (NM 427266)
All year

Situated at the western end of the Ardmeanach peninsula, this site is famous for its fossil tree, believed to be 50 million years old. Known as McCulloch's tree, it is embedded in columnar basalt and can be seen only at low tide. The area is notable for its rich and varied plant life, and also for the butterflies which are attracted by the wealth of summer flowers.

Carradale

NR 8137; 70ha; SWT reserve
Coastal grassland, low cliffs and island
April–June

There is rich coastal and marine life around this grassy peninsula, which affords good views over Kilbrannan Sound. Otter frequent the shoreline and porpoise, white-beaked dolphin, bottle-nosed dolphin and killer whale are regularly seen offshore. A variety of seabirds can be seen in summer, and there is a small though long-established herd of white feral goats, as well as a herd of sika deer.

Carradale Forest

NR 8038; 700ha; FC
Conifer plantations and moorland
All year

This is probably the only area in Scotland with both sika and fallow deer, as well as roe deer.

The sika deer originated from an enclosure at CARRADALE, and have colonised the Kintyre peninsula. Fallow deer occur only in the Deerhill section of the forest (NR 8039).

Crinan Wood

NR 790940; 40ha; WdT reserve
Scrub oak woodland
Summer

Lying on a prominent series of rocky ridges at the western end of the Crinan Canal, this wood is part of the Knapdale National Scenic Area. Its rocky crags, scrub oak woodland and damp grassy clearings provide a rich wildlife habitat.

Fairy Isles

NM 7688; 21ha; SWT reserve
Woodland and small islands
Spring, summer

The Fairy Isles consist of 6 small islands at the head of Loch Sween in the small sea loch north of Rubh'an Oib and east of Caol Scotnish. All the islands except one are tidal but access to some is difficult, even at low tide, due to the very soft, muddy substratum. The reserve also consists of a narrow coastal strip of broadleaved woodland. All the islands are slightly different but generally have a cover of oak, birch and rowan together with a few 'exotic' trees. Woodrush, bilberry, heather and bluebell are some of the components of the ground layer, which also includes penny-wort and Scots lovage.

Treecreeper and willow warbler are found but more evident are the birds of the coast – eiders, herons, terns and red-breasted mergansers. Loch Sween itself is an area of exceptional marine biological interest.

Glasdrum Wood

NN 0545; 169ha; NCC reserve
Hanging woodland
Access restricted: contact NCC, Ardchattan, by Oban
Leaflet from NCC, Balloch
May–August

This trackless, closed-canopy woodland rises steeply from just above sea level to an altitude of 530m; above it lies open hill. A band of alder occupies the damp lower slopes; ash and hazel dominate the middle section, in which lime-rich rocky outcrops occur; and above the main escarpment sessile oak and birch gradually give way to moorland. The herb-rich ground flora includes a variety of ferns, and such typical woodland flowers as dog's mercury, wood anemone and enchanter's-nightshade. Many maritime bryophyte and lichen species are present and the reserve has an interesting insect population.

Glen Nant

NN 0128; 200ha; NCC-FC reserve
Native deciduous woodland
Access restricted: contact NCC, Ardchattan, by Oban
Nature trail (4km) on forest nature reserve
April–July

The mark of man's past activities is still apparent in these woods, once the source of charcoal for the iron furnace at nearby Bonawe. Stumps of coppiced oaks, some around 400 years old, and the levelled circles of charcoal hearths, are widely scattered through the mixed woodland that clothes the slopes of Glen Nant today. A variety of tree species is now present, including oak with abundant ash, hazel and birch. Bird cherry, rowan and holly are well represented, with the occasional wych elm and wild cherry, and alder and willow in the wetter areas.

The shrub layer is minimal – only a few blackthorn, hawthorn and guelder-rose. In some places ferns dominate the ground vegetation. Elsewhere feathery clumps of tufted hair-grass tower above a carpet of ramsons, primrose and wild strawberry. Both living and fallen tree trunks carry a luxuriant growth of mosses, and there are many lichens.

Wood warbler, redstart and great spotted woodpecker are among the breeding birds in the wood. Roe deer are common – the ground cover is networked by their tracks – and voles, fieldmice and hedgehogs are plentiful. Insect life is also varied. Beneath the trees wood ants work around their mounded nests, some of which have been there sufficiently long for bilberry to colonise their summits.

The Forest Nature Reserve accounts for considerably more than half of the total woodland area. It lies on the west side of the valley, and is separated by the River Nant from the NNR, which is in private ownership and not open to the public.

Inverliever

NM 9410; 13,383ha; FC
Conifer plantations, oakwood and open hill
Forest walks; further information from forest office, Dalavich, Taynuilt (NM 970126)
All year

The large stretches of untouched heathery hill ground support red deer and such typical moorland plants as purple moor-grass, deergrass, bog asphodel and bog myrtle. Hen harrier nest on the moorland, and golden eagle and peregrine can sometimes be seen flying over. The forest itself holds breeding buzzard, sparrowhawk, jay and crossbill, and there are red, roe and sika deer and badger in the area. Several remnants of the old oakwoods remain along the shores of Loch Awe and a variety of other native species, such as alder, ash, wych elm and hazel, are present. The woods and wet gullies are rich in ferns, mosses and lichens and hold many smaller birds and mammals.

Loch Gruinart, Islay

NR 280670; 1654ha; RSPB reserve
Farmland, estuary, saltmarsh and moorland
View from road on south and west side of loch
Autumn, winter, spring

The reserve consists of farmland and moorland on the south and west sides of Loch Gruinart and

Argyll Forest Park: the semi-natural woodlands support a more varied bird life than do the plantations.

is one of the two most important wintering areas for barnacle geese in Britain. Islay is renowned for its wintering geese: the 18,000 barnacles form two-thirds of the Greenland race, while up to 4000 Greenland white-fronts represent one-third of the world population. A significant proportion of both these species can be seen on or around the reserve. Other birds include nesting lapwing, redshank, eider and shelduck on Gruinart flats and around the shore, while on the moor black and red grouse and curlew breed. Peregrines, golden eagles, merlins and hen harriers all hunt over the reserve.

Loch Lomond

Described under Central.

Mealdarroch

NR 8868; 205ha; NCC reserve
Deciduous woodland, ferns and bryophytes
Access difficult: advice from NCC Warden, Glenview Cottage, Kilmichael, Glassary, Lochgilphead
All year

An area of scattered woodland on steep slopes above the sea which are separated by several small but deep gorges. The trees are mainly oak and birch with ash, hazel and elm in richer places. The reserve is of international importance for its Atlantic bryophytes and ferns.

Moine Mhor

NR 8292; 501ha; NCC reserve
Raised bog
Access difficult: advice from NCC Warden, Glenview Cottage, Kilmichael, Glassary, Lochgilphead
June–August

One of the best examples of a raised bog left in Britain. It includes wetland habitats from acid peat to saltmarsh and is the finest site in the country to see this transition. The plants found include two species of cranberry. The best place to see the reserve is from the top of nearby Dunadd hill fort.

Taynish

NR 7384; 370ha; NCC reserve
Woodland, heath, bog and foreshore
Visitors welcome but are asked not to use vehicles on Reserve track
Leaflet from NCC, Balloch
April–July

The oakwoods clothing the schist ridges of this reserve represent one of the largest remnants of this type of woodland surviving in Scotland. Ash, hazel, rowan, honeysuckle and holly occur among the even-aged oaks, and there is a luxuriant growth of mosses on the boulders littering the woodland floor. Between the ridges open areas of boggy ground, heath and wet meadow fringed with mixed woodland increase the habitat diversity. Heath spotted-orchid and northern marsh-orchid grow in these areas, which attract a wide variety of butterflies – Scotch argus are abundant in late summer.

Taynish is rich in lichens as well as mosses; many of the tree trunks are completely swathed in luxuriant growths – which often represent several species. Lungwort is common and other species confined to the Atlantic coast also occur.

There is unusually little tidal variation in the sheltered waters around the Taynish peninsula, and the warm shallows hold a variety of marine species normally found over a much wider range of depth. Herons stalk over the tangles of golden-tawny seaweeds, and sea-urchins, starfish and various species of sponge flourish in the unpolluted water. Common seal and otter frequent the nearby islets, and wigeon visit Linne Mhuirich in winter to feed on the eelgrass.

Strathclyde South

Southern Strathclyde extends from the inland hills and valleys of Lanark north to the shores of the Clyde Estuary and west to the coast of the Firth of Clyde. In the lowlands of Lanark, Renfrew and Ayrshire, once deciduous woodland, the important dairy industry developed to meet the expanding demands of nineteenth-century Glasgow. Farming today is less intensive than in eastern Scotland, and the abundant wildlife reflects the sheltered habitats created by the hedgerows, copses and rough pastures of the less fertile areas.

The uplands are largely rolling hills and moorlands, mountains being found only in the south. Rough grass and bracken clothe the well-drained steeper slopes, while heaths dominate the rocky outcrops and great peat bogs cover the flat, poorly drained areas. This is sheep country, though conifer plantations are becoming more evident. Rural depopulation has made its mark, and isolated ruined cottages bear witness to a more dynamic past.

The Clyde coast provides habitats ranging from rocky shore, raised beaches and cliffs to sand dunes. Despite increased pressures from man these habitats remain generally unspoilt, and even the shore of the inner Clyde Estuary between Port Glasgow and Erskine is still nationally important for waders.

The climate is temperate throughout the year. Prevailing south to south westerly winds maintain a warm, damp airstream and relatively high rainfall in the uplands; areas around Ayr and Troon, however, have the lowest rainfall (around 890mm per annum) on the west coast of Scotland. The Gulf Stream is responsible for the relatively mild winters; snow rarely lies long, particularly along the coast.

Southern Strathclyde's geology is reflected in its scenery and vegetation. The uplands of the south and Galloway comprise hard, relatively acidic rocks of the Ordovician and Silurian periods, exemplified by the granites of the Loch Doon area. To the north of Loch Doon, across the Southern Upland Fault, the old red sandstone of Ayrshire and Lanark has been more readily eroded to produce a rolling landscape, while the

sandstones, shales and limestones of the central basin of Ayrshire form low-lying, gently undulating ground.

During the later ice ages the Merrick region in Galloway was an area from which glaciers moved north and west, creating U-shaped valleys such as the upper Nith Valley and features such as drumlins and moraines. Glasgow's steep streets are the result of its being built on drumlins while the rushy upland grassland to the south may reflect moraine and boulder clay deposition resulting in poorly drained soils. Post-glacial raised beaches formed by wave action during glaciation are prominent along the Clyde coast, particularly at BALLANTRAE, Dunure, Portencross and the CLYDE ISLANDS.

Deciduous woodland is now largely confined to copses and river banks. The trees are generally beech, sycamore, wych elm, ash or oak; shrubs and herbs are more diverse under the last two, since they come into leaf last and have an open leaf canopy. In spring the drier woodlands are coloured by wood anemone, wood-sorrel, lesser celandine and bluebell, followed by avens, herb-Robert and other shade-loving species. Wetter soils are dominated by alder and willow, with which are associated marsh-marigold, golden-saxifrage, ramsons, meadowsweet and marsh valerian. The woodlands shelter roe deer, foxes, badgers, shrews, field mice and voles, and occasionally heronries.

Notable deciduous woodlands include the FALLS OF CLYDE reserve near Lanark, and further to the west ENTERKINE WOOD; both are rich in woodland birds and have a spring carpet of bluebells. The country parks of CULZEAN and BRODICK also include woodlands: at Brodick, the grounds contain mature oak and beech, which provide a shady habitat for mosses, liverworts, lichens and ferns, while Culzean has extensive policy woodlands and formal ponds. The cliffs at Culzean support heathland and maritime species, and the pebble or sandy beaches are rich in marine life and shore birds.

The Culzean seashore is typical of the Clyde coast: sand dunes or shingle beaches are often flanked by rocky headlands and cliffs. The dunes contain sea lyme-grass and marram, red fescue, sand sedge, silverweed and bird's-foot-trefoil. The shingle beaches are often colonised by salt-loving plants such as sea sandwort, grass-leaved orache or silverweed, among which may be found the nests of oystercatcher, ringed plover or terns. At Ballantrae, about 24km south of Culzean, a reserve has been established on a shingle spit at the mouth of the River Stinchar. Little, common and arctic tern nest on the shingle, while shelduck, red-breasted merganser, common sandpiper and gulls frequent the lagoons. Plant life includes the salt-loving sea campion, sea sandwort and oysterplant.

Rocky shores form a micro-habitat for seaweeds, shellfish, crabs, sea anemones and fish. The shoreline south of Girvan is particularly unspoilt, while Turnberry, Dunure and Portencross have a raised beach and cliffs with interesting flora and fauna. In mid-May the cliffs of south Ayrshire are tinged by brilliant blue spring squill, occasional patches of rock-rose, bitter vetch and spotted-orchids which complement the bird's-foot-trefoil, sea campion and sea pink.

Inland again is a birdwatchers' reserve at LOCH-WINNOCH. Beds of reed canary-grass and sedges, with scattered willow scrub, provide good cover for breeding black-headed gull, great crested grebe, mallard, tufted duck, coot, moorhen and the occasional teal and shoveler. Marsh plants include common spotted-orchid and lesser butter-fly-orchid, marsh valerian, meadowsweet and purple-loosestrife. Among winter wildfowl are wigeon, pochard, goldeneye, greylag goose and whooper swan. A similar habitat is found at LOCH LIBO where the plant life includes sedges, pondweeds, and white and yellow water-lilies. POSSIL MARSH, similar in character to these two wetland reserves, is remarkable since it lies within the boundary of the city of Glasgow.

Base-rich meadowland is scarce in the west of Scotland, and two meadow reserves have recently been established south of Ayr – AUCHALTON MEADOW and FEOCH MEADOWS. Both support greater and lesser butterfly-orchid, fragrant and frog orchid and field gentian; a wide variety of butterflies has been recorded at Feoch Meadows, including large skipper.

In the moors and hills of the Clyde coast the most interesting areas are often the gullies and glens, colonised by ferns and other shade-loving species. The fringes of Shielhill Glen above Inverkip are typical moorland, while the birch, oak and alder within shelter brown and mountain hare, fox, stoat, weasel and roe deer, as well as a variety of small mammals. Wood pigeon, willow warbler, tawny owl, chiffchaff, wood warbler, spotted flycatcher, carrion crow and buzzard are among the breeding birds.

Southern Strathclyde contains a wealth of wild-life interest, reflecting the climate, geology and traditional farming practice. While the development of Glasgow and the associated urban and industrial complexes have had a marked effect locally, the greater part of the area is relatively unspoilt and has suffered less from man's inter-ference than has much of lowland Britain.

RALPH KIRKWOOD

Auchalton Meadow

Permit only; 7ha; SWT reserve
Lime-rich grassland
Mid-June–July

At one time three lime kilns were in operation on this site, which supports a wide variety of herbs and grasses. Adder's-tongue, common twayblade, greater and lesser butterfly-orchid, frog orchid, field gentian and quaking-grass are among the more interesting of the 98 plant species present.

Ayr Gorge Woodland

NS 4524; 19ha; SWT reserve
River valley woodland
Path along west bank of river
Spring, summer

The sessile oak woodland lies on steep slopes where the river has cut through the soft beds of Permian sandstone, and there is also birch, rowan, holly and hazel. Woodland plants include hairy wood-rush, Yorkshire fog, wood-sorrel and blue-bell; in acid areas heather, bilberry and the local cow-wheat grow in carpets of moss. Many interesting insects and spiders have been found on the warm, south-facing slopes, and there is a good variety of mammal and bird species.

Ballantrae

NX 0882; 22ha; SWT reserve
Shingle spit and lagoons
Access restricted mid-May–mid-August, when terns are breeding
Leaflet from warden on site May–August
April–August

Sea campion, mats of fleshy sea sandwort and blue-grey oysterplant crown this shingle spit, composed largely of grey stones worn flat by the waves. The ridge of the spit lies parallel to the tideline; behind it the waters of the River Stinchar mingle at high tide with the sea in a series of brackish lagoons.

A colony of little tern, small in number but still the largest in the Clyde Estuary, breeds on the spit, where common and arctic tern, ringed plover and oystercatcher also nest. Shelduck, red-breasted merganser and common sandpiper frequent the lagoons, and common gull roost at the river mouth.

Around the landward fringe of the reserve bird's-foot-trefoil, meadow crane's-bill and natu-ralised *Rosa rugosa* provide patches of bright colour to contrast with the background greys and greens, and in early summer the area between the river and the lagoons is covered with the frothy white flowers of wild carrot.

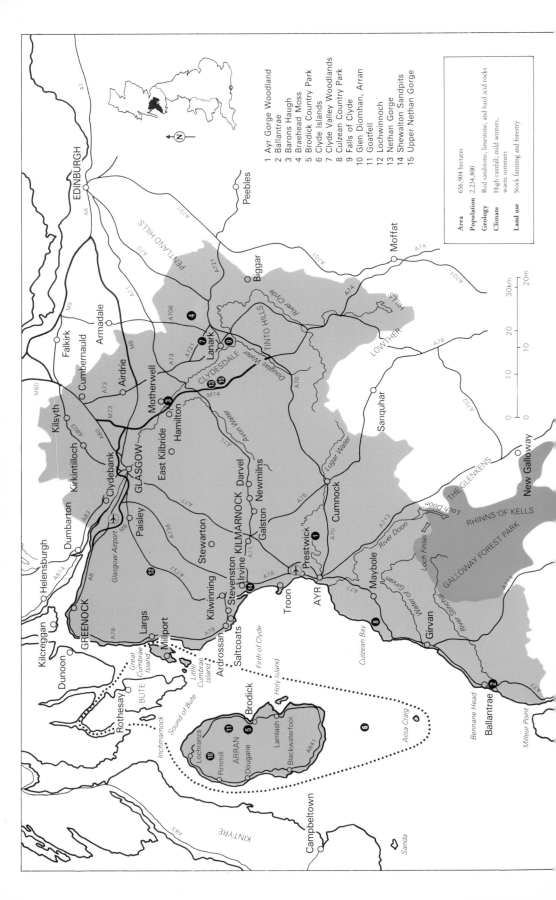

1 Ayr Gorge Woodland
2 Ballantrae
3 Barons Haugh
4 Brodick Country Park
5 Brodick Country Park
6 Clyde Islands
7 Clyde Valley Woodlands
8 Culzean Country Park
9 Falls of Clyde
10 Glen Diomhan, Arran
11 Goatfell
12 Lochwinnoch
13 Nethan Gorge
14 Shewalton Sandpits
15 Upper Nethan Gorge

Area	656,904 hectares
Population	2,234,800
Geology	Red sandstone, limestone, and hard acid rocks
Climate	High rainfall; mild winters, warm summers
Land use	Stock farming and forestry

Barons Haugh

NS 755552; 107ha; RSPB reserve
Woodland, parkland and marsh
All year

This reserve lies on the outskirts of Motherwell and consists of woodland, parkland and marshes running down to the River Clyde. On the marshes and parks along the riverside whooper swans winter, along with a variety of ducks, including teal, pochard and goldeneye. In summer mute swan, little grebe and water rail breed, while kingfishers, grey wagtails and sand martins nest in the river banks. Whinchats and reed buntings are plentiful on the marshland. The woodlands support the common bird species, as well as willow tit at the northern edge of its range. Red squirrels and roe deer are present.

Braehead Moss

NS 9551; 87ha; NCC reserve
Raised and blanket bog
Information from warden, 22 Muirpark Way, Drymen
All year

This reserve represents the best example of its type in southern Strathclyde, having remained largely free from agricultural operations, severe burning or forestry in the recent past. Its major interests are typical peat bog plants and less common species of *Sphagnum*. There are no tracks or paths and most parts are very wet underfoot.

Brodick Country Park

NS 0138; 72ha; NTS–Cunninghame DC
Mature policy woodlands
Nature trail; guided walks; access path to Goatfell; visitor centre; ranger-naturalist
April–August

The wide variety of trees includes some particularly fine mature specimens of oak and beech. Mosses, liverworts, lichens and ferns flourish in the damp shade of the woodland paths. The combination of tall trees and rhododendrons provides a habitat for birds such as chiffchaff, garden warbler and blackcap; nightjar breed in the more open woodland nearby.

Cander Moss

Permit only; 24ha; SWT reserve
Bog, heather moor, mixed woodland and grassland
Summer

This 10,000 year-old raised peat bog is the best example of its kind in the area, and is rich in wildlife. Tormentil, bog asphodel, cross-leaved heath and round-leaved sundew are among the characteristic plants. The bog is fringed with birch and Scots pine; heather and lichen grow on the drier moorland ridges, with the marshy hollows dominated by *Sphagnum*, rushes and marsh bedstraw. Nesting birds include snipe, redshank and curlew, and small heath, peacock and small tortoiseshell butterflies can be seen in summer.

The mild, damp climate encourages lush wildflower growth on the scree slope below Ailsa's cliffs.

Clyde Islands

See map; includes 16 sites
All year

From the rugged grandeur of Arran to the almost featureless plateau of Great Cumbrae, and from the bird-dominated rock of Ailsa Craig to the fertile farmland of Bute, the Clyde Islands offer a remarkable variety of scenery and natural history. Each of these islands, and many of the smaller ones, too, has its own distinctive character and wildlife.

Arran, at 427sq.km by far the largest in the group, exhibits a greater geological complexity than any other British island of comparable size. The discovery, in 1975, of the fossil trail of a giant centipede preserved in the rock of one of the island's quarries added yet another aspect to Arran's geological interest.

Lying astride the Highland Boundary Fault, the island is part highland and part lowland, and is sometimes described as a microcosm of Scotland. GOATFELL and its attendant granite peaks, with their ice-carved corries and jagged ridges reaching to nearly 900m, give the northern half an impressively wild character. Here eagle and raven fly, arctic–alpines flourish. South of 'The String', the road which bisects the island, lies a gently undulating plateau seldom exceeding 400m in height. Much of this area has been afforested in the last 20 to 30 years, providing extensive stretches of new habitat for woodland birds. Crossbill first bred in these plantations in 1980, goldcrest and siskin are well established, and sparrowhawk and buzzard are on the increase. Hen harrier hunt over the adjoining moorlands, and several pairs of peregrine breed on the island. Both red-throated and black-throated diver occur.

Red deer are present in large numbers on the Arran hills, but are absent from all the other Clyde Islands. Badgers also occur on Arran, having been introduced at the end of the last century, but there are neither mountain hares nor foxes on any of the islands. Red squirrels were introduced to Arran in the 1920s and are still present, but grey squirrels have not yet reached the islands.

The cliffs at Drumadoon have held breeding fulmar since 1948 and this species now nests at several places on the west coast. One or two pairs of black guillemot breed among the boulders at Dippen Head, but there are no breeding records of guillemot, razorbill or kittiwake, and the small colonies of common and arctic tern can perhaps most appropriately be described as 'of no fixed abode'. Pladda, the smaller of Arran's two off-lying islands, once held large numbers of breeding terns, including a few pairs of roseate tern. However, its close proximity (only 1.5km offshore), and popularity for picnickers, have resulted in such disturbance that the tern colonies are now much reduced. Large numbers of duck breed on the island, however; eider, shelduck, mallard and red-breasted merganser are all plentiful.

Holy Island, Arran's other offlier, is much larger, steeper and rougher than Pladda, and rises to over 300m. Buzzard and raven nest on the cliffs, while there is a sizeable mixed colony of gulls and a large population of stonechat, whinchat and wheatear. A herd of white wild goats and a few Soay sheep roam the rocky hills, a few grey seal have bred, and the island shares with Arran the distinction of supporting adder, a species absent from all the other islands in the group.

The isolated rocky hump of Ailsa Craig is the Clyde's premier seabird station. With 150m vertical cliffs, crowned with a grassy dome rising to 350m and fringed by a narrow, boulder-strewn foreshore, Ailsa holds a population of around 35,000 pairs of seabirds, nearly half of them gannets. The Ailsa gannetry has existed since at least 1526, and was for long a locally important source of human food. Other seabirds breeding on Ailsa Craig include several thousand kittiwake, guillemot, razorbill and gulls, with smaller numbers of fulmar, puffin and black guillemot.

Bute has hummocky acid moorland, rising no higher than 278m and covered with bracken, heather and grass. Sycamore dominates much of the woodland on the steep inland cliffs, but there is ash and elder too. These woods, and the tangled scrub on the uncultivated sections of Bute's raised beaches, hold good populations of tits and other small birds as well as buzzard and sparrowhawk.

The island is well endowed with freshwater lochs, several of them large, secluded and with adjacent marshy ground which provides nesting cover for waterbirds. Tufted duck breed regularly in some numbers and shoveler do so occasionally. The larger lochs are important roosts for the substantial winter population of greylag geese, which reaches a maximum of around 4000. On Greenan Loch there is an attractive summer show of water lilies.

Much of Bute's shoreline is rocky, and carved by the sea into a series of ridges and contorted pinnacles. Eider, red-breasted merganser, oystercatcher and ringed plover are frequent around the coast but the biggest gatherings of both duck and waders occur in the beautiful sandy bays of Kilchattan, Scalpsie, St Ninian's and Ettrick. Many curlew, oystercatcher, wigeon and mallard use the mudflats here, and a wide variety of waders is recorded in migration periods. There are also significant numbers of turnstone on the nearby rocky shores in winter.

The small island of Inchmarnock is farmed, but subject to much less disturbance than the popular holiday resort of Bute. Several species of bird breed there in impressively large numbers, notably eider and gulls. Fulmar and black guillemot also nest on Inchmarnock, as do peregrine, buzzard and raven. Access to the island is from Straad on Bute, by private arrangement.

Perhaps not surprisingly, in view of its extensive farmland, Bute has a large population of moles, absent from both Arran and Great Cumbrae. Hedgehogs are also abundant on Bute and were introduced to Inchmarnock in 1972, resulting in a population explosion about five years later. Numbers have since declined, but hedgehogs are still occasionally seen on the shore at dusk, where they have been observed eating winkles. A small herd of multi-coloured wild goats lives at the northern end of Bute and there are substantial numbers of roe deer in the woodlands. The displays and trail guide available at the Buteshire Natural History Society's Museum in Rothesay provide a useful introduction to the island's natural history.

The last of the larger Clyde Islands, Great Cumbrae, is capped with heather moor and girdled by an inland cliff of red sandstone conglomerate. Below the cliff the flat rim of the island is marshy, with spears of yellow iris alternating with newly unfurled bracken in early summer. A jungle of gorse, bramble, rowan, hawthorn and elder straggles up the cliff face, often neatly shaped by the wind, and clumps of sycamore give additional shelter. This scrubland is busy with stonechat and whitethroat, common gull nest in the bog, and all around curlew and redshank engage in their display flights.

In June the road verges are colourful with yellow rattle, marsh lousewort, heath spotted-orchid and a few northern marsh-orchids. The rocky shoreline is equally colourful, with patches of grey-green lichen adorning the red rocks, and clumps of pink thrift, yellow bird's-foot-trefoil and pinky-white English stonecrop.

It is, however, for marine life that Great Cumbrae is best known. The Marine Biological Station at Keppel, near Millport, runs a museum and aquarium which is open to the public; there the visitor is given some idea of the complexity of marine communities and also of the varied, and surprisingly exotic, forms of life found in the waters around the Clyde Islands.

Clyde Valley Woodlands

NS 9045; 51ha; NCC reserve
Deciduous woodland
Information from warden, 21 Ardmore Gardens, Drymen
April–July

Cleghorn Glen, part of the Clyde Valley Woodlands, is a nationally important site whose main conservation feature is its diverse and varied woodland cover. The woods, largely of elm, ash, oak and alder, support a range of interesting plants. Uncommon species such as rough horsetail, wood fescue, herb-Paris and stone bramble add to the reserve's importance.

Culzean Country Park

NS 2310; 229ha; NTS
Woodland, ponds and coastline
Visitor centre open April–October; exhibition and audio-visual programme; guided walks programme covering specialist and children's interests; publications; ranger-naturalist
May–September

The extensive policy woodlands and formal ponds within this country park support a very varied population of plants and animals, offering excellent opportunities to study many aspects of natural history. It is along the 5.5km of coastline, however, that the richest natural communities are found.

Low cliffs back the beach. For 2km southwards from the castle they are composed of lava, and rise from a rock platform pitted with a multitude of pools. To the north, the cliffs are of old red sandstone, heavily vegetated, and support relics of the pre-improvement heathland flora, such as heather and tormentil, as well as the typical maritime species sea campion and thrift. Caves in the lava cliff, now well above the high-tideline, house hibernating herald moths in winter.

The pebble beach is rich in agates and the rock pools are well populated with seaweeds, as well as with animals such as beadlet sea-anemone, sea-slug, brittle star, sea-urchin, butterfish and chiton. At Port Carrick the shore is sandy, and several pairs of shelduck take up territory in spring before nesting in rabbit burrows on the cliffs. Most of the more usual shorebirds can be seen in summer; winter visitors include occasional less common species such as great northern diver and long-tailed duck.

Dalmellington Moss

Permit only; 28ha; SWT reserve
Peat bog, fen and fen woodland
June–September: mosses; October–March: roosting birds, plants

Heather, *Sphagnum* mosses and cottongrass, together with great sundew and bog-rosemary, are of special interest on this reserve. The fen-carr of birch and willow is undisturbed and in many places impenetrable, being a tangle of fallen and half-fallen trees and dissected by numerous water-filled channels and pools. The Moss is also home for many unusual insects and is a safe refuge in winter for roosting birds of prey.

Enterkine Wood

Permit only; 5ha; SWT reserve
Mixed woodland
Nature trail (1km): leaflet from SWT
April–October

This attractive and varied mature woodland contains 16 broad-leaved tree species, including lime, and three species of conifer. Many of the trees were probably planted, but natural regeneration of several species is now occurring. Bramble, hazel, hawthorn, honeysuckle and sapling trees give good nesting cover for a large population of woodland birds. Thirty-four species breed, among them blackcap, chiffchaff, goldfinch and woodcock. Bluebells carpet parts of the wood in spring; wood anemone, enchanter's-nightshade, dog's mercury, comfrey, woodruff and great wood-rush all cover considerable areas; and in one place the feathery wood horsetail is common.

A stream runs through the wood, forming a pond where it is checked in its progress by a dam. Hart's-tongue ferns adorn a second dam, now in disrepair, and marsh-marigold, yellow iris and golden-saxifrage flourish nearby.

Above the south banks of the stream, where the ground slopes steeply, is a badger sett overlooked by two tree hides.

Secluded pools, like this at Aird Meadows, attract the more secretive ducks such as teal and shoveler.

Falls of Clyde

NS 8841; 67ha; SWT reserve
River gorge and surrounding woodland
Access restricted in Corehouse section of reserve
Visitor centre in New Lanark, tel. Lanark 65262;
ranger service; reserve leaflet
April–August

The spectacularly stepped gorge of the River Clyde separates the two distinct sections of this reserve: Bonnington on the north east bank and Corehouse to the south west. Above the uppermost fall, Bonnington Linn, the river flows deep and still, edged by overhanging banks and small sandy beaches which attract mink and otter. Much of the flow is diverted for hydroelectric purposes at Bonnington and returned to the river below Cora Linn. This middle fall drops 30m in two steps and when the Clyde is in spate, or the water is deliberately released, spray drenches the basin below and rises mist-like above the level of the gorge.

Dundaff Linn, the lowest of the three falls, lies just above New Lanark, once famous for its cotton mills powered by the Clyde, and now being refurbished. Dipper haunt the old mill stream as well as the river; grey wagtail flick their immaculate yellow tails as they flutter from rock to rock; and occasionally a kingfisher streaks over the dark water. The Clyde, here clean and healthy, is well stocked with minnow, trout, grayling and pike, while lamprey have been seen in the mill stream.

Inaccessible ledges on the precipitous gorge sides afford secure nesting sites for kestrel and safe lodging for such interesting plants as purple saxifrage, butterwort and meadow saxifrage. Ferns and mosses abound in the wetter sections.

Although much of the Bonnington reserve is under conifer plantation there are many deciduous species, and the ground vegetation reflects the fact that this is an area of long-established woodland. Near New Lanark the spring flowers are typical of oakwood – lesser celandine, dog's mercury, bluebell and red campion, with wood avens and marsh marigold in the damper areas. Further upriver, where the soil is more acid, bilberry, great wood-rush, heather and wood anemone carpet the woodland fringe. Northern marsh-orchid, with its wine-purple flowers, wood vetch and the slender and graceful grass wood millet are among the less common plants on the Bonnington bank.

The Corehouse reserve, originally formal policy woodlands, contains introduced species such as *Sequoia* and rhododendron, as well as native species including oak, alder and yew. Several hundred flowering plants have been recorded here and the variety of the vegetation is increased by marshland and an artificial lake.

Garden warbler, chiffchaff and spotted flycatcher are among summer visitors to the woodlands, both green and great spotted woodpecker occur and five species of tit, including long-tailed and the very local willow tit, are present. The woods are rich in fungi and insects – the latter also well represented in the gorge. Badger, roe deer, red squirrel, pipistrelle and Natterer's bat are among the mammals recorded.

Feoch Meadows

Permit only; 16ha; SWT reserve
Meadow on lime-rich rock
May–August

An unusually rich vegetation – some 140 species of herbs and grasses have been noted – reflects the fact that this site is ancient meadowland. Orchids include fragrant, frog and small-white, and greater and lesser butterfly-orchid. The area attracts a variety of butterflies: 14 species have been recorded, among them the very local large skipper.

Glen Diomhan, Arran

NR 9246; 10ha; NCC reserve
Woodland
No access to fenced part of reserve
Information from NCC, Cairnbaan,
by Lochgilphead, Argyll
May–September

This remote woodland remnant, situated in a steep-sided gorge at over 300m, contains two rare native species of whitebeam, *Sorbus arranensis* and *Sorbus pseudofennica*; both are restricted to north Arran. The scrub includes rowan, birch, juniper, willow, holly and aspen, together with a few specimens of burnet rose.

Goatfell, Arran

NR 9941; 2673ha; NTS
Mountainous country, woodland on lower slopes
Guided walks programme; access path from
Brodick Country Park; ranger-naturalist
All year

Sheer slabs, huge hunks of rock and jagged, knife-edge ridges are features of these peaks, many crowned with blocks of granite intricately fissured in all directions.

Raven haunt the high corries, and golden eagle are quite often seen over the glens. On the moorland slopes of Beinn a Chliabhain a few golden plover breed, and redpoll nest in the woodlands of lower Glen Rosa. Moorland plants such as heath milkwort and heath spotted-orchid grow on the lower ground and in the glens, where dwarf juniper also occurs. High on the peaks starry saxifrage, mountain sorrel, goldenrod and alpine buckler-fern are among the plants of the granite pavement.

Merkland Wood (NS 023385), with its mature birch, pine, beech and oak, attracts many different woodland birds. Breeding warblers include blackcap, chiffchaff, garden warbler, and wood warbler, and there have been sightings of pied flycatcher.

Loch Libo

Permit only; 18ha; SWT reserve
Loch, wetland and woodland
May–July: flowers; October–March: wildfowl

White and yellow water-lilies grow in the mineral-rich water of the loch; mare's-tail and several species of pondweed also occur. The surrounding marshland vegetation includes nine species of sedge – among them the very local lesser pond-sedge – bogbean, marsh cinquefoil and cowbane. Moorhen, coot, mallard and mute swan breed on the reserve, the woodland attracts a variety of small birds, and wintering wildfowl include species such as tufted duck, pochard, wigeon, goldeneye and whooper swan.

Lochwinnoch

NS 3558; 230ha; RSPB reserve
Open water, marsh and woodland
Open all year; school parties welcome: contact warden,
Largs Road, Lochwinnoch; access limited to marked
paths
Nature centre with displays etc.; two hides; leaflet
from centre or RSPB, Edinburgh
April–June: breeding birds; October–March: wildfowl

The panoramic windows of a tower at the Nature Centre offer commanding views of this reserve and the surrounding countryside. To the north lies Aird Meadow, a stretch of shallow open water surrounded by varied marshland. Barr Loch, larger, deeper and more open, lies to the south west, on the far side of the A760, where a hide is available.

Dense beds of reed canary-grass and sedges, with scattered willow scrub, give good cover around Aird Meadow, and additional nesting sites have been provided in the form of small, floating raft-islands. Located within easy viewing distance of the hides, these help visitors to observe breeding species such as black-headed gull and great crested grebe. With a population of around 11 pairs, the chances of seeing the grebes performing their elaborate courtship display are unusually good for a Scottish site. Mallard, tufted duck, coot and moorhen can often be watched at close range as they lead their broods through the patches of bogbean in front of the hides. A few teal and shoveler also breed, but they tend to be more secretive and spend much of their time in thick cover.

The strip of mixed woodland along the eastern side of Aird Meadow contains oak, birch, beech and lime with an understorey of rhododendron, hawthorn and dog rose. Many common woodland birds can be seen here, and typical plants such as wood-sorrel, red campion and ramsons are present. Common spotted-orchid and lesser butterfly-orchid occur, and meadowsweet, valerian and purple-loosestrife flourish along the edge of the marsh. Where the water level is higher yellow iris, marsh-marigold and marsh cinquefoil add colour among the sedges and rushes.

In winter Aird Meadow and Barr Loch attract substantial numbers of wildfowl. Wigeon, pochard and goldeneye are usually present as well as mallard, teal and tufted duck, and Barr Loch is used as a roost by greylag geese and whooper swans. As long as the marshes remain unfrozen

The familiar kestrel, equally at home in town or country, often hunts along roadside verges.

snipe and heron feed in the shallows; cormorants are also among the regular visitors. Over 154 bird species have been recorded on the reserve in recent years, and 65 species are known to have nested.

Nethan Gorge

NS 8246; 7ha; SWT reserve
Gorge woodland
Path through reserve to Tillietudlem Castle
Spring, summer

The Clyde Valley woodlands are of classic conservation interest as remnants of the mixed deciduous forest that once clothed much of the Scottish Highlands. High above the river, a fringe of oak and birch trees marks the more acid soils along the top of the wood, but the major part of the reserve is on unstable slopes of lime-rich carboniferous rocks where the trees are predominantly ash and elm and the spring flowers are a lush carpet of wood anemone and bluebell, ramsons and dog's mercury.

Possil Marsh

NS 585700; 28ha; SWT reserve
Open water, marsh and scrub
All year

On the northern edge of Glasgow, this exciting, well-known loch with its surrounding marshland and scrub of willow and birch has long been recognised for its variety of plants and animals. The marshland has bulrush beds, marsh cinquefoil meadows and bottle sedge swamp in which greater spearwort, mare's tail and tufted loosestrife all occur. Sedge warbler, reed bunting, and whitethroat breed and the reserve attracts many wintering and migrant birds. Eight species of Tardigrade have been recorded here.

Shewalton Sandpits

NS 326370; 17ha; SWT reserve
Scrub, grassland and lagoon
June–August: plants and insects; October–March: wildfowl

The sandy grassland around this worked-out sand and gravel pit forms a suntrap for numerous species of insects, many of which are at the northern extremity of their range. Grasshoppers, grayling butterflies, darter dragonflies, six-spot burnet, cinnebar moths and green tiger beetles are all found on the reserve. The pools and scrapes are important for wildfowl and waders, and attract migrants such as bar-tailed godwits, ruff and greenshank in the autumn.

Upper Nethan Gorge

NS 801442; 35ha; SWT reserve
Woodland and meadows
Spring, summer, autumn

The sides of the gorge are covered in mixed deciduous woodland dominated by oak, ash and elm, with a scrub layer of hazel, birch and rowan. Alder is more common towards the bottom of the valley alongside the river Nethan. Great wood-rush is plentiful in the reserve, while two of the less common species are great horsetail and broad-leaved helleborine.

Tayside

Like much of Scotland, Tayside is a region of contrasts, with the imposing Grampians to the north and the green lowland straths and coastal strip to the south and east. This diversity of scenery and habitat is reflected in the variety of wildlife in the region, which includes species characteristic of the mountains, glens and coast. The hills are the home of rare alpine plants and the lowlands are memorable for the vast numbers of grey geese and wildfowl which winter on the many lochs. The hand of man has largely fashioned the lowlands of Tayside, but his impact has been much less in the uplands. A small area around Dundee is industrial, but agriculture predominates in the lowland south, and sporting interests such as deer stalking, game shooting and salmon fishing are catered for farther north.

The scenery and habitats of Tayside relate to its geological skeleton which is dominated by the Highland Boundary Fault, running south west to north east. To its north lie the uplands, mainly metamorphic in origin and composed largely of schists which are locally lime-rich. A band of limestone crosses this area. To the south of the faultline are Devonian sandstones and conglomerates forming the straths, and upwellings of volcanic lavas which have produced the Sidlaw and Ochil hill ranges. Superimposed on the geological skeleton is the reshaping produced by the last glaciation. After the ice sheets melted colonisation by tundra vegetation took place, followed by vast forests of oak, elm and hazel in the lowlands, pine and birch in the highlands. Above these forests grew montane scrub of dwarf birch, dwarf willow and juniper.

Man's impact began with clearance of this forest and scrub, and has continued ever since; now the remaining areas of wildlife habitat are very fragmented, and in the lowlands virtually islands in a sea of intensively farmed land. The other main influence on Tayside is its climate, which has an exceptional range, from the wet, relatively mild, semi-oceanic west to the drier, more continental east. The weather on the mountains can be truly arctic while the sheltered straths are basking in balmy sunshine.

Visitors to the highland area of Tayside find high mountains alternating with sheltered glens.

The mountains in the west, the part known as Breadalbane, consists of very lime-rich rock on which grow many rare alpine plants. Queen of these mountains is BEN LAWERS, renowned for its flora, and in the east CAENLOCHAN is of equal interest, although supporting different species partly because of its more continental climate. Other hills have limestone outcrops and Schiehallion even boasts limestone pavements, the quarrying of the best of which has now been made illegal throughout Great Britain. In the north the hills are less lime-rich and so more heathery; here breed peregrine falcon, golden eagle, and the rare but trusting dotterel. Red deer can be seen on most of these hills and are important to the economy of local estates, such as ATHOLL. However this traditional use of the hills is increasingly being replaced by afforestation, skiing, and even mining, with consequent threat to wildlife. In the far west lies the desolate, boggy RANNOCH MOOR, from which the last ice sheet is thought to have radiated.

The highland glens are largely pasture, enhanced by many large lochs – most are harnessed for hydroelectric power, and many enlarged or even created specially for this purpose. In these glens most of the remnants of primeval forest and scrub are to be found, their survival reflecting the attitude of large estate owners who have retained them for their amenity and sporting value. There are Caledonian pinewoods at the BLACK WOOD OF RANNOCH, mixed gorge woodlands at the PASS OF KILLIECRANKIE, LINN OF TUMMEL and KELTNEYBURN, oakwoods such as at Queen's View and juniper scrub at BALNAGUARD GLEN. These woods, where not in nature reserves, are gradually being either felled or converted to faster-growing conifers as in parts of the HERMITAGE. The pastureland in between has largely been fertilised or reseeded, but here and there untouched areas retain a rich flora with many orchids, as at Keltneyburn, or an old hayfield mixture, as at BRERACHAN MEADOWS.

In the lowland area are many small lochs formed in hollows after the ice sheets retreated. These lochs are spectacular for the thousands of grey geese which roost there on winter evenings after feeding on nearby farmland during the day. Many species of duck also winter on these lochs, the

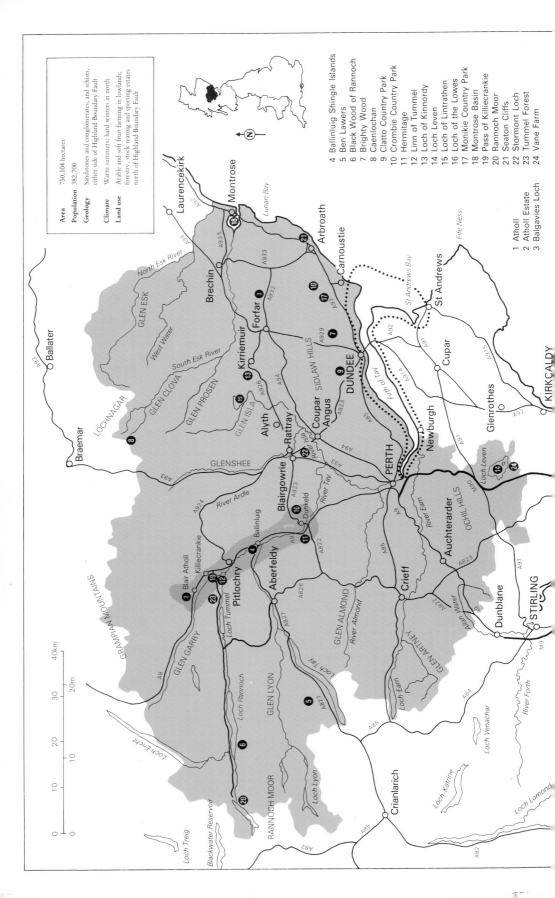

Area 750,104 hectares

Population 382,700

Geology Sandstones and conglomerates, and schists, either side of Highland Boundary Fault

Climate Warm summers; hard winters in north

Land use Arable and soft fruit farming in lowlands; forestry, stock rearing and sporting estates north of Highland Boundary Fault

4 Ballinluig Shingle Islands
5 Ben Lawers
6 Black Wood of Rannoch
7 Brighty Wood
8 Caenlochan
9 Clatto Country Park
10 Crombie Country Park
11 Hermitage
12 Linn of Tummel
13 Loch of Kinnordy
14 Loch Leven
15 Loch of Lintrathen
16 Loch of the Lowes
17 Monikie Country Park
18 Montrose Basin
19 Pass of Killiecrankie
20 Rannoch Moor
21 Seaton Cliffs
22 Stormont Loch
23 Tummel Forest
24 Vane Farm

1 Atholl
2 Atholl Estate
3 Balgavies Loch

largest of which, LOCH LEVEN, is of international importance and has the VANE FARM Nature Centre alongside. Other places worth a winter visit are BALGAVIES LOCH, LOCH OF KINNORDY ,LOCH OF LINTRATHEN, LOCH CRAIGLUSH and the LOCH OF THE LOWES. Many are important for breeding ducks and grebes, but their best-known breeding bird is osprey which has nested at the Loch of the Lowes since the early 1970s. Their plant life is also of interest: in the case of a few lochs high up the stream system it is still relatively unaffected by pollution. Increasingly the sands and gravels surrounding the lochs are being exploited, but afterwards flooded pits can become wildlife habitats in their own right.

The lowlands are bounded to south and east by the sea. Estuaries, sea cliffs and extensive sand dunes are all represented, together with the largest reedbeds in Britain. MONTROSE BASIN is an almost unique landlocked tidal basin whose mudflats are home to large flocks of waders at low tide, and also to ducks and geese. Almost as fine is the TAY ESTUARY (Fife), whose vast reedbeds are now being harvested for thatch. Also worth seeing, especially in summer, are the red sandstone cliffs north of Arbroath, where seabirds nest and many northern and southern plants meet in a blaze of colour. Part of these cliffs is included in the reserve at SEATON CLIFFS. North Sea oil and gas put much of this coastline, particularly the dunes and estuaries, under threat from industrial development and pollution. Recreation too has a considerable impact: many dune systems have been flattened for golf courses and caravan sites.

ROSALIND A.H. SMITH

Atholl

See map; includes 12 sites
All year

This stretch of country provides a wealth of natural history interest. Varied rock types, glacial deposits and river conditions have resulted in a diversity of plant communities. Woodlands of contrasting types clothe the lower hill slopes and fringe the lochs and rivers, and physical difficulties limit cultivation.

Although it looks like a single entity the valley has, in fact, three rivers running through it. The two northernmost, the Garry and the Tummel, have been greatly affected by hydroelectric developments. Beyond Blair Atholl the Garry is reduced to a trickle of water in summer, and can no longer support brown trout. By the time it reaches Killiecrankie tributaries have added greatly to the river's volume, but the flow through the pass, although impressive in spate, is still small in comparison with its former scale. Similarly, the construction of the Clunie Dam has reduced the flow in the Tummel. However, the Faskally Dam at Pitlochry, fed by both the Tummel and the Garry, created a new, large and very beautiful loch. Provision of a fish ladder ensured that the dam did not prevent the movement of salmon upstream to their spawning grounds, while the loch itself attracts a variety of wildfowl.

Below Pitlochry the Tummel spreads itself over a shingly bed and meanders from one side of the valley floor to the other. The same pattern is maintained after it has joined the Tay at Ballinluig, with a variety of oxbow lakes, backwaters and marshy hollows marking the river's earlier routes. Although the River Tay is free of dams and generating stations it has been affected by the reduced flow in its tributaries and by the periodic artificial spates when surplus water is released by the power stations, giving sudden fluctuations in level, even in summer.

A notable feature of the Pitlochry to Dunkeld stretch is the shingle islands. Continuously influenced by erosion and deposition, these islands represent habitats in a constant state of flux. They vary greatly in size and degree of permanency, and carry widely differing plant communities. Many have well-established cover of willow and alder scrub; on some, Scots pine is regenerating naturally, with seedlings and young trees of various ages; yet others support colourful stands of blue nootka lupin, yellow broom, red campion, comfrey, stone bramble and melancholy thistle.

Road realignment has threatened some of the surviving remnants of meadowland along the valley. Most of the riverside meadows have long been under cultivation, and it is only on steep banks and in odd pockets that the attractive, varied meadow vegetation remains. Where such pockets survive they are often rich in orchids, and sometimes support such locally uncommon species as maiden pink, giant bellflower, cowslip, kidney vetch and purple milk-vetch. The meadow flora is especially rich where limestone occurs, as it does near Blair Atholl.

In contrast to the situation in many other parts of Scotland, planted conifers have been a familiar sight in this area for well over 100 years. Some 15 million conifers, mostly larches, were planted around Dunkeld by successive dukes of Atholl between 1738 and 1830; trees were even established on the rocky slopes of Craig a Barns, using a cannon to sow the seed! The dukes also carried out extensive amenity planting of hardwoods at Dunkeld and Blair Atholl. Horse-chestnut, beech, walnut and maple were chosen for their form and colour as much as for their timber value.

The largest oakwood in the area, Craig Wood, on the ridge between Dunkeld and the LOCH OF THE LOWES, was probably also planted and was at one time coppiced. Invading sycamore, rhododendron and beech are now making it less like an oakwood but offer more cover for birds and animals in the shrub layer. Roe and fallow deer regularly visit this wood, the latter – like the larches – introduced to the area many years ago by a duke of Atholl, and wood warbler, jay and great spotted woodpecker breed here.

Some quite large areas of semi-natural birch-wood also still exist, and at BALNAGUARD birch and juniper grow together on the hillside. These woodlands of little or no commercial value are gradually dwindling, their place being taken by conifers. Even the once heather-covered plateaus are beginning to be encroached upon.

The inaccessibility of some of the steeper slopes, together with a series of woodland reserves, should help to ensure that some sizeable areas of semi-natural tree cover survive, however. Such areas are important not only for breeding and wintering birds, but also for migrants. In spring many small, insectivorous migrants, such as warblers and flycatchers, work their way northwards through these sheltered valley woodlands well in the vanguard of the main arrival. The almost continuous tree cover has also allowed green woodpecker, a resident woodland species currently expanding its range, to colonise as far as Blair Atholl without encountering treeless areas.

It is not only woodland species that use this valley as a migration route. Swallow, martin and wagtail follow the river itself, and wheatear and whinchat move along the hillsides above. Geese, both greylag and pink-footed, regularly use this route through the high hills in autumn and in spring. And osprey – including, perhaps, some of those reared at the Loch of the Lowes – follow the rivers, fishing as they go northwards to Speyside.

Atholl Estate

NN 8666; 54,000ha; Atholl Estates
Woodland and mountainous countryside
Access restricted to waymarked routes unless accompanied by countryside ranger
Nature trails leaflet from Blair Castle or caravan site
May–June

This very large estate includes policy woodlands, extensive conifer plantations and a vast area of open hill ground. Particularly notable is the arboretum at Blair Castle, known as Diana's Grove, which contains an exceptional collection of large conifers. Red deer are plentiful on the hills and the estate as a whole supports a varied collection of plants and animals. Nature trails follow the banks of the River Tilt; the middle section of Glen Tilt is a classic geological site.

Balgavies Loch

NO 534508; 46ha; SWT reserve
Loch, fen, carr and woodland
Hide open to public on first Sunday of month, 1–4p.m. groups welcome: apply SWT; access to areas other than hide restricted: apply SWT
April–July: flowers and breeding birds;
October–March: wildfowl

Woodland and marsh fringe this sheltered loch, which is important for plants and winter wildfowl. Mixed woodland, willow carr and reedbeds add to the habitat diversity, and a stretch of abandoned railway track demonstrates the rapidity with which the succession towards woodland proceeds. The hide (for which members may obtain a key) overlooks open water, an island and part of the marsh and woodland near the shoreline.

Yellow water-lily and amphibious bistort cover substantial areas of the water surface, bogbean and bulrush also occur, and the fringing vegetation includes yellow iris and cowbane. Osier and crack willow are among the several willows represented. Tufted loosestrife and coralroot orchid grow in the sedge-dominated fen and fen carr.

Greylag geese coming in at dusk to roost on the loch provide one of the reserve's most spectacular sights and sounds. Other wintering wildfowl include wigeon, shoveler, pochard, goldeneye and goosander. Heron and cormorant often roost in the larger trees near the water, and water rail, woodcock and snipe are regular in winter. Many of the duck species breed in small numbers and great crested grebe are usually present in summer. Kingfisher, whooper swan and ruddy duck visit, the latter probably arriving from LOCH OF KINNORDY.

Otter have been seen on the reserve, and there is a resident population of roe deer. The loch's very rich population of aquatic invertebrate animals has been the subject of intensive study; at least 10 species of pond snail are known to occur.

Ballinluig Shingle Islands

NN 9753; 29ha; SWT reserve
River islands
Path along river bank
June–August

These shingle islands are found along the western bank of the River Tummel. They support a great array of different habitats, from bare open shingle through 'unimproved' herb-rich grassland to mixed woodland with alder, birch, Scots pine and some juniper. Over 350 species of plants have been recorded – goldilocks buttercup in the woods, thyme, meadow rue, globeflower, meadow saxifrage, cowslip and yellow rattle in the grassland, with sea campion and mountain sorrel also present. Common tern, ringed plover, common sandpiper, common gull, redshank, oystercatcher and lapwing are found on the reserve. Scotch argus and common blue butterflies fly in the meadows and there are a number of interesting species of cranefly.

Balnaguard Glen

Permit only; 55ha; SWT reserve
Birch–juniper woodland and wooded gorge
Information sheet with permit
April–July

The birch and juniper woodland on the higher ground represents one of the finest examples of this habitat in Tayside. Prostrate and upright forms of juniper are scattered through the open birchwood. Grazing pressure in the past has discouraged regeneration, but some young plants are present, especially on the steep eroding slopes of glacial drift on the northern side of the gorge. Heather and bilberry dominate the ground cover, and there is abundant harebell and bird's-foot-trefoil. Common blue and Scotch argus butterflies are plentiful.

The gorge itself is thickly wooded, with dense thickets of blackthorn, hawthorn and tall bracken on the steeper north west facing slopes. Tree species include alder, ash, oak, elm, hazel, rowan and wild cherry, with occasional whitebeam, aspen, field maple and guelder-rose. The ground flora is richest near the stream, especially around the waterfall. Stone bramble, burnet-saxifrage, alpine bistort, cowslip, rock-rose, fragrant orchid and both mountain and wood melick are among the species present. The site is rich in fungi, and many species of bryophyte are also found.

Birds known to breed include green woodpecker, sparrowhawk, redstart and grey wagtail. Short-eared owl and black grouse frequent the adjoining moorland, and wood warbler and pied flycatcher have been recorded in the woodland. Roe deer are resident in the area, red deer occasionally visit, and both brown and mountain hare have been seen.

Ben Lawers

NN 6138; 3974ha; NTS–NCC reserve
Mountain and moorland
Access to area north of Beinn Ghlas–Ben
Lawers–Meall Garbh ridge, and to Meall nan
Tarmachan area, restricted 12 August–15 February
Visitor centre open Easter–end September, with display:
nature trail; guided walks programme; publications
May–August

Ben Lawers has long been renowned for its arctic–alpine flora. The schists of which this mountain and its neighbours Beinn Ghlas and Meall Garbh are largely composed are rich in lime and other minerals, and very friable. One result is an extensive area of steep, constantly eroding cliff face which supports a varied plant life. The altitude (Ben Lawers' summit is 1214m) and exposure of these hills, on which snow often lies late, particularly favour montane species, represented here in great variety. Scree slopes, mountain springs and the grassy sides of corries also hold plant communities of great interest, including several species of very local distribution.

The most luxuriant vegetation is found on the cliff ledges, inaccessible to sheep and deer. Roseroot, angelica, wood crane's-bill and red campion flourish in such places, alongside less common species such as alpine forget-me-not, alpine cinquefoil and alpine saw-wort. Shady crevices among block scree hold woodland plants such as oak fern, wood anemone and moschatel, while yellow saxifrage, hairy stonecrop, alpine scurvygrass and various sedges favour wet gravel springs with a high proportion of bare ground. Even on the lower slopes many of the commoner mountain species are widespread among both the mat-grass-dominated grassland of the glacial drift soils and the bilberry- and lichen-rich vegetation at the lower edge of the schists.

Bird life is comparatively sparse on these rather bare hills, but golden eagle and peregrine are seen occasionally, and buzzard and kestrel more often. Ring ouzel frequent the gullies, and raven sometimes play over the high ridges. A few red grouse and ptarmigan are present, but the species most certain to be visible are carrion and hooded crow, meadow pipit, skylark and wheatear.

Red deer, which move freely between the reserve and the adjacent hill ground, are occasionally seen on the south-facing slopes. Mountain hare are found on high ground, but brown hare on the lower slopes only. Common shrew and mole can penetrate to surprisingly high altitudes.

The insect fauna is rich; northern eggar, fox moth, emperor moth and yellow underwing are among the larger moths likely to be seen. One of the most interesting insects is small mountain ringlet butterfly, for which the Breadalbane hills represent its Scottish headquarters.

Black Wood of Rannoch

NN 5755; 2350ha; FC reserve
Pine forest
Access restricted to forest tracks, starting at
NN 589561 and 536540; there is no vehicular
access to these points
April–August

This important remnant of the Caledonian pine and birch forest is managed as a Forest Nature Reserve, with the aim of conserving, and where necessary restoring, the natural pinewood ecosystem. In parts of the reserve the woodland is open, with fine mature pines from 160 to 250 years old, and a good sprinkling of birch and rowan. Some natural regeneration is occurring, and the trees are of mixed ages. Exotic species planted prior to declaration of the reserve will gradually be removed. Much of the ground cover is bilberry and long heather, with abundant mosses in the damper hollows. Chickweed wintergreen, common wintergreen and lesser twayblade are among the more interesting plant species.

Substantial populations of capercaillie and black grouse inhabit the forest, siskin are common, and Scottish crossbill are known to breed. Summer visitors include redstart, spotted flycatcher and tree pipit. Roe deer are plentiful, and in winter a few red deer are sometimes present.

The Black Wood and the birchwoods on its western fringe are internationally important for their insects; many rare and local species are recorded. The Camghouran birchwoods are particularly noted for their moths.

Many of the species in the Black Wood can also be seen along the forest trails starting from Carie (NN 617573), where there is ample car parking. From there it is also possible to join the right-of-way path leading from Loch Rannoch over the hills to Innerwick in Glen Lyon.

Boat Brae and Sunny Brae

NO 028426; 2.5ha; WdT reserve
Oak and mixed woodland
Summer

Part of the woodlands of Dunkeld, both areas consist mainly of oak, with a mixture of other species. Boat Brae is too steep for easy access.

Brerachan Meadows

Permit only; 0.5ha; SWT reserve
Uncultivated meadow
May–July

Globeflower, spignel, melancholy thistle and quaking-grass are among the 119 plant species recorded in this remnant of former hay meadow, part of which is subject to periodic flooding.

Brighty Wood

NO 445378; 5.3ha; WdT reserve
Mixed woodland
Spring, summer

Originally this reserve was a birch wood but some parts have been replanted with a mixture of hardwoods and conifers. The latter will be eventually replaced with broadleaves to make it attractive to a broader range of birds and wildlife.

Caenlochan

NO 2070; 925ha; NCC reserve
Mountains and steep glens
Access restricted June–October; contact NCC, Angus
April–May

Stretching north-west from Glen Clova, this reserve includes a high level plateau and steep corries with exposures of lime-rich rocks. The cliff ledges in these corries support a very varied flora including many arctic-alpine species; among them are montane willows, purple saxifrage, alpine bistort, alpine meadow-rue and northern bedstraw. *Cladonia* lichens, stiff sedge and woolly fringe-moss are widespread on the summit plateaus, each dominating the plant community where it occurs.

Large numbers of red deer frequent the corries and plateau, and fox and blue hare are not uncommon. There are ptarmigan on the reserve, golden plover and dunlin breeding on the plateau, ring ouzel haunt the corries, and golden eagle are quite often seen over the glens.

Clatto Country Park

NO 368346; 16ha; Tayside RC
Reservoir and plantations
Leaflet available on site
Summer

The reservoir supports common breeding water birds such as coot, moorhen and mallard. There is also a good variety of fish including carp.

Crombie Country Park

NO 523405; 97ha; Tayside RC
Woodland and reservoir
Leaflet available on site
Summer, winter

The woodland is mainly conifer plantations but there are areas of mature broadleaves. Roe deer, fox and stoat are present. The reservoir attracts breeding great crested and little grebe and goldeneye and smew in winter, when it is also used by large numbers of greylag and pink-footed geese.

Hermitage

NO 0142; 15ha; NTS
Woodland, gorge and falls
Booklet from Pass of Killiecrankie Visitor Centre, The Ellshop, Dunkeld or NTS, Edinburgh; guided walks, nature trail; ranger-naturalist
April–October

There is a long history of conifer planting around Dunkeld and the trees close to the River Braan include many particularly fine specimens of Douglas and silver fir, Norway spruce and larch. Along the river bank alder, birch and wild cherry attract birds such as long-tailed tit and willow warbler. Dipper and grey wagtail nests can often be watched from the bridge over the gorge, as can salmon making vain attempts to leap up the falls.

Keltneyburn

Permit only; 34ha; SWT reserve
Meadow and wooded gorge
Parties by arrangement with SWT
Reserve booklet
Mid-May–mid-July

The Black Wood of Rannoch represents a habitat that once covered much of the Highlands.

In the meadow section of this reserve – part of which is marshy – comparatively lime-rich soil and minimal management for agricultural purposes have resulted in a very varied flora. Greater butterfly-orchid, frog, small-white and fragrant orchid are among the abundant orchids recorded. Other species of interest include field gentian, globeflower, spignel, burnet-saxifrage, mountain everlasting and the curious little fern, moonwort. Encroaching bracken and birch scrub are a potential threat to this attractive meadow, and active management is needed to keep them from taking over.

The gorge section of the reserve, the Den of Keltney, is precipitous and difficult of access, with much loose material on the steep upper slopes. Broad-leaved woodland – predominantly ash, hazel, wych elm and oak at the lower end, and birch above – clothes the sides of the den. Typical woodland herbs such as dog's mercury and ramsons occur, and lily-of-the-valley is also present. The humid conditions deep within the gorge are reflected in a rich growth of ferns, mosses and liverworts.

Killiecrankie

NN 907627; 380ha; RSPB reserve
Deciduous woodland, cliffs and moorland
May–July

Stretching from the rock-strewn bed of the River Garry to the heather moorland over 300m above, this reserve encompasses a wide variety of habitats. On the lower oak-clad slopes wood warbler, redstart, green woodpecker and great spotted woodpecker breed. The birch-clad hillside and rugged cliffs above hold redpoll, tree pipit, buzzard, kestrel and raven, while on the moorland curlew nest and blackcock gather to display at the lek.

The reserve is of considerable botanical interest. A variety of ferns grows among the jumble of rocks and moss-covered tree trunks in the gorge, and other plants include wood vetch, yellow saxifrage and shining crane's-bill. Many of the species on this reserve can also be seen in the PASS OF KILLIECRANKIE, to which there is unrestricted access and which in turn is linked by trail to the Linn of Tummel.

Linn of Tummel

NN 9160; 20ha; NTS
Wooded river banks
Nature trail (3.5km); booklet from Pass of
Killiecrankie Visitor Centre and The Ellshop,
Dunkeld; car park at NN 913610; ranger-naturalist
April–October

Varied woodland, largely deciduous, covers much
of this area, which lies at the confluence of the
Rivers Garry and Tummel. Oak and beech are
dominant in some places, a mixture of birch, hazel
and alder predominates in others, and there is a
stand of Scots pine on the north bank of the
Tummel. Many exotic conifers are also present.
The ground vegetation varies with the tree cover,
being quite rich in the most natural areas of the
woodland. Here mountain and wood melick,
stone bramble, primrose, common wintergreen,
goldilocks buttercup, lily-of-the-valley and common dog-violet occur. Elsewhere heather is dominant, and there is abundant bilberry and bracken.

Red-breasted merganser, goosander, dipper and
grey wagtail are among the birds regularly seen
along the rivers, while greylag geese from the
feral flock on Loch Fasdally often graze on the
fields beside the path. Breeding woodland birds
include siskin, redpoll, long-tailed tit and treecreeper; capercaillie visit the heathery glades, and
great spotted and green woodpecker frequent the
area. Roe deer and red squirrel are also quite
common.

Loch of Craiglush

Permit only; 35.5ha; SWT reserve
Loch with fringing marsh and woodland
All year

Similar in many ways to the neighbouring LOCH
OF THE LOWES, and linked to it by a wide canal,
this loch can be viewed from the A923. The area
around the loch is kept as free from disturbance
as possible, and permits are granted only to bona
fide research workers.

Loch of Kinnordy

NO 3653; 81ha; RSPB reserve
Loch with surrounding marsh and woodland fringe
Reserve visiting April–August, all days;
September–November, Sunday only; December–March
closed.
Hours: 9a.m. to 9p.m. or sunset when earlier
Two hides with information display
April–June: breeding birds; October–November: wildfowl

Birds dominate the scene virtually all year round.
In summer there is the constant noise and
movement of the several thousand-strong colony
of black-headed gulls and in winter up to 5000
greylag geese flight in at dusk to roost on the
loch.

Vast mats of the tangled rhizomes of bogbean
and cowbane form floating islands on which the
gulls nest. There is constant bickering between
adjacent birds for the available space. Amidst all
this activity the presence of other waterbirds can
easily be overlooked, but patient scanning of the
open water between islands is likely to reveal at
least six duck species as well as coot, moorhen,
dabchick and great crested grebe. Shovelers,
mallard, teal, gadwall, pochard and tufted duck
are regularly present in summer. A much more
surprising record is that of breeding ruddy duck.
This dumpy, stiff-tailed duck is a North American
species which now breeds wild in England; to
date Kinnordy is its only Scottish nesting site.

Reeds and willow scrub, with a windbreak of
spruce and an isolated group of pines, fringe the
loch and provide habitat for woodland birds.
Sedge warbler and reed bunting nest in the willow
scrub, while waders such as snipe, curlew and
redshank breed in the drier areas of the marsh.
The mud exposed by the low water levels of
summer is an ideal feeding ground for waders.
Waders on passage are attracted to the mud, too:
ruff, greenshank and spotted redshank have all
been recorded here in autumn.

Much of the summer marshland vanishes under
a sheet of water in winter. Many more duck are
on the loch at this season, including sizeable
flocks of wigeon. From October onwards the
greylag geese appear at dusk: clamorous flocks
flight in from their feeding grounds on the
surrounding farmland and whiffle down on to the
tree-fringed loch, to bathe and rest until dawn.
Only when ice covers the water do wildfowl
numbers drop right away, leaving only a few
mallard, with coot and moorhen sheltering in the
willow scrub. It is in this kind of weather that
birds of prey such as hen harrier and short-eared
owl are most likely to be seen, hunting over the
tall marsh vegetation for mice and voles.

Loch Leven

NO 1501; 1597ha; NCC reserve
Large freshwater loch
Access restricted to Kirkgate Park, Findatie,
Burleigh Sands and Loch Leven Castle; permit
required to visit other parts of reserve and granted
only to bona fide research workers: apply NCC
(SE Region), Edinburgh
*Late September–March: wintering wildfowl;
April–August: breeding duck*

Loch Leven is one of the most important wildfowl
sites in Europe and holds the greatest concentration of breeding duck in Britain. Its shallow
waters and the surrounding fertile farmland provide rich winter feeding grounds for a wide
variety of wildfowl species, and its islands offer
a relatively safe nesting place for large numbers
of duck. Loch Leven also serves, through the
RSPB's activities at VANE FARM, as a valuable
resource for conservation education. This site is
listed under the Ramsar Convention for the
conservation of wetlands.

The loch is one of a small number of major
arrival points for pink-footed geese in autumn,
and in years when they arrive in daylight a
continuous stream of skeins can be seen coming
in from the north and dropping on to the water.
Once down, the geese rest on and around St Serf's

Island before dispersing to feed on nearby fields or moving on to their wintering grounds elsewhere. Greylag geese arrive later and in smaller numbers, but a much larger proportion of the birds remain in the area all winter. Barnacle, brent, Canada, white-fronted and snow geese appear as stragglers in most seasons, and whooper swan are present throughout the winter.

Most of the 1000 or so pairs of breeding duck nest on the 42ha St Serf's Island, the majority among tussocks of tufted hair-grass or reed canary-grass, and often surprisingly close together. Many of the 500–600 pairs of tufted duck choose sites within the several thousand-strong colony of black-headed gull. Mallard, gadwall, wigeon, shoveler and shelduck also nest on the island.

Although the once-extensive areas of marsh were greatly diminished when the water level was lowered 150 years ago, the wetter fields around the loch still hold quite large numbers of breeding waders, such as lapwing, oystercatcher, snipe, curlew and redshank. A few common sandpiper and ringed plover also nest near the shore. In late summer large areas of mud are exposed along the north side of St Serf's Island, attracting a variety of passage waders. Dunlin, jack snipe, greenshank and ruff occur regularly in small numbers, and golden plover are found in flocks of up to 500. Other species, such as green sandpiper, black-tailed godwit and spotted redshank, are occasionally recorded.

Many changes in Loch Leven's animal and plant populations have been noted in recent years, largely resulting from enrichment of the loch by run-off from the surrounding farmland. Only small patches of common reed and reed canary-grass now remain where there used to be extensive reed-beds. Once-dense beds of Canadian pondweed and stonewort have virtually disappeared, pondweed species of value as waterfowl food plants have much decreased, and thick algal blooms have become a frequent occurrence. There have also been associated changes in invertebrate life; dragonflies and mayflies are no longer seen, and freshwater shrimps are less abundant, but there are still vast numbers of the non-biting chironomid midge, upon whose larvae many of the duck feed.

Loch Leven is also famous for its fish, especially brown trout. Perch, pike and stickleback are also present, and there are roach and brook lamprey in the inflow stream. Both fishing and wildfowling on the loch are carried out on a commercial basis and under strict control, as they have been for many years.

Loch of Lintrathen

NO 2755; 162ha; SWT reserve
Reservoir
Access to hide restricted to members except on advertised open days; no access elsewhere on reserve
October–April: wildfowl

Very large numbers of wildfowl visit this deep loch during the winter. In late October and November the numbers of greylag geese coming in from neighbouring farmland to roost may be as high as 5000, and their arrival and descent on to the water at dusk looks and sounds impressive. The number of mallard occasionally exceeds 3000; like the geese they leave the loch to feed elsewhere. Diving ducks, dependent on the loch for their food supply, are less numerous, although several hundred tufted duck are sometimes present along with smaller numbers of goldeneye. Shoveler generally appear for a short time in October and teal, wigeon and whooper swan all occur regularly. There is a heronry near the loch, and at times as many as 30 of these handsome birds gather in the vicinity of the hide.

Loch of the Lowes

NO 0544; 98ha; SWT reserve
Loch with fringing woodland and marsh
Access limited to centre, hide and unfenced section of south shore
Visitor centre open April–September (see below); hide open at all times; handbook and leaflets, parties and educational groups should book, tel. Dunkeld 337; ranger service
April–June: breeding birds; July: young ospreys, if present; late October–March: geese

Although the view from the hide is always attractive, with a backdrop of rugged hillside setting off the reed- and tree-fringed loch, the most rewarding times for a visit to this reserve are early morning and late evening in midsummer. Then mallard ducklings may feed almost under the hide, diving terns may make an audible splash as they hit the water, and water rails may be screaming in the reedbeds. By mid-July the fat buds of white water-lilies are opening, and if the ospreys have nested successfully the young birds are likely to be indulging in energetic bouts of wing flapping. It is even possible that the observer will share the hide with a treecreeper busily feeding its brood.

Here, at the very edge of the Highlands, plants and animals typical of both upland and lowland Scotland occur. Most of the reserve is water, much of it shallow, but the narrow fringe of woodland and marsh are significant in contributing towards species diversity. In the loch aquatic plants typical of nutrient-poor Highland lochs – quillwort, shoreweed, water lobelia and bogbean – grow near species characteristic of silts rich in nutrients, such as yellow water-lily and amphibious bistort. Common reed, reed canary-grass and sedges border the western bay, and provide cover for nesting grebes and for resident roe deer as they come down to drink.

The loch's wealth of invertebrate life supplies food for brown trout, perch, pike and eels, as well as diving ducks. Over 1000 greylag geese usually roost on the loch in late autumn.

The Loch of the Lowes has been noted for its great crested grebes since the first Scottish breeding was recorded there in 1870. The normal population is now four or five pairs, and their display dance is a fascinating sight. Little grebe

Looking east from Loch Ba, Argyll, the wet wilderness of Rannoch Moor stretches away into Perthshire.

also breed on the reserve, and in 1973 the very decorative Slavonian grebe nested here, the first recorded breeding south of the Grampians.

The bird most people hope to see from the hide is the handsome osprey. These birds have not nested successfully every season, however, since they first appeared in 1969 shortly after the reserve was established, but they have reappeared at the loch and spent some time there every year.

Scots pine, the species most favoured by nesting osprey, is just one of the wide range of native trees in the reserve's fringing woodland. Oak, ash, hazel, holly, alder and five species of willow are present, and juniper, wild cherry and bird cherry are frequent. Because the woodland strip between loch and road is so narrow, the ground flora includes not only the expected species, such as wood anemone, wood-sorrel and primrose, but also plants much more commonly associated with disturbed ground, for example pineappleweed and colt's-foot.

The mixed woodland attracts a varied bird population. Both green and great spotted woodpecker occur; common redstart, spotted flycatcher, grasshopper and wood warbler are among the summer visitors and siskin and redpoll are common in winter. Capercaillie occasionally visit the reserve; black grouse can be heard at their lek on a nearby hillside; and goldcrest and long-tailed tit frequent the birch and juniper near the Centre. In the summer, high-powered binoculars are provided in the hide.

Few of the reserve's mammals are likely to be seen during the day, but badger, otter, wild cat, fox and red squirrel are known to occur. Roe deer appear quite often at dawn and dusk and fallow deer, from a long-established herd on the hills to the north, sometimes forage in the woodland.

Milton Wood

Permit only; 24ha; NCC reserve
Alder wood
Permit from NCC, 9 Castle Street, Forfar DD8 3AE
May–July

One of the largest remaining examples of a mixed alder wood in Tayside. It displays an almost unique range of alder and oak stands which were managed as coppice until about 1900. The ground flora is herb-rich.

Moncreiffe Hill Wood

NO 130200; 13ha; WdT reserve
Mixed wooded hill

A magnificent wooded hill occupying a prominent position on the north side of Strathearn. The wood is a plantation of deciduous and conifer species, but it also contains some scattered ancient oak and beech, and fine specimens of Douglas fir.

Monikie Country Park

NO 505385; 75ha; Tayside RC
Woodland, grassland and reservoirs
Leaflet available on site
Summer, winter

The reservoirs are the most interesting areas for wildlife with mute swan, tufted duck, coot and little and great crested grebe all breeding. In the winter they are used by large numbers of pink-footed and greylag geese as a roost.

Montrose Basin

NO 6957; 1012ha; SWT–Angus DC reserve
Large estuarine inlet
Permit only to hides
Leaflet and ranger
October–March

At low tide this almost circular basin is a vast expanse of mud, with the deep trough of the River South Esk winding near the southern shore, and minor channels patterning the main flats. Emerald-green sea lettuce provides splashes of colour on the mud, and the mussel beds along the course of the Esk give a strong contrast in textures. Many thousands of wildfowl and waders come to this estuary in autumn and winter, some soon moving on while others remain throughout the winter.

The Basin is particularly noted for its populations of redshank, knot, oystercatcher, curlew and dunlin. Each species reaches peak numbers at a different time: curlew in August and March; redshank in September and March; oystercatcher in October and November; knot in January; and dunlin in February. Although birds are widely scattered over the mud at low tide, the feeding area most favoured is near the river channel. Most birds roost at the north west corner of the Basin, with curlew, redshank and dunlin moving on to the fields behind the seabank during very high tides, although oystercatcher tend to gather in the south east corner, where there is a shingle ridge. Many other wader species are recorded on migration, often being found in the pools and marshy mud channels around the Lurgies. Small numbers of oystercatcher, redshank and snipe breed in the area.

The presence of glasswort and three species of eelgrass helps to draw large flocks of duck to the area. Several thousand wigeon are often present, with smaller numbers of mallard, teal and pintail; this is one of the few Scottish east coast sites where pintail appear regularly. There is a sizeable winter population of shelduck, which also breed on the reserve. Eider, too, are year-round residents, nesting on the seabanks and around the edges of the fields, and feeding on the mussels. A group of nonbreeding mute swans is also present throughout the year, the numbers peaking in July and August when the area is an important moulting ground. Both greylag and pink-footed geese use the estuary for roosting; the site is of national importance for the latter. Numbers are smaller than in the past, but it is hoped that the flocks will build up again as disturbance decreases.

Other birds of the Basin include cormorant – often seen 'hanging out to dry' on sandbanks – and both common and arctic tern, fishing in the shallows. Sedge warbler breed in the area and both they and swallow use the reedbeds at the west side as a migration roost; water rail have also been recorded here. Salmon and sea trout pass up the South Esk – there is an old-established salmon-netting station near the mouth of the estuary – and seals occasionally follow them into the Basin. Eels are trapped as they make their way down to the sea, and local fishermen farm the mussels and dig in the mud for bait. To reconcile these traditional activities with wild-fowling and the more recently introduced recreational sailing and wind-surfing presents a great challenge to those responsible for managing and conserving this relatively new reserve.

Pass of Killiecrankie

NN 917627; 22ha; NTS
Wooded gorge
Visitor centre, open Easter September
guided walks, ranger-naturalist
April October

Oak dominates this woodland on the steep banks of the River Garry, but many other tree species, including bird cherry, are also present. The ground flora includes very local flowering plants such as wood vetch, bird's-nest orchid, stone bramble, melancholy thistle and giant bellflower, as well as many more widespread species.

Wood warbler, redstart and spotted flycatcher are among the small birds breeding in the oakwood; dipper and grey wagtail frequent the rocky gorge; and woodcock and great spotted woodpecker are also regularly recorded. The gorge itself is of considerable geological interest.

Paths from the pass link up with the LINN OF TUMMEL trail.

Rannoch Moor

NN 4053; 1499ha; NCC reserve
Peaty moorland, lochs and bogs
April-July

This is an area of trackless, hummocky terrain with an intricate mosaic of bogs, peat hags, lochans and small pools occupying the hollows. The reserve which includes part of Loch Laidon,

Containing both highland and lowland species, the Loch of the Lowes is of particular interest.

lies at an altitude of about 360m and is notoriously bleak in bad weather. Plants associated with the mires and of particular interest include Rannoch-rush, for which Rannoch Moor is now the only British site. All three species of bladderwort are present, and dwarf birch also occurs. Red and roe deer graze the reserve, and a variety of moorland birds and waterbirds breed there.

Seaton Cliffs

NO 667416; 10.5ha; SWT reserve
Coastal cliffs
Nature trail (5km); booklet from information centre,
105 High Street, Arbroath
May–August

There is colour here whatever the weather or season, with the sandstone cliffs glowing richly red against grey sea and green grass. In early summer sweet-smelling white scurvygrass cascades down the slopes, and clumps of thrift and bird's-foot-trefoil provide splashes of pink and yellow. Primroses and violets bloom in the most sheltered corners, and where springs create marshy conditions there is a lush growth of meadowsweet and meadow crane's-bill. In a few places scattered spikes of marsh-orchid, early-purple orchid and heath spotted-orchid occur. The vetches growing along the cliff top represent an interesting mixture of maritime and non-maritime species.

The cliff vegetation attracts a variety of butterflies and moths. Green-veined white butterflies are among the earliest to appear, visiting the scurvygrass; common blue and meadow brown are abundant in summer. The vividly coloured six-spot burnet moth flaunts its metallic green and red body in leisurely flight, and in the sandy bank alongside the path solitary bees excavate their burrows. Several species of snail occur among the vegetation of these lime-rich cliffs, many of them attractively banded or mottled.

Seaton Cliffs harbour few seabirds since the alternating layers of coarse sandstone and pebbly conglomerate, which slope to seaward, do not provide suitable nest sites. They do, however, weather to form spectacular arches, blow-holes and caves, some of which are occupied by breeding house martin. Fulmar, kittiwake and guillemot can be seen offshore in summer, while eider and seals are regular visitors to the bays. Many migrant birds have been recorded in the area in autumn and winter. The flat shelves of seaweed-strewn rock exposed at low tide attract waders, as well as being of interest for the marine life contained within the pools.

Stormont Loch

NO 193422; 48ha; SWT reserve
Open water, fen and woodland
Autumn, winter, spring

These two shallow lochs with their adjoining fen and willow scrub and fringing woodland are important for wintering wildfowl. Stormont Loch is one of a series of greylag roosts, while the more interesting duck include shoveler and gadwall. Extensive areas of fen are uncommon in Perthshire and here contains many unusual plants such as water plantain and yellow water-lily.

Tummel Forest

NN 865597; 6800ha; FC
Woodland and lochs
Visitor centre open April–September; guided walks programme; audio-visual programme; leaflet
All year

Below the famous Queen's View overlooking Loch Tummel a walk leads through the mixed deciduous woodland which still clothes the steep slopes. Oak, ash, hazel, alder and birch are the most abundant trees in this area, over dog's mercury, wood anemone, wood-sorrel, marsh hawk's-beard, herb-Robert, climbing corydalis and broad buckler-fern. Redstart, wood warbler, spotted flycatcher and great spotted woodpecker breed.

Limestone ridges are exposed around Lochan na Leathain at 400m on the hills above Queen's View, where the vegetation includes thyme, quaking-grass, fairy flax, bearberry and common reed. The more acid lochs nearby support water horsetail, water lobelia and common spike-rush. Mallard, teal, wigeon and Canada geese breed near these lochs, and there is a colony of black-headed gulls on Lochan na Leathain. There are capercaillie and goldcrest in the conifer forest, with black grouse along the fringes.

Vane Farm

NT 1699; 185ha; RSPB reserve
Loch shore, woodland, moor and farmland
April–December: open daily except Friday,
10a.m.–5p.m.; January–March: open weekends
only 10a.m.–4p.m.; parties should book, tel.
Kinross 62355; nature trail accessible all times
Nature centre open all days April–Christmas, on limited basis January–March; school parties welcome by appointment with warden; Vane Farm Nature Centre,
Kinross KY13 7LX
Nature centre; trail; hide; educational facilities
October–March

From the upper floor of the reserve's nature centre, using the high-powered binoculars provided, the late autumn spectacular of LOCH LEVEN's vast flocks of geese and duck frequenting the area between Vane Farm and St. Serf's Island can be enjoyed in comfort whatever the weather.

Much of the farmland included in the reserve is managed at least partly for the benefit of birds, and the two main arable crops, barley and potatoes, provide good autumn gleanings for the geese and attract them close to the centre. Another feature that brings a variety of species within easy viewing distance is a lagoon, complete with islands, created some years ago in a low-lying marshy field. This offers shelter, feeding grounds and nesting sites for both ducks and waders where the loch shore is rather bare and exposed.

The lower slopes of Vane Hill behind the Centre carry rather sparse birch woodland, which gives way to heather moor above. It is through this area that the nature trail is routed. A programme of fencing and planting is under way with the aim of increasing the woodland cover. Many of the commoner small woodland birds breed either among the birches or in the nearby conifer plantation. Insects include digger bees and wasps which burrow in the trailside sandy banks; and several species of aquatic invertebrates inhabit the small streams. From the viewpoint high on the moorland the view of Loch Leven and its surrounding hills is spectacular.

Although the range of habitats is limited, and the bird life not particularly rich, there is much here of value for educational purposes – and education is a primary aim on this reserve. Details of special facilities and displays from centre or RSPB Edinburgh.

Abbreviations Used in the Guide

Note: county councils are given in the following form, e.g. ACC for Avon County Council; the county is always the same as the section title unless otherwise stated, and these abbreviations do not appear in the list below. All county names beginning with the letter N are spelt out to avoid confusion with the NCC (Nature Conservancy Council); CC alone stands for the Countryside Commission. For convenience the managing body named in line 1 of each entry is sometimes given an obvious abbreviation in line 3, when indicating for instance the availability of a leaflet (e.g. KAMT for Kenneth Allsop Memorial Trust). Such abbreviations are not listed below.

BC	After a place name: Borough Council
BR	British Rail
BTCV	British Trust for Conservation Volunteers
CC	Countryside Commission/after a place name: County Council
CEGB	Central Electricity Generating Board
DNS	Deeside Naturalists' Society
FC	Forestry Commission
HIDB	Highlands and Islands Development Board
HMSO	Her Majesty's Stationery Office
LNR	Local Nature Reserve
MBC	After a place name: Metropolitan Borough Council
MOD	Ministry of Defence
NCC	Nature Conservancy Council
NNR	National Nature Reserve
NTS	National Trust for Scotland
RC	After a place name: Regional Council
RSNC	Royal Society for Nature Conservation
RSPB	Royal Society for the Protection of Birds
RSPCA	Royal Society for the Prevention of Cruelty to Animals
SSSI	Site of Special Scientific Interest
SWT	Scottish Wildlife Trust
WdT	Woodland Trust
WT	Wildfowl and Wetland Trust

Addresses

The following is a list of the major wildlife organisations in Scotland, together with those owners and managing bodies from whom information and/or permits may be obtained, but whose addresses are not already given in the text. All requests should be accompanied by a stamped addressed envelope, and readers should understand that permits may be refused at the managing bodies' discretion.

The nature conservation trust of Scotland

Scottish Wildlife Trust
Headquarters
25 Johnston Terrace
Edinburgh
EH1 2NH

Northern Office
Pitgaveny House Flat
Elgin
Moray
IV30 2PQ

Other organisations

Barvas Estates Ltd
c/o Smiths Gore
The Square
Fochabers
Moray

Borders Natural History Society
The Reenes
Bellingham
Hexham
Northumberland
NE48 2DU

Borders Regional Council
Planning Dept
Newton St Boswells
Roxburghshire
TD6 0SA

British Waterways Board
Melbury House
Melbury Terrace
London NW1 6JX

Central Electricity Generating Board
The Surveyor
Sudbury House
15 Newgate Street
London EC1A 7AU

East Lothian District Council
Recreation and Tourism Dept
Brunton Hall
Ladywell Way
Musselburgh
EH21 6AE

Fair Isle Bird Observatory Trust
21 Regent Terrace
Edinburgh
EH7 5BT

Warden
Bird Observatory
Fair Isle
Shetland

Forestry Commission

Headquarters for England, Wales and Scotland
231 Corstorphine Road
Edinburgh
EH12 7AT

Scotland
South
Greystones Park
55/57 Moffat Road
Dumfries
DG1 1NP

Mid
Portcullis House
21 India Street
Glasgow
G2 4PL

North (North Sunart woodland, Highland)
21 Church Street
Inverness
IV1 1EL

Glen Tanar Estate Office
Aboyne
AB3 5EU

Her Majesty's Stationery Office

Government bookshop
13A Castle Street
Edinburgh

Moray District Council
Planning Dept
High Street
Elgin
Morayshire
W30 1BX

National Trust
42 Queen Anne's Gate
London
SW1H 9AS

There are also 15 regional offices in England and Wales: their addresses are obtainable from the address above

National Trust for Scotland
5 Charlotte Square
Edinburgh
EH2 4DR

Nature Conservancy Council

Headquarters
Northminster House
Peterborough PE1 1VA

Scotland
North East (Grampian, Orkney, Shetland and Speyside)
17 Rubislaw Terrace
Aberdeen
AB1 1XE

North West (Highland (except Speyside), Outer Hebrides, Skye and the Small Isles)
9 Culduthel Road
Inverness
IV2 4AG

South West (Dumfries and Galloway, Strathclyde)
The Castle
Loch Lomond Park
Balloch
Dunbartonshire
G83 8LX

South East (Borders, Central, Fife, Lothian, Tayside) and headquarters
Research Avenue 1
Research Park
Riccarton
Edinburgh
EH14 4AP

Royal Society for Nature Conservation
The Green
Witham Park
Lincoln
LN5 7JR

Royal Society for the Protection of Birds

Scotland
17 Regent Terrace
Edinburgh
EH7 5BN

Royal Society for the Prevention of Cruelty to Animals
Causeway
Horsham
West Sussex
RH12 1HG

Wildfowl and Wetland Trust

Scotland
Eastpark Farm
Caerlaverock
Dumfriesshire
DE1 4RS

Woodland Trust
Autumn Park
Dysart Road
Grantham
Lincolnshire
NG31 6LL

Index